BATTLES AND CAMPAIGNS

BATTLES AND CAMPAIGNS

MALCOLM SWANSTON

CARTOGRAPHICA

A CARTOGRAPHICA BOOK

This book is produced by
Cartographica Press
6 Blundell Street
London N7 9BH

Copyright © 2007 Cartographica Press

This edition printed 2008

ISBN: 978-1-84573-324-7

QUMBAMC

Printed in Singapore by
Star Standard Industries Pte Ltd

CONTENTS

INTRODUCTION 6

PART 1: WARFARE IN THE CLASSICAL AGE 25

PART 2: DARK AGES TO THE RISE OF ISLAM 59

PART 3: MEDIEVAL TO RENAISSANCE WARFARE 71

PART 4: KINGS AND REVOLUTIONS 87

PART 5: WARS OF THE INDUSTRIAL AGE 105

PART 6: WARFARE IN THE TECHNOLOGICAL AGE 127

MAP AND RECONSTRUCTION LIST 158

INTRODUCTION

THE EMERGENCE OF WAR

EARLY SIGNS OF MAN'S AGGRESSION

After the end of the last Ice Age, 12,000 years ago, the ice retreated, glaciers melted, sea levels rose and climates warmed. Signs of increasing population and social complexity brought with it the first evidence of organized warfare. In Offnet Cave in Germany, 34 skulls were discovered, all showing damage made by stone axes and in Upper Egypt the remains of 59 people were discovered, all killed by arrows.

A MORE SOPHISTICATED APPROACH TO DEFENSE

As the human population continued to multiply, settled groups began controlling their surrounding hinterlands and complex defenses appeared. Jericho, near the Dead Sea, had the oldest fortifications in the world, with stone walls 6 feet thick and towers 12 feet high that defended a community of perhaps 2000. Similar cities became common around the Middle East.

IMPERIAL AGGRESSION

Cities such as these struggled with each other for power, but a new pattern evolved sometime after 2400 BC. The new imperial visionary was Lugalzagesi, King of Umma. He went on to expand his rule over the cities of the Euphrates and the Tigris rivers, possibly extending his rule to the Mediterranean coast.

DEVELOPMENT OF WEAPONS

Well-made weapons were necessary to be successful in battle. The original weapon was a club that was gradually refined into an instrument with sharpened edges. This was the Stone Age prototype of the sword. The first missile was a rock that could be hurled at an enemy. The velocity of the missile was much improved by the development of the simple leather sling. From these two basic concepts, weapons continued to develop; the javelin for throwing, the pike for thrusting, and the bow and arrow with its high rate of fire; were all valuable assets for the fighting man. Sometime around 2000 BC, metallurgy developed and this enabled the evolution of the sword, probably introduced by the Assyrians.

Alongside the development of offensive weapons, attention was also given to defense. Wicker, leather, or wooden shields began to appear, alongside leather and quilted cloth armor. With metallurgy came breastplates, helmets, and other forms of body armor.

WARFARE IN THE CLASSICAL AGE

INTO BATTLE

Thus equipped, men marched to meet their enemies, intent on conquest or defense. The tactics they deployed consisted of large masses of infantry employing little protection other than a simple shield and carrying a spear to thrust at a similarly equipped enemy. These men usually came from the poorest group in society around which a noble or professional warrior elite could operate. There would also be troops armed with slings and bows to deliver missiles. Alongside the infantry came early chariots. These were slow and ungainly at first, but in time they became the striking force of many armies, until cavalry began to take over this role.

The sole objective of these early armies was to find a suitable place of battle and overwhelm the enemy before they could do the same. Objectives became greater and local struggles turned into campaigns as geographical horizons widened. Except for the military elites, the men who made up these armies had little training and went into battle motivated by fear of their commander, as well as the prospect of booty.

When armies met on the battlefield, the main group, usually spearmen, stayed together in groups. Their commanders were in their chariots, or on horseback. On the flanks or in front, groups of archers or slingers formed a forward skirmish line, maintaining a harassing fire until the chariots or cavalry sensed the right moment to charge. The skirmishes then moved to the flanks and rear through the massed infantry who were, by now, moving forward.

Occasionally the initial charge would drive the enemy terror-stricken from the battlefield but more usually the opposing forces would converge and hand-to-hand butchery would begin, ending only when one side sensed defeat. Usually only a small proportion of the defeated army escaped death or enslavement.

THE WORLD'S FIRST PROFESSIONAL ARMY

Egyptian Pharaoh Amosis is credited with creating the world's first permanent professional army, c.1525 BC. He adopted the war chariot and his well-disciplined infantry was accompanied by contingents of highly trained archers. The Assyrians took this new professionalism to a new level, building a highly militaristic state.

ASSYRIA – THE FIRST MILITARY STATE IN HISTORY

The Assyrian people were located on the upland plains of north-eastern Mesopotamia in an area with little or no natural frontiers, so they were constantly threatened by surrounding peoples and states. This made them the most warlike people in the region. After Tiglath-pileser III created a superbly trained, well-paid professional army in 745 BC, Assyria's principal income started to come from the results of warfare, not just from booty, but also from taxes levied both on conquered territories and the control of trade across the region. A large part of this income was lavished on the army, where no expense was spared in continually providing it with the best weapons and training that contemporary technology could supply. Assyria had become the first truly military state in world history.

THE CHINESE PICTURE

In China the art of war was also well advanced. As early as 1400 BC chariots were first used and before long the strength of a state was judged on the number of chariots it could deploy.

THE CHARACTERISTICS OF WARFARE

Around 600 BC clear military trends had begun to emerge that would remain unchanged for the next 2000 years. Armies approached each other in a set battle formation, almost always in parallel lines with the infantry in the centre and cavalry or chariots on each flank. Occasionally chariots would be deployed in front of the infantry to disrupt the enemy and attempt to screen the approach of the main force. As the main bodies closed, these skirmishers would withdraw through the main body leaving the more heavily armed infantry and cavalry to the decisive engagement. Occasionally one army would stand on the defensive awaiting the approach of the enemy, but more commonly both sides marched towards each other resulting in a clash of arms with both armies urging each other with their war cries, creating a violent and terrible noise. The Persian armies, under Cyrus the Great, adapted and developed

MACEDONIAN DOMINANCE
Alexander the Great, also known as Alexander III of Macedon, northern Greece, has gone down in history as one of the greatest military commanders of all time. By the time of his death in 323 BC, at the age of 32, he had managed to conquer most of what was then regarded as the civilised world, including the mighty Persian Empire, and had left a monumental military legacy.

His battles to win the Persian territories are some of his most famous, culminating in the Battle of Gaugamela, where he defeated the Persian emperor Darius. Over the next decade he continued his legendary conquests, founding over 70 cities along the way and securing an empire that stretched across three continents.

PROFESSIONAL WARFARE
PROFESSIONAL WARFARE
The world's first permanent professional army dates back to 1525 BC, led by the the Egyptian Pharaoh Amosis, founder of the 18th dynasty and member of the Theban royal house. With the help of his army, Amosis finally managed to expel the alien dynasty of the Hyksos from Egypt and regained power over the Egyptian territories, Nubia and Canaan.

their cavalry, turning the Persian heavy cavalry and their mounted archers into the best horse soldiers in the world.

GREEK IDEAS

In Greece a new style of warfare was developing based on the Greek Phalanx. This was a disciplined formation of heavy infantry formed into lines between 8 and 16-men deep. Each man was armed with a long pike and was protected by a large shield, helmet, breastplate, and shin guards, or greaves. Physically fit, well trained, and highly disciplined, the front rank would point their spears towards the enemy, the next rank pointing their spears over the shoulder of the man in front, and so on, to create a bristling hedge of points aimed at the enemy. These elite, well-armed men came from the middle and upper classes of society. The flanks of the Phalanx were protected by lightly armed troops, not as well trained or disciplined. They could include slingers and archers and came from the lower classes of society or were often mercenaries.

SPARTA

Sparta, the capital of the Peloponnesian State of Laconia, developed a society based on creating the best trained and most determined army in Greece. Young males were passed to the State at the age of seven to begin a rigorously disciplined and mainly military education lasting 12 years. At the completion of his education, a period of military service would begin.

THE ATHENIANS AND THE DEVELOPMENT OF MARITIME WARFARE

The Athenians, in addition to maintaining a capable army, also developed a navy. The Athenian trireme, based on an improved version of the Phoenician galley, was a long, low, narrow warship powered by three banks of oars on each side. Capacity and comfort were sacrificed to achieve speed and maneuverability. The ship's main weapon was a 9 to 12 ft long pointed bow or ram, usually tipped in metal. A favored tactic was for Athenian vessels to advance towards their enemies at speed, swerving at the last moment to come alongside. The Athenians would quickly withdraw their banks of oars and smash the opposition's oars, rendering that vessel unmaneuverable and making it a sitting target for the Athenians to either capture or sink. Very few Athenian enemies could match this ability at sea.

ATHENS VERSUS SPARTA – THE FIRST AND SECOND PELOPONNESIAN WARS

From the 470s BC, there was a growing rivalry between Athens and Sparta. The Greek City States had established the Delian League to defeat a Persian invasion, but the Spartans were alarmed by the growth in Athenian power and its domination over smaller Greek States. A war broke out in 460 and lasted until 445, when Pericles of Athens managed to secure peace. Spartan land power and Athenian sea power were both undefeated.

The Second Peloponnesian War raged from 432 until 404. The end came following the total destruction of the Athenian fleet and the final surrender of Athens, leaving Sparta the dominant force in Greece.

THE RISE OF MACEDONIA

In 359 BC a new power emerged in Macedonia, northern Greece, under the leadership of its new King Phillip II. His first act was to set about reorganizing the Macedonian army and he produced the finest fighting force the world had yet seen.

This was bequeathed by Philip II to his son Alexander the Great, who continued to develop an army that would have held its own against any other until the development of gunpowder. Alexander the Great's campaigns across Asia demonstrated time after time both his own skills in leadership and the Macedonian military system.

THE MARCH OF ROME

As the Empire of Alexander the Great declined, a new power was emerging in the Mediterranean. The Roman army was originally a militia organization but as Roman power expanded, by 250 BC a professional standing army had evolved with the Legion as its main unit.

When on the march, the Roman Legion was completely self-contained, with a baggage train of about 500 mules carrying food supplies and all necessary equipment, including dismantled ballistae and catapults.

On the field of battle, the Romans attempted to gain the advantage of high ground to give their arrows and spears greater range. The highly trained infantry remained the backbone of the armies throughout most of the Roman period, but there was an increasing reliance on mobile heavy cavalry. Horsemen had dominated warfare over most of Asia and it became evident to Roman commanders that it would be necessary to develop cavalry capable of meeting this threat. By the 4th century AD, cavalry made up about a quarter of the typical Roman field army. A higher proportion of infantry were now dedicated to delivering missiles, either by operating the ballistae or as archers or slingers, reducing the level of hand-to-hand combat.

Rome reached its greatest geographical limit during the 1st and 2nd Centuries AD. The Pax Romana (the long period of relative peace experienced by the Roman Empire) spread from the Atlantic to the Persian Gulf. The Empire had almost stable frontiers, while the provinces were firmly controlled and protected with frontier lines, from Hadrian's Wall in northern England to the Danube delta.

By the late 3rd and 4th Centuries, the eastern and western parts of the Empire were growing apart. At the beginning of the 5th century the West was failing to defend itself against barbarian attack and by the end of the century most western provinces were virtually lost to the Empire.

In contrast in the East, Diocletian (285–305), had introduced reforms, restored efficiency to government and laid the foundation of an Empire that would last into the mid-15th century.

Attempts were made in the 6th century by Justinian to reunite the eastern and western parts of the Empire. He was inspired by the ideal of a Christian Roman Empire with the Mediterranean Sea as its epicenter and he reestablished Roman control over the Germanic peoples who had settled in Italy, France, Spain, and North Africa. However, he was the last true Roman Emperor and his reign (527–556) marks the end of the Late Roman period and the beginning of the Byzantine Empire that would last until 1453.

Early in 772, Charlemagne began to build a mighty European Empire and in 800 Pope Leo III crowned him Emperor, acknowledging that all Christians in Europe, apart from those in the British Isles, owed allegiance to him. His position was recognized by Byzantine Emperor Michael I in the 812 Treaty of Aix-la-Chapelle.

This Empire brought relative peace and stability and ensured that most of western and east-central Europe was protected from outside raids. Christianity spread and this led to the growth of churches and religious communities, but the wealth of these institutions, together with associated merchant settlements, proved an attractive target for three marauding groups: Magyars, Vikings, and Arabs.

ROMAN RULE
By 250 BC a professional standing army had evolved with the Roman Legion at its core. In an effort to build on its already considerable might, the army's cavalry was expanded and the reliance on hand-to-hand combat reduced. By the 4th century cavalry made up one-quarter of the typical Roman field army.

DARK AGES TO THE RISE OF ISLAM

MAGYARS, VIKINGS, AND ARABS

The nomadic Magyars were mainly horse archers who attacked in small, loose groups rather than large formal armies. They were skilled in ambushes, sometimes feigning retreat before counter-attacking. Their tactics were to confuse an enemy, weaken it with accurately fired arrows and then attack with a final destructive charge. A Magyar attack in 924 resulted in the capture of a Magyar prince, enabling King Otto I of Germany to arrange a truce that lasted nine years. Otto finally crushed them at the Battle of Lechfeld in 955.

Further north, bands of Scandinavian Viking warriors, using ships of technically advanced design, set about raiding Western Europe in the final years of the 8th century. Some Vikings were colonists, reaching the northern islands of Britain early in the 7th century and the Faeroes 100 years later. During the 9th century Norwegians settled or attempted to settle many parts of the British Isles and traveled as far south as Lisbon and Seville. They reached North America around the year 1000.

Other Vikings were more warlike. Viking dragonships, each carrying a crew of 40 to 100 warriors would attack the coasts of northern Europe, shaking the very foundations of the Christian states. They penetrated rivers, using these routes to loot towns and monasteries, seizing many captives who were later sold as slaves. At the mouth of the River Seine a base settlement was established by a Norse chieftain named Rollo. Within a hundred years this settlement had grown into the Duchy of Normandy, where the population spoke Norman French and had rebuilt a Carolingian administration while working closely with the Church. Duke Robert II used his warriors and the power of the Church to control Normandy in both political and religious senses. A direct descendent of Rollo later became King William I of England after his success at the Battle of Hastings in 1066. To the east, a new power was growing, built around the relatively new religion of Islam. Muhammad was the founder of Islam and is regarded by Muslims as the last messenger from God and the greatest of the prophets.

Although initially Muhammad gained few followers, by the time of his death most of Arabia had been converted to Islam.

Muhammad's death left the Muslim community without an obvious leader. One of his oldest companions, Abu Bakr (632–634), was acknowledged by several leaders as the first caliph, or successor. Under Abu Bakr and his successor Umar (634–644), the tribes that had begun to fall away on the death of Muhammad were reunited under the banner of Islam and converted into a formidable military and ideological force. Motivated by desire for plunder, as well as religious faith, the

Arabs broke out of the Arabian peninsula. Sweeping everything before them, they soon had control of half of the Byzantine provinces, Persia, Jerusalem, and Egypt and were moving into the Mediterranean region.

Southern Europe began to defend itself with fortifications built by local warlords who established a feudal independence. Likewise, the Viking raids promoted the devolution of power to local elites, leading to the growth of self-interested feudalism.

GROWTH OF FEUDALISM

Feudalism was a hierarchical system where a lord protected his people in exchange for services. Every lord held his lands from an overlord who, in turn, held his from a great and powerful noble family. At the top of the chain was the king. The lord was required to be a trained warrior, capable of turning out, ready and equipped to fight, at the command of the overlord from whom he held his lands. If he had an extensive holding, his obligation would extend to the provision of a number of trained fighting men, and the wealthier he was, the larger, better equipped, and more highly skilled the force he provided had to be.

In theory this system enabled a well-regulated kingdom to mobilize an efficient fighting force against a common enemy for the protection of society. In practice it depended on the authority of the person at the top. If the king was weak this tended to encourage the growth of power among the nobles, who would then fight for dominance among themselves.

NORMANDY

King William I of England was of doubtful parentage and as a result was often called William the Bastard, although history knows him better as William the Conqueror. He was born into an era of intrigue and violence, but he was well educated, both academically and in matters of warfare and battle, which undoubtedly helped when he invaded England in 1066.

BATTLE OF HASTINGS
King Harold II of England never stood much of a chance against William of Normandy and his army in the famous battle of 1066. He had little choice but to fight defensively, relying on the shield-wall method of protection. A meager 5,000 Saxon soldiers were pitted against the Norman's 15,000-strong infantry and they were soon defeated, despite putting up a brave fight. The battle was famously depicted in the Bayeux tapestry (pictured).

MEDIEVAL TO RENAISSANCE WARFARE

THE CAVALRY

Knights, their armor, and weapons are associated with the period between the Viking invasions and the Hundred Years' War (1337–1453). Knights were cavalrymen, mounted shock troops, who were deployed by most European peoples. The Normans and Crusaders both made use of cavalry in their campaigns and battles and a knight's armor was more than just protection; it was very much a status symbol. Many surviving suits of armor have been preserved as works of art. In battle a tight formation of cavalry, 20 horses wide, could move with immense force, like a battering ram against which few infantry could stand.

A huge variety of weapons would be used by knights and cavalry. There were many types of sword, both for use by cavalry and by foot soldiers for close hand-to-hand fighting. Originally the chief weapon of a knight would be a lance, but axes and maces were other favored weapons.

Many lethal weapons were developed that were designed to unseat cavalrymen, either by attacking the horse, or the rider. Once the man was on the ground he could usually be speedily dispatched.

Weapons and means of defense developed over the centuries. Various types of shield were popular at different times and these changed over the years depending on the weapons of the opposing army.

The longbow or war bow was used with devastating effect against men and horses. Although these weapons were used throughout Europe, it was only in England that the monarchy demanded regular practice from all able-bodied men. English archers were trained from boyhood and a volley-shooting technique was developed where large numbers of archers would fire arrows along a high trajectory at the rate of 15 arrows a minute. The sky turned dark as they rained down on the enemy, creating carnage. Crossbows were introduced in the 11th century and although they had the advantage of a longer range and greater effectiveness against armor, the war bow had a greater rate of fire.

Up to the 13th century, cavalry dominated the battlefield, whether they were the heavily armored horsemen of western Europe or the lighter-armored, fast-moving Mongol cavalry from the grasslands of Asia.

The Mongol armies, under their leader Genghis Khan, were a model of discipline and training. The armies were made up of about 60 per cent light cavalry, who wore little or no armor except a helmet. They were equipped with the powerful reflex bow and carried two quivers of arrows, a javelin, and a lasso. The heavy cavalry, about 40 per cent of the army usually wore complete armor made of leather and later mail captured from defeated enemies, in addition to a basic helmet. Their horses were also equipped with some protective leather armor; the main offensive weapon was the lance.

The Mongol Army, having first successfully invaded China, moved westward toward Europe conquering Russia and parts of Central Europe. The army never exceeded 150,000 men in total, but moved with a speed and efficiency that would be difficult for even a modern army to match.

RETURN OF THE INFANTRY

During the 13th and 14th Centuries new trends emerged which saw a return of the infantry soldier to dominate the battlefield. The Battle of Crécy, in 1346, is considered by many as symptomatic of this change; here the dreaded English longbow was instrumental in destroying a French army of almost 60,000. Most were disabled or killed in an area between 50 yards and 400 yards in front of the English line. There are no accurate figures but it is thought that French losses were more than 21,000 compared with some 200 on the English side. Offensive power was now in the hands of the infantry; archers backed by disciplined men-at-arms could now dominate the battlefield. The role of the cavalry was to complete the victory if and when required. It is also possible that Crécy saw the first use of gunpowder weapons. These spread rapidly and by the beginning of the 15th century were part of the equipment of almost every European army.

The formula for gunpowder had been perfected by the Chinese by the middle of the 9th century AD and within the next 200 years they had harnessed this explosive and developed the first guns, but the first true cannons did not appear until the 13th century.

By the beginning of the 14th century the ability to manufacture cannons had arrived in Europe. These early weapons were deployed on the battlefield alongside the traditional catapults. Early artillery was noisy and exciting but capable of little else. However, development continued and by the middle of the 15th century cannon had replaced the catapult over most of northern Europe.

By the beginning of the 16th century, recognizable field artillery had appeared.

AMERICAN VENTURES

On 7 June 1494, a treaty was signed between Spain and Portugal establishing a line that would give Spain exclusive rights of exploration and colonization on its western side, while

BATTLE OF CRÉCY
The English army, led by Edward III of England, was victorious at the Battle of Crécy, despite being outnumbered by the French by up to 2,000 men. The English victory is generally attributed to the superior weaponry used, which included the deadly English longbow, effective even when used against armored cavalry.

The battle, which took place in 1346 in Crécy, northern France, was one of the most significant battles of the Hundred Years' War between France and England.

Portugal would have the same rights to the east. For the first time since the Crusades, Europeans had made military decisions beyond their homeland. Around this time the Aztec Empire controlled all of Southern and Central Mexico and parts of Central America. Hernan Cortés attacked this immense domain with a force of 600 men, 17 horses and 10 cannon. He quickly overcame local tribes, which he turned into allies before marching on the Aztec capital. Here, Montezuma, the Aztec Emperor, allowed him to enter, thus giving the Spaniard virtual control of the city. This was the first example of a number of European military dominations of the peoples of the New World.

THE WAR AT SEA

The Europeans began putting guns in ships that had a trans-ocean capability. This development fundamentally changed war at sea. From classical times enemy ships closed for action with each crew boarding the enemy or attacking from very close range. Now, led by the English, maritime countries built galleons, ships that could bombard the enemy to a standstill then close-in to capture or destroy the enemy vessel.

IMPROVED INFANTRY WEAPONS

Meanwhile back in Europe, the Continent was transforming itself into a bloody proving ground of advancing technology. Gustavus Adolphus, King of Sweden 1611–32, transformed the musket. He redesigned the weapon to weigh as little as 11 pounds and also adopted the cartridge, which was a measure of gunpowder with the ball attached. The result was the infantry now had a weapon that was lighter, easier to handle, easier to load and with a rate of fire of one round per minute. The pikeman was entirely replaced by the musketeer and disappeared from the military scene.

Gustavus Adolphus also influenced the deployment of artillery, redesigning the artillery pieces in detail and insisting on three sizes of weapons: 3-pounder regimental guns, 12-pounders and 24-pounders. Contract mercenary gunners were replaced by professionally trained cannoneers.

KINGS AND REVOLUTIONS

MILITARY STRUCTURE

The Thirty Years' War provided a major turning point in warfare and military organization. The basic infantry unit consisted of around 500 men and was called a battalion by the French, a term that persists to the present day. Three battalions became a regiment to be commanded by a colonel, and the battalion by a lieutenant colonel; companies by captains and smaller units by lieutenants. Officers, usually drawn from the upper or educated classes, had completed their evolution from chivalric knight and marched at the head of armies still drawn from a largely rural society. Science and technology continued to develop, providing accurate clocks, telescopes and maps that were increasingly important for coordinating military campaigns.

PROFESSIONAL ARMIES

The traditional mercenary troops were gradually being phased out in favor of standing professional armies. After 1648 this trend intensified with France emerging as the dominant political, military, and cultural force in Europe. Forms of conscription began to emerge.

Through the wars of the early part of the 17th century, there emerged a new culture of militarism. Military colleges were established all over Europe including specialist colleges, such as the French Royal Corps of Artillery, which opened in 1679. It was from these colleges that practical courses on the study of warfare emerged.

The medieval castle with its high curtain walls was now vulnerable to artillery. These were adapted and became forts with a low profile, thick walls and ditches. They were equipped with their own permanent guns and crossing lines of fire to discourage infantry attack. Notable architects and military engineers constructed massive defensive works aimed at dominating and protecting strategically important points.

NORTH AMERICA

Warfare in the Americas was driven either by expanding European colonies at the expense of the native peoples, or as a consequence of war between rival nations in Europe being carried over to their respective colonial possessions.

Apart from the Spanish conquest of the Aztec and Inca empires, few formal armies were encountered. From north to south the Americas presented an immense variety of tribes and cultures, all with differing levels of military or fighting skills, which were usually adapted to their immediate environment.

The relative simplicity of the native peoples' weapons left them at some disadvantage when facing Europeans, but knowledge of their environment, together with hunting skills, went some way to restoring the balance.

The colonies were encouraged by their political masters back in Europe to defend themselves. Britain and France maintained few regular troops in North America and the early settlers therefore developed a militia system. In 1643 Massachusetts instituted compulsory military training for all males and most other colonies followed suit. Their initial composition was two-thirds musketeers and one-third pikemen, but the pike soon proved itself useless in the conditions prevailing on the frontier and was rapidly discarded. There was also a cavalry element of the militia and although it was almost useless in the dense forest of the region, it remained the most prestigious branch of the militia in which to serve. The native tribes' military operations usually consisted of the raid, surprise attack, or ambush but their inability to maintain long-term discipline and their reluctance to exploit tactical victories placed them at a great disadvantage when facing colonial forces. The rare exception was the Iroquois Confederacy, which produced an ordered form of military and political organization. They also developed assault tactics, which, together with the cult of personal bravery, proved difficult for many part-time colonial militias to face.

THE GROWTH OF EUROPEAN POWER

During the 18th century, Europe had emerged preeminent in world affairs. Only three non-European military powers still existed: the Ottoman Empire, Mogul India and Manchu China. None of these states had transoceanic military reach, and all were declining in power. In Europe, Britain, France, Spain, Russia, Portugal, and the Netherlands all to a greater or lesser degree enjoyed intercontinental reach, Russia by land, the rest by sea.

BRITANNIA RULES THE WAVES

Sea warfare and naval issues became dominated by Britain, whose unchallenged position is almost unmatched in subsequent history. The galleon had become a ship of the line. This required opposing fleets to sail in a single column on parallel courses and each ship in the fleet would attempt to engage its opposite number. Ships fired broadside after broadside until one side gave in and "struck their colors." Britain's domination of the seas was based on nautical experience and tradition and by its numerical superiority in fighting ships. Each ship was equipped with multitiered broadside batteries that allowed her to fight it out in the line of battle. The ships averaged around 2000 tons each and were about 200 feet in length, into which were packed up to 1000 men. They carried between 64 and 100 guns. Beyond the line of battleships were frigates; of lighter construction and carrying between 20 and 40 guns, these vessels were built for reconnaissance, screening, and commerce raiding. Beyond these

NAVAL MIGHT
Multi-decked sailing ships known as galleons were used by European nations throughout the 16th and 18th centuries. By the 18th century Britain was far ahead of the competition when it came to its naval might, using ships of the line that could hold up to 1000 men and 100 guns.

Made largely of oak, these warships were expensive to construct and equip but their effectiveness in the line of battle and as a projection of power on behalf of their owners was priceless.

13

came smaller ships of war designed for local defense, escorts, and specialist missions. Living conditions on board these overcrowded warships were harsh in the extreme.

EUROPEAN ARMIES—THE SWEDISH EXAMPLE

Land warfare in the first half of the 18th century rested on the example of Gustavus Adolphus, but changing social conditions in 18th-century Europe began to exert an influence on the prevailing military systems. The beginnings of the Industrial Revolution influenced the available manpower for the recruitment of armies. Although officers continued to be recruited from the nobility, ordinary soldiers were now generally being recruited from the unemployed and unproductive. Once recruited, these men were subject to a fierce discipline that involved complete mental and physical control. This was regarded as the only way for recruits to be made into soldiers. They would enjoy little freedom and almost no leave. Major engagements were infrequent. However, when battles did occur, as at Blenheim in 1704, they were generally fought with a bloody tenacity that produced very high casualty figures.

THE NEW PRUSSIAN ARMY

Frederick II was crowned King of Prussia on 21 May 1740. He inherited a reasonable-sized typical army of the day and within seven months he marched into Silesia, beginning the War of the Austrian Succession. Although defeated in this campaign, he gained the territory by treaty in 1742. With an expanded Prussia, Frederick forged ahead with economic reforms in agriculture and manufacturing, but it is his reforms

in the army for which he is best remembered. Through incessant drill, the individual Prussian soldier merged into a disciplined unit that was maneuverable on the battlefield, being able to move seamlessly into battle formation from a marching column over almost any terrain. A Prussian soldier could load and fire his musket at twice the rate of any enemy. Frederick the Great was enthusiastic in encompassing all military developments into his army, abandoning reliance on the military supply depot; Prussian soldiers carried three days' rations in their knapsacks with a further eight days' supply in the regimental train and up to a month's supply in the army trains. Modern armies had now developed a far more sophisticated, disciplined, all-arms capability that could be sustained on campaign for much longer periods.

THE EFFECTS OF THE AMERICAN WAR OF INDEPENDENCE

The American War of Independence of 1776 was the culmination of a series of irreconcilable differences between Britain and her North American colonies. Although the war was not particularly revolutionary in military ideas or practice, the Americans realized that a disciplined regular force would need to be created if the British were to be defeated. The Americans, though proud of their dedication to liberty and republicanism, were pragmatic enough to accept help from the French King Louis XVI.

This war provided the French with a great opportunity to seek revenge after the Seven Years' War, when Britain had succeeded in dismantling much of France's overseas empire and almost all of France's North American territories had fallen into British hands.

The war formally ended with signing of the Treaty of Paris in 1783. The War of Independence had succeeded.

THE FRENCH REVOLUTION AND ITS AFTERMATH

The French Revolution of 1789 also had an enormous effect on the world. Following the Revolution, France found herself with many enemies. Napoleon Bonaparte had been appointed Commander of the Army for the Interior and he first moved against the Piedmontese in 1796, knocking them out of the war at the Battle of Mondovi on 21 April. Under his command, the French Army of Italy went on to drive the Austrians out of Lombardy. Napoleon then began to advance on Vienna, at which point the Austrians sued for peace.

Two years later, following a coup d'etât on 9 November 1799, Napoleon Bonaparte declared himself First Consul, effectively becoming dictator of France and enjoying complete

REVOLUTIONARY FERVOR
The French Revolution officially began in May 1789 with the meeting of the States General, but not until the Bastille was stormed in October did the Revolution begin in earnest. King Louis XVI was not executed until January 1793, some four years later.

All able-bodied men were requisitioned to defend the nation under an edict known as the "levée en masse." Although it was not popular, it increased the size of the French army sufficiently to turn the tide of the war in the Revolution's favor.

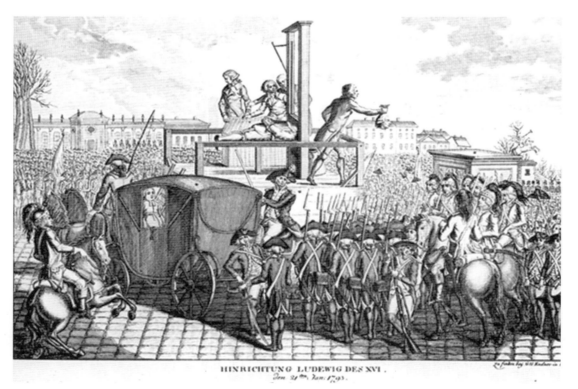

HINRICHTUNG LUDEWIG DES XVI.
Den 21ten Jan. 1793.

NAPOLEONIC REIGN
After declaring himself First
Consul of France in 1799,
Napoleon Bonaparte began
to develop increasingly
sophisticated methods of
war making.
   Bonaparte was victorious in
many campaigns. He started by
defeating the Austrians at the
Battle of Marengo, but was
finally defeated by the British
and their allies at the Battle
of Waterloo

control of the State. He developed innovative techniques of war making. These were clearly demonstrated in his early campaigns in Italy and Egypt. Although he never committed his ideas to paper, from his remarks and writings it has been possible to collate a number of his ideas on tactics and strategy. He always attempted to develop plans that suited each campaign, thus keeping his enemies off-balance and never knowing what to expect.

Wherever possible, Napoleon tried to seize control of a campaign before the first engagement was ever fought. Using a combination of deception and rapid marching he would attempt to move around the enemy's flanks and to seize the hostile line of communication, then maneuver to make the enemy fight at a disadvantage.

Napoleon would keep his forces spread out until the last possible moment, then rapidly concentrate them at a critical point. This also deceived his enemies, whose military strength almost always exceeded his own. Another of Napoleon's favored moves was to concentrate his army between two opposing armies, then defeat each in turn, but this particular move proved to be a spectacular failure at the Battle of Waterloo in 1815.

WARFARE IN THE INDUSTRIAL AGE

THE ADVANCE OF MILITARY TECHNOLOGY

In the post-Napoleonic era, steam power became critical in strategic planning. First there was a race to build the best and most powerful steam-driven ship. In 1858 the French launched the first – screw-driven, steam-powered, and iron clad. Three years later the British launched HMS *Warrior*, which was even more powerful. This still had guns down each side, but within a few years rotating turrets were developed. Warships were also now firing explosive shells.

On land the spread of railways, together with the electric telegraph, had an effect upon both strategy and tactics. By 1860 railways had spread across most of Europe and the eastern half of North America, and were beginning to make an appearance in other parts of the world. Railways enabled commanders to move their armies swiftly when required. Growing industrial capacity and technology provided better weapons and equipment that could be mass-produced for the ever-expanding armies.

A leader in the development of this new technology was the United States, but the Americans at that time saw no need for a professional army. It was considered that a citizen militia was quite sufficient.

THE AMERICAN EXPERIENCE

Between 1815 and 1846, the US Army mainly fought Indian and frontier wars, but in 1846–47 the United States found itself at war with Mexico. This proved to be a major training ground for officers who would be in senior positions at the beginning of the Civil War 14 years later.

When the Civil War began, the South had about half as many small arms, cannons, and military equipment as the North, but in spite of this they managed to keep their troops relatively well-armed throughout the war. The Union's overwhelming industrial might and greater source of manpower made the outcome of the war largely inevitable and the South's only real hope was to inflict enough casualties on the Union to make it sue for peace.

In the first year the South seemed to be at the height of its success, but in reality the war was steadily draining the Confederacy of its limited resources. The battlefront continued to swing to-and-fro, with each battle bringing thousands more casualties. The number of replacements available to the South was beginning to dry up.

At the Battle of Gettysburg in July 1863, despite Southern hopes of victory, they suffered a massive defeat losing 28,000 out of their 70,000-strong army and the Confederacy's fortunes withered away.

The armies of the Civil War were gigantic when compared with armies of the past: the North had fielded almost 2.2 million soldiers and the South 900,000. This represented one-tenth of all Americans and total deaths came to 665,000.

THE CRIMEAN WAR

Meanwhile in Europe a war began in 1854 between Russia on one side and the Ottoman Empire, Britain and France on the other. This war was centered on the little-known Crimean peninsula on the Black Sea, and for the first time war reporters were able to telegraph dispatches back to their papers. The result was a major outcry, particularly in Britain, at the way the troops were being treated, especially the wounded. During the war some 252,000 allied soldiers lost their lives, more than half of these from neglect and disease.

THE RISE OF GREATER GERMANY

In Germany Bismarck had created and consolidated the North German Confederation and wished to place a Hohenzollern Prince on the Spanish throne. Napoleon III of France regarded this as an anti-French threat and, believing the French Army to be invincible, on 15th July 1870 he declared war on Prussia. German mobilization followed a well-conceived plan using Germany's railway network to the full. German artillery was available in large numbers and manned by extremely well-trained troops, so the French had no real chance.

Between 2 and 12 August, German armies consistently defeated the French in every battle. Napoleon, shaken by these defeats, relinquished command and moved to the fortress town of Verdun. The Prussians outmaneuvered the French and Napoleon III was forced to surrender. The Second Empire crumbled and a provisional government was set up.

On 15 January 1871 the bombardment of Paris began and France sought terms of surrender. On 10 May the Treaty of Frankfurt was signed and France was forced to give up the provinces of Alsace and Lorraine to the new German Empire.

COLONIAL CONFLICTS

European colonial armies continued to extend their territory and put down the occasional rebellion.

In South Africa conflict arose between the British and the Boer states of the Orange Free State and the South African Republic. For the first time the British met with concentrated, well-aimed rifle fire from a highly mobile force, which had the ability to inflict heavy casualties on the generally slower-moving British columns. Although the British outnumbered the Boers by about 12 to 1, it still took two years and eight months to subdue the Boer States.

NAVAL DEVELOPMENTS

The steamers of the Royal Navy were now a major force in the world. To support the fleet, a chain of coaling stations and a fleet of colliers were set up, enabling the Navy to operate anywhere in the world and never be far from a source of fuel. Meanwhile the German Kaiser was developing a German battle fleet and this posed a particular threat to Britain's interests.

In the Far East, the Japanese launched a surprise attack on a Russian fleet at anchor in Port Arthur. The Russians sent their Baltic Fleet to aid their stricken Pacific Fleet. After a seven-month voyage they met the Japanese Fleet. The Russian ships were very quickly battered and put out of action in a crushing defeat.

ORIGIN OF WORLD WAR I

The Balkan conflict was rumbling on, but it was only after the heir to the Austro-Hungarian throne was assassinated in Serbia on 28 June 1914 that a crisis developed.

The outraged Empire of Austria-Hungary delivered an ultimatum to Serbia on 23 July; Serbia mobilized on 25 July. Three days later, the Austro-Hungarians declared war. Russia followed, declaring war against Austria. On 1 August Germany declared war on Russia and in accordance with her own Schlieffen Plan, mobilized in preparation for an invasion of the West, that would pass through the neutral states of Belgium and Luxembourg. Germany also declared war against France on 3 August. Britain declared war on Germany on 4 August, initially in protection of neutral Belgium. Catching up with events, Austria-Hungary now declared war on Russia on 6 August. Italy remained neutral, stating that her alliance was void because the Austrians had initiated the war.

Germany's Schlieffen plan was designed to cope with a war on two fronts. Russia would be slower to mobilize, so would be held in check in the east, while the major part of the German army would be thrown against France in the west. Most of the German field forces would move through Belgium and the Netherlands, thus enveloping the entire French army. The advancing spearhead would then pass just west of Paris and turn eastward attacking the remaining French forces in the rear. The concluding part of the German campaign would be to drive the French army against prepared positions in Alsace-Lorraine. While this was being carried out, the small forces deployed in East Russia would slowly give ground in the face of a Russian advance, buying time for a German victory in the west. As soon as this had been achieved, the bulk of the German armies in the west would be transferred to the east using its excellent railway system and the Russians would be defeated by another systematic campaign.

THE BEGINNINGS OF THE WESTERN FRONT

The initial offensive by the French armies was thrown back in

TRENCH WARFARE
A British photographer is thought to have taken this picture of Australian soldiers by a breastwork trench near the French town of Amentiéres. World War I is remembered for its trench warfare, which resulted in long and arduous campaigns and catastrophic losses on both sides. Conventional transport infrastructure, such as roads and railroads were eschewed in favor of a network of trenches and tramlines.

Frontline trenches were typically about 7 ft deep and 6 ft wide and the front of a trench was known as a parapet, where sandbags would be piled up to absorb bullets and shrapnel.

The bottoms of the trenches were lined with duckboards in an effort to prevent disease and afflictions, such as trench foot, but conditions were frequently wet and insanitary.

disorder with shocking loss of life. On 23rd August, a small British Expeditionary Force came into contact with the German 1st Army. Though outnumbered, The British fought back fiercely, using its famous rate of aimed rifle fire to take a terrible toll on the massed German ranks.

What became known as the Battle of the Marne began around 2.30 in the afternoon on 5 September, but there was to be no swift victory for the Germans as envisaged by the original Schlieffen Plan. From the middle of September both sides attempted to outflank each other, extending their operations northward to the Channel coast. The Western Front settled down along the lines that it would occupy for the next four years.

IN THE EAST

On the Eastern Front, the Russian army had advanced into East Prussia but thanks to uncoded radio signals the Germans had an extremely good idea of Russian dispositions. The Germans completely destroyed the Russian 2nd Army before turning northeast and destroying the Russian 1st Army. Between 26 August and 14 September 1914, the Russian armies lost approximately 250,000 men and 650 guns and approximately half of their transport; German losses were around 40,000.

TURKEY JOINS IN

On 29 October 1914, the Ottoman Empire declared war, joining Germany and Austria-Hungary. With access to its Black Sea ports now in enemy hands, Russia was now effectively isolated from the south and there was much pressure to attack Turkey to open the Dardanelles and restore communications to Russia.

On 25 April 1915 the Allies landed a hastily gathered force of largely Australian and New Zealand troops on the Gallipoli peninsula. The Allies, suffering from poor command and control, failed to reach their objectives. Further landings were made in August and these turned out to be equally unsuccessful. Lacking real commitment and supply from Allied High Command and also lacking capable command on the spot, the operation failed. On 23rd November the new Commander's recommendation for evacuation was approved. Casualties for the campaign amounted to 251,000 Turkish and 252,000 Allied soldiers.

MOUNTING LOSSES ON THE WESTERN FRONT

Along the Western Front, the Allies launched various offensives, none of which achieved any great success; tiny amounts of land exchanged hands usually for horrific losses of men. During 1915 German losses reached 615,000; French and British together totalled around 1,579,000.

THE FIRST AIR RAIDS

The night of 19 January 1915 saw the first German air raids on Britain. These were launched by Zeppelin airships under command of the German navy. Though they caused relatively minor casualties and damage, the effect on the British population was out of all proportion. Great anger developed among the population at what were seen as barbaric attacks. There would be 18 further air raids during the year.

ITALY JOINS IN

On 23 May Italy declared war on Austria, seeking to gain territory from the Austro-Hungarian Empire, but by the end of the year none of its strategic objectives had been achieved.

BACK IN THE EAST

On the Eastern Front, Russian losses in 1915 reached more than two million, of whom around half became prisoners. The Central Powers suffered just over one million casualties.

THE U-BOAT WAR

In February 1915 an unlimited German submarine campaign was launched against merchant ships operating in British waters. On 7 May, the British luxury liner *Lusitania* was torpedoed without warning off the Irish coast. Among the 1000 casualties were 124 Americans. Feeling ran high in the United States where the US Government issued a strongly worded protest to the German Government. However, submarine warfare continued until mid-August, when the sinking of the British liner *Arabic* involved the death of yet more Americans. American feelings became so hostile that Germany announced the cessation of unlimited submarine warfare, however, by this time almost one million tons of Allied ships had been sent to the seafloor.

HEAVY FIGHTING ON THE WESTERN FRONT

The year 1916 witnessed two gigantic battles on the Western Front. On 21 February, a huge German attack was launched in the vicinity of Verdun. Although the battle lasted until November, at the finish there had been virtually no change in the front line. True casualty figures will never be known, but the Germans lost approximately 434,000 soldiers, and the French approximately 544,000.

About halfway through the Battle of Verdun, on 1 July, the first Battle of the Somme was launched. After a massive seven-day artillery barrage, the British advanced from their trenches following a supporting curtain of shellfire. By the end of the first day the British Army had lost 60,000 men, the greatest loss in its history. In spite of these horrific losses,

British reserves continued to move forward. The British used tanks for the first time, but these were underpowered and unreliable. In November the battle ground to a halt. The British and French both claimed substantial territorial gains, but these amounted to as little as 8 miles. British losses were 427,000, the French lost 195,000, and the Germans lost an appalling total of 650,000, mostly in endless counterattacks to retake lost ground.

RUSSIA'S 1916 OFFENSIVE

From early June to the end of September Russia launched a massive offensive over a 300-mile front. The offensive finally petered out as ammunition shortages and sheer exhaustion began to tell on the Russian army. This was perhaps the most successful Russian offensive of the war; it had severely weakened Austria and would have even knocked Austria out of the war had it not been for German reinforcements at the last moment. Although the Russians had lost more than one million casualties, the rickety Empire of Austria-Hungary lost a similar number. This defeat was a major contributory factor to the Empire's eventual disintegration.

THE BATTLE OF JUTLAND

On 30 May 1916 the German High Seas Fleet put to sea, but the British soon picked up its unguarded radio chatter. The German Fleet had 21 battleships and battle cruisers with 6 older battleships and 72 other major vessels, while the British had 37 battleships and battle cruisers with 114 other ships in support.

This led to the only great fleet action of World War I, which became known as the Battle of Jutland. The British lost 3 battle cruisers and 11 other warships and the Germans lost one battleship, one battle cruiser, and 9 other ships.

From now on the main German naval effort concentrated on submarine operations, where a horrifying toll was taken on British and Allied shipping; losses reaching 300,000 tons per month by December 1916.

THE ENTRY OF THE UNITED STATES

Despite the losses experienced in 1916, the Allies had grown relatively stronger by early 1917 and had agreed to give priority to the Western Front. The new French commander began planning a gigantic Allied offensive.

German High Command became aware of the Allies' preparations and adopted a defensive posture. It also approved the resumption of unrestricted submarine warfare. This angered the American Government and on 3 February the United States severed diplomatic relations with Germany.

The last straw came on 1 March when the Zimmermann note was published. This proposed an alliance between Germany and Mexico, with a promise to assist Mexico in recovering former Mexican territories lost to America in the war of 1846–1847. This was too much for the Americans and on 6 April 1917 the United States declared war on Germany and Austria-Hungary. Immediately, the United States mobilized hundreds of thousands of men, with a long-range plan to have three million men in Europe by 1918.

MORE SET-PIECE BATTLES

The British launched the Battle of Arras on 9th April 1917, which was a preliminary to the grand French offensive that was launched on 16–20 April. The French attacked with 1,200,000 men supported by 7000 guns. The French Infantry managed to capture the German first line but that is where they stopped. The whole plan turned out to be a colossal failure with French losses of almost 120,000.

On 24 October the Central Powers launched a new offensive on the Italian Front. Though the Italians were badly shaken by this offensive, losing 40,000 battle casualties and 275,000 prisoners, they managed to hold the line as French and British reinforcements arrived.

THE RUSSIANS GO BUT THE AMERICANS ARRIVE

In March the Russian Revolution began with the mutiny of the Petrograd garrison. By the end of October the Bolsheviks, led by Lenin and Trotsky, succeeded in seizing power and opened peace negotiations with Germany. By 15 December, the armistice of Brest-Litovsk had been agreed, ending the war on the Eastern Front.

The year 1917 ended with Russia out of the war and the United States in the war. The German High Command realized their last hope of winning the war would be a decisive victory in the West but that this must be achieved before new American armies could operate on the battlefield. With peace on the Eastern Front, large numbers of German troops could be transferred to the West. It would be these troops who would spearhead a series of planned attacks stretching from the Channel coast almost to Verdun.

The first attack was launched on 21 March and for two months it looked as though this strategy might have been successful, but on 28 May the first American division arrived. This proved the turning point. Further American divisions stopped the German advance and by July the Americans were arriving at the rate of 300,000 a month, by which time the German forces were exhausted.

By October the German Army had begun to fall apart. With its armies in retreat, disorders at home and mutiny in the High Seas Fleet, Germany requested an armistice and terms were agreed, becoming effective at 11.00 a.m. on 11 November 1918.

AFTERMATH

A feature of World War I was the amazing growth in air power. In 1914 the British Royal Flying Corps was a group of enthusiastic amateurs numbering 1429 men and 63 aircraft. By 1918 it had become the Royal Air Force made up of some 292,000 men and 22,000 aircraft. The formation of the RAF recognized that now, not only was there a capability of maintaining air superiority over the battlefield but also the ability to reach out over enemy lines of supply and to its industrial bases beyond.

This "War to End All Wars" had seen the mobilization of more than 65,000,000 men, of whom about 8,000,000 were killed and 21,000,000 wounded. The war officially ended with the signing of the Treaty of Versailles in 1919.

THE RISE OF THE NAZIS

There was little or no consultation with Germany about the terms of the Treaty and when these became known, particularly the acceptance of war guilt and the loss of territory, many Germans were astounded. A myth grew that the country had been "stabbed in the back" by defeatist Germans. When the Nazis came to power, demands for restitution soon arose. The Nazis speeded up the rearmament programme and in March 1936 Hitler reoccupied the demilitarized Rhineland. In 1938, after stage-managing a union between Austria and Germany, Hitler demanded the annexation of the German-speaking borderlands of Czechoslovakia, the Sudetenland. The alarmed Western Allies had no wish for another major

European war and agreed. Sudetenland was occupied in October 1938 and the rest of Czechoslovakia was swallowed without negotiation in March 1939.

In the East, Japan continued to develop expansionist policies having been at war with China since 1933. Italy had begun a policy of expansion with its invasion of Abyssinia in 1936. Germany, Italy and Japan created a global military alliance, the Rome–Berlin–Tokyo Axis, which would ultimately connect wars in Europe, Africa, and Asia, and eventually draw in the majority of sovereign nations of the world.

WARFARE IN THE TECHNOLOGICAL AGE

WORLD WAR II

On 1 September 1939, Germany launched its invasion of Poland in the first demonstration of the technique of *Blitzkrieg*, or "lightning war."

By 3 September, with large areas of Poland overrun, the Western Allies declared war and mobilized. On 17 September, in line with a previous arrangement between Germany and the Soviet Union, the Red Army attacked eastern Poland. Although in a hopeless situation, Poland resisted until 5 October. Many thousands of Poles escaped, determined to fight on.

For several months very little happened in the West. This period was called the Phoney War. Germany needed raw materials for its war effort so in April 1940 Hitler decided to occupy both Denmark and Norway. Denmark was occupied with relative ease, but in Norway the Germans met Allied forces intent on the same objectives. However, the Allies, faced by an army with better air support, better equipment, and better training, had no option other than to evacuate on 9 June 1940.

Meanwhile, on 10 May, the German assault on the West had been launched, crossing the Dutch and Belgian frontiers. Within four days the Netherlands fell, following the brutal bombing of Rotterdam. The Germans moved with great speed through the "impassable" Ardennes and on 16 May they turned west toward the Channel coast, which they reached on 21 May. The Belgians surrendered on 27 May while the British began an evacuation from the beaches and harbour of Dunkirk. By 4 June, 338,000 Allied soldiers, two-thirds of them British, had been rescued.

The Germans now concentrated on completing the conquest of France and 16 days later, despite desperate resistance, France surrendered on 21st June.

BRITAIN ALONE

Britain now stood alone, expecting invasion at almost any time but despite her seemingly impossible position, she still

THE WAR AT SEA
During the course of the Second World War the balance of power at sea changed from the large armored warship to the aircraft carrier. At the beginning of hostilities Germany had no aircraft carriers available, they chose to deploy a large submarine force and surface raiders, some disguised merchant ships others like the *Scharnhorst*, classic gun-armed battlecruisers. This ship, commissioned in 1939 met her end in one of the few big gun actions of World War Two. She was sunk by *HMS Duke of York* and the accompanying cruisers *Norfolk, Jamaica* and *Belfast* when attempting to intercept an allied convoy off northern Norway on the 26th December 1943.

SCHARNHORST
Germany - BB
(GNEISENAU Class)
(1939)

held two major trump cards: the seas around her shores were controlled by the most powerful navy in the world; and the Royal Air Force, backed by its remarkable radar-equipped command and control system, commanded British airspace.

In order to be successful, a German invasion would have to beat both the Royal Navy and the Royal Air Force and would still be faced with having to transport a large force over the unpredictable waters of the English Channel. In spite of this, on 5 June Hitler made the decision that Britain was to be invaded. The first phase of the battle, aimed at gaining air superiority over England, began in mid-July with attacks on Channel targets and early assaults on coastal airfields. Radar-directed British fighters almost always intercepted these. From 24 August, the Germans shifted their main targets to British airfields. This was the critical phase of the battle. After some bombs probably mistakenly fell on London, British bombers retaliated by bombing Berlin. Hitler and Goering were infuriated and shifted their targets from British airfields to Britain's cities in general and London in particular. From 7 to 30 September, London was attacked continuously. This actually simplified the defense arrangements for the British because they could concentrate resources in a smaller area, bringing a relatively greater firepower to bear on the German bomber formations and their fighter escorts. By the end of this period, German losses were so great that the daylight-bombing offensive was called off.

Hitler suspended invasion plans and finally cancelled the operation altogether on 12th October 1940.

Britain had survived, though for many months she would face the nightly bomber raids known as "the Blitz" and a protracted battle in the Atlantic against German submarines.

AFRICA AND THE MEDITERRANEAN

On 11 November, the British launched a daring air attack by 21 aircraft from the carrier H.M.S. *Illustrious* against the Italian naval base of Taranto. This one attack restored British naval supremacy in the Mediterranean and pointed the way for the development of carrier-borne air power.

In Africa, the British had enjoyed considerable success against the Italian Empire, first liberating Ethiopia before driving the Italians back into Libya. Italy's poor performance persuaded Hitler to send reinforcements and Rommel arrived at the Italian-held port of Tripoli, where he organized his soon-to-be-famous Afrika Corps.

In the Balkans, German forces invaded Yugoslavia and Greece and on 20 May 1941 launched the first major airborne-led assault in history on the island of Crete. Regardless of heavy casualties, the Germans managed to capture an airfield and

immediately flew in supplies and further troops. The Royal Navy had managed to hold back attempts to send reinforcements by sea, but German air superiority and the absolute determination of the airborne troops decided the outcome of the battle. The British withdrew most of their forces and the remaining units surrendered on 31 May. Though the operation was successful from the German point of view, Hitler was so shocked at the loss of life in his elite airborne division that he never again ordered an airborne assault on a comparable scale.

THE EASTERN FRONT

On 21st June 1941, the largest invasion army in history assembled along the western borders of Soviet Russia. The Germans, together with Finnish, Romanian, and Hungarian units had amassed almost 3.6 million men with some 3600 tanks and almost 2800 aircraft. Facing them was a Soviet army of approximately 2.9 million strong with somewhere between 10,000 and 19,000 tanks, though many were obsolete. There was also the Red Air Force of some 8000 aircraft, though this was in the process of being reequipped.

To begin with the Red Army responded slowly and ineffectively and the German army managed massive offensives led by the four main Panzer groups. Although it soon became clear that a major problem was going to be maintaining lines of supply, in the first few weeks the Germans achieved vast encirclements and captured hundreds of thousands of Soviet prisoners. In spite of these massive losses, the Soviets seemed to have vast reserves of manpower and there was no collapse.

Although beset by supply problems, German units continued deep into Russia. One group was slowly approached Leningrad and another group was aimed at Moscow, but at this point Hitler changed his policy. Moscow was "put on hold," with one of the Panzer groups being sent south to support the army that was approaching Kiev and another being sent to aid the advance toward Leningrad.

By the end of October, after fighting a battle where they took around 667,000 Russian prisoners, the Germans reached the Crimea and the River Don.

In the north, Leningrad was now under siege. In the center, after another change of emphasis, Hitler ordered an all-out effort on Moscow. At this point the weather changed. Heavy rains slowed the German advance giving the Russians time to bring up reserves.

Before long the Russian winter had arrived. The Germans were completely unprepared for this. On 5 December 1941 the Soviets launched their offensive and in bitter weather both sides fought to the death. Little by little the Soviet forces gained ground and the German commanders asked Hitler for permission to fall back. Hitler's response was to sack them all and on 19 December he took command of the army himself.

THE AMERICAN ENTRY

In March 1941 President Roosevelt approved the Lend Lease Act in which the United States could provide services and supplies to any country considered to be vital to the defense of the still neutral United States.

Toward the end of the year, at the beginning of December, a Japanese Carrier Fleet was sailing in great secrecy towards the US Pacific base at Pearl Harbor in Hawaii. The United States Navy was the only real threat to Japan's ambitions in the Pacific and the logic was that by wiping out this fleet Japan would gain enough time to seize the territory containing the strategic supplies it so desperately needed.

The air attack was launched at 7.40 a.m. on Sunday, 7 December 1941. By the end of the attack, the Japanese Carrier Fleet had lost only 29 aircraft, but had inflicted horrific damage on the American fleet, sinking 6 battleships, 3 light cruisers, 3 destroyers, and damaging several more ships. By coincidence the US Carrier Fleet was absent on the day of the attack, which was fortunate, because it would be from this fleet that the American counteroffensive would be launched.

America was instantly united in its desire to defeat what it saw as a deceitful and vicious enemy. Due to the alliance between Japan, Italy, and Germany, when the US declared war on Japan it immediately became part of the European War. This war was now truly global.

The day after the Pearl Harbor attack the Japanese launched their campaign against Malaya, the Dutch East Indies, and the Philippines. On 10 December, two major British warships were sunk off the coast of Malaya and by 15 February, the fortresses and bases of Singapore had fallen. Sixty-two thousand Allied troops were taken into Japanese captivity.

After a campaign of three months, virtually all of the Dutch East Indies and its valuable assets were in Japanese hands. Early in 1942 Burma fell, with British forces being driven back to, and sometimes beyond, the Indian border. The Japanese continued south toward the Solomon Islands and New Guinea. It was here that the first critical battle of the Pacific War was fought. This became known as the Battle of the Coral Sea. It was the first major naval engagement between two carrier forces and was the first sea battle where neither side saw each other. It was considered a tactical victory for Japan because American losses were greater, but it was a strategic victory for the Allies because it caused the Japanese to abandon their plans to take New Guinea.

THE 1942 RUSSIAN OFFENSIVE

With the arrival of the Russian spring, the German generals were hoping to take Moscow and bring the war in the East to a swift end, but Hitler had other ideas. He wanted the army to drive to Stalingrad, take the Caucasus oil fields, and eventually link up with Rommel's Afrika Corps. Toward the end of 1942, German forces had reached the foothills of the Caucasus Mountains and were fighting in the streets of Stalingrad. Despite this desperate situation, the Soviets refused to give in and, slowly, street-by-street, a truly horrific battle unfolded. By the time it was over only estimates of casualties could be made, but these came close to 850,000 German and 1,130,000 Soviet troops, making it the single most costly battle in human history.

MASS PRODUCTION

By 1942 the United States was producing arms on a massive scale. In addition to supplying at least part of the needs of Britain, its Commonwealth, and Soviet Russia, it was also building up its own strength for deployment in Europe and across the Pacific, but this immense productive effort still had to be delivered across thousands of miles of often-hostile oceans. Britain and Soviet Russia were also both producing weapons on a huge scale. Britain was producing thousands of bombers for its air war against Germany and the Soviet Union had reequipped its armies with the famous T-34 tank, which was being built in vast numbers. The Axis powers could not match this capacity no matter how hard they might try.

THE BATTLE OF KURSK

After holding the Germans at Moscow, driving them from the Caucasus and beating them at Stalingrad, the Soviets were growing in strength and confidence.

The area around Kursk then became the focus of attention. The Soviets, expecting an attack and determined not to lose any ground, packed the area with almost 1,300,000 troops ready for the Germans' launch of Operation Zitadelle on 5 July 1943. After brutal fighting the Germans advanced only a few miles and the battle developed into one of attrition and involved the biggest tank battle in history. On 12 July the Soviets launched their own offensive, but this coincided with Allied landings in Sicily and Hitler was persuaded to end the operation. Within days the Germans were in retreat.

ALLIED LANDINGS IN ITALY

In Africa Rommel had proved to be a master of mobile warfare, supporting his armored forces with motorized troops and air support. Although the Afrika Corps was finally placed on the defensive after the Allied victory at the Battle of el Alamein in

October 1942, it remained a thorn in the Allied side until it was finally driven out of Africa in May 1943 as the Allies were starting to prepare for their invasion of Sicily.

The invasion of Sicily was the first large-scale Allied landing on European territory and marked the beginning of a long and arduous campaign. After clearing Sicily in August 1943, there would be two major landings on the Italian mainland; Salerno in September and Anzio in January 1944. The armies continued north and on 4 June reached Rome. This was the first Axis capital to fall into Allied hands.

For a further 11 months the allies slogged on until they eventually linked up with Allied forces moving south from Germany on 4 May 1945.

THE AIR WAR AGAINST GERMANY

The war against enemy-held Europe in general and Germany in particular began as early as 1940. From its bases in Britain RAF Bomber Command slowly built up its strength. In the early days little impact was made, but gradually a series of tactics evolved that involved huge air raids. By 1942 Britain had launched its first 1000-bomber raid and in the same year the US deployed its 8th Air Force to Britain. With better aircraft and improved technology, the bombers managed to stay ahead of the ever-more sophisticated German air defense system. By 1943 some 10,000 flak guns served by 500,000 men and hundreds of fighter aircraft defended the Reich. Without the bomber campaign the bulk of these forces would undoubtedly have found their way to the battlefronts.

By 1944 US daylight raids were supported by a full fighter escort to and from the target. Although losses were reduced, there were still many bitter air battles to be endured. At night the RAF developed its own techniques. By late 1944 both air forces operating together had the power to "take out" any given target. The bombing of Germany remains controversial to this day. It did not beat the country into submission as many of its supporters had promised it would, but it played a decisive role in disrupting industrial production and tying down valuable resources that would otherwise have been used elsewhere.

THE BATTLE OF THE ATLANTIC

To keep Britain supplied with food, fuel and the raw materials for the war effort, the Atlantic supply lines had to be maintained. From 1940 to early 1943 the German U-boat force had the upper hand. Hunting in packs, they were able to decimate an intercepted convoy. Eventually the Allies developed the ability to read German codes, which enabled many convoys to be routed clear of U-boat concentrations.

New radar was developed, with more escort vessels equipped with better weapons. Long-range aircraft capable of patrolling the Atlantic sea-lanes were another important development. All of these finally controlled the U-boat menace, although it was never completely eliminated.

THE NORMANDY INVASION AND THE ADVANCE INTO GERMANY

The true invasion point of mainland Europe was a closely kept secret and a program of misinformation was devised to keep the enemy guessing. The final plan was to launch an invasion of Normandy. It called for combined airborne and seaborne landings over five beaches. By 5.30 a.m. on 6 June the invasion fleet lay off the coast and thousands of transports and landing craft closed with the beaches. After bitter fighting in some places, the troops were ashore.

By that evening there were 150,000 Allied troops in Normandy, and over the following weeks the German forces were driven back in a series of major battles. By September the German armies were in retreat and Paris, then Brussels, were liberated. During September Hitler had begun to prepare a counterattack in the west, which was launched on 16 December 1944. Initially American divisions were forced into a hasty retreat but resistance grew as reinforcements were rushed to the front. German supplies ran short and American counterattacks finally restored the front by 7 February 1945. In this defeat the Germans had lost their last reserve of armored and mobile troops in the west.

BATTLE ON THE GROUND Armored fighting vehicles, or "tanks," first appeared in the battlefield during World War I. Although they made a significant impact they were unreliable. By World War II tanks had reached a much greater level of sophistication. German tanks were largely inferior to opposition models at the beginning of the war, but after coming up against Soviet tanks during Operation Barbarossa they set about designing a new model, the Panzer V Panther, which was much more capable and reliable. On the British side, the Sherman tank prevailed, accompanied by the Cromwell, which was very fast, but undergunned and somewhat temperamental.

By March the western Allies were able to cross the Rhine. The road to Berlin lay open but it was the Soviets who got there first.

On 15th April 1945, just before dawn, 2.5 million Soviet soldiers, more than 6000 tanks, and 41,000 guns and mortars, supported by 7500 aircraft launched a series of huge attacks. Against this the Germans could only deploy the remains of 33 war-torn divisions. The Germans were in a hopeless situation and, despite fanatical resistance, on 25 April Berlin was surrounded. Hitler committed suicide on 30 April and Berlin officially surrendered on 2 May.

The war in Europe was almost over.

THE END IN THE FAR EAST

In August 1942 US forces had landed on Guadalcanal. Here the Japanese, at the extreme extent of their advance in the South Pacific, were constructing an airbase that could threaten communications between the US and Australia. In what was to be a hard fought and expensive campaign, the Americans emerged victorious. They then proceeded to drive the Japanese back, island by island. In spite of enormous casualty rates, the Americans slowly captured the islands. Once made secure, airfields could be put to use as the forward bases for B-29 bombers and in 1944 the bombing of the Japanese homeland began in earnest.

War in the Far East finally came to end with the dropping of atomic bombs on Hiroshima and Nagasaki, instantly killing hundreds of thousands of people. This new type of warfare was to become one of deterrent rather than direct action, sowing the seeds of the Cold War.

THE COLD WAR

The end of World War II also saw the separation of former Allies in to two ideological camps, one led by the United States and the other by the USSR.

NUCLEAR ATTACK
More than 73,000 people were killed when an atomic bomb was dropped on Nagasaki, Japan, on 9th August 1945. Just a few days earlier a nuclear bomb had been dropped on Hiroshima, also resulting in the immediate death of tens of thousands of people. The death toll rose substantially, in both instances, in the aftermath of the attacks due to the effects of radiation.

The war between North and South Korea was a war fought with the support of the superpowers. Very quickly the North almost overran the South. This was a shock to the predominately American UN troops. The Chinese entered the conflict in 1951 and the Russians lent some of their pilots to the northern cause to give them much needed experience against their Cold War enemies. The war ended with a ceasefire in July 1953, but no formal peace treaty was ever signed.

The nearest the world came to obliteration was during the Cuba Crisis in 1962, where the US and USSR both accused the other of intense provocation. Fortunately skillful diplomacy prevailed.

The Vietnam War could be seen as another conflict between western ideals and Communist regimes, with the US Government not wanting to see Communism spread throughout Southeast Asia, intervening to help the South Vietnamese defeat the Communist North. In spite of the US throwing vast amounts of personnel and hardware at the conflict, slowly the North Vietnamese began to take a heavy toll on the US army and with animosity at home against the war, the US Government eventually pulled out of the region.

The Soviet Union had a similar experience when it invaded Afghanistan in the late 1970s. Again, equipped with the latest technology and weapons, the Soviets were still unable to defeat a guerrilla force hiding in rugged terrain.

The Gulf War was authorized by the United Nations after Iraq had invaded Kuwait in August 1990. US forces led a coalition of about 30 other nations to secure Kuwait's liberation. The result was a swift and decisive victory, with a minimum number of casualties.

THE POST-COLD WAR WORLD

Since the collapse of the Soviet Union, the threat of global oblivion has declined but proliferation of nuclear weapons continues and the chances of a terror group using such a device one day is a new challenge to the security forces of the world.

Since the 1970s there have been some 80,000 terrorist attacks around the world with the most outstanding being America's 9/11 attacks in 2001 that killed more than 3,000 people.

The International War on Terror was initially given as one of the reasons for the invasion of Iraq in 2003. Another reason was to seek out and destroy Iraq's stock of weapons of mass destruction, which never materialized. The third reason was to topple Saddam Hussein and restore democracy. Saddam was successfully removed, but with his iron hand also removed and nothing put in its place, much of the country rapidly descended into lawlessness.

PART 1

WARFARE IN THE CLASSICAL AGE

*T*HE EARLIEST ARMIES CONSISTED largely of spearmen, who stayed together in groups; their commanding officers rode in chariots or on horseback, while on the flanks were placed the cavalry. In front of the main body of spearmen, archers and slingers were deployed to maintain a harassing fire upon the enemy until the right moment arrived for the chariots and the cavalry to charge. While the mobile chariots and cavalry charged, the massed infantry moved forward, with skirmishers moving through the ranks to the rear. Occasionally the initial charge would drive the enemy from the battlefield, but more commonly opposing forces would clash and hand-to-hand butchery would ensue, ending only when one side sensed defeat. In the Classical period, iron weapons appeared on the battlefield for the first time, and these overwhelmed earlier bronze weaponry. Other than this metallurgical development the implements of war remained largely unchanged for almost 2,000 years. In the mountains of Greece, where the terrain was unfavorable to cavalry, there evolved an improved and highly disciplined infantry formation, the phalanx. Soliders within the phalanx were called hoplites, and these physically fit, well-trained and highly-disciplined troops ensured the domination of the phalanx on the battlefields of Greece and the Near East. From around 400 BC Rome emerged as a capable military power; as in Greece, at the heart of its armies were disciplined infantry. The professional Roman legion would be the dominant military force in the region for the next 800 years.

THE EMPIRE OF HAMMURABI

1750 – C. 1500 BC

THE EMPIRE OF HAMMURABI c. 1750 BC
In wars between ancient cities, the siege was common. Unless overwhelming power could be effected quickly in the attack on a fortified site then the defenders could often hold out. Warfare was therefore limited and, to some extent, indecisive.

This system was disturbed by the emergence of a new and ambitious player on the scene, King Hammurabi of Babylon. In a series of highly focused campaigns he removed and absorbed his rivals and developed an empire that ranged from the Persian Gulf to the foothills of Anatolia in modern-day Turkey.

Hammurabi is also remembered for establishing his code of law, which contained 282 rules that were applicable across his empire. It was an attempt to create a unified empire operating under the same laws. The city of Babylon, which was elevated to the capital of the empire, became the religious and cultural capital of the region, a position it would maintain for the following 15 centuries.

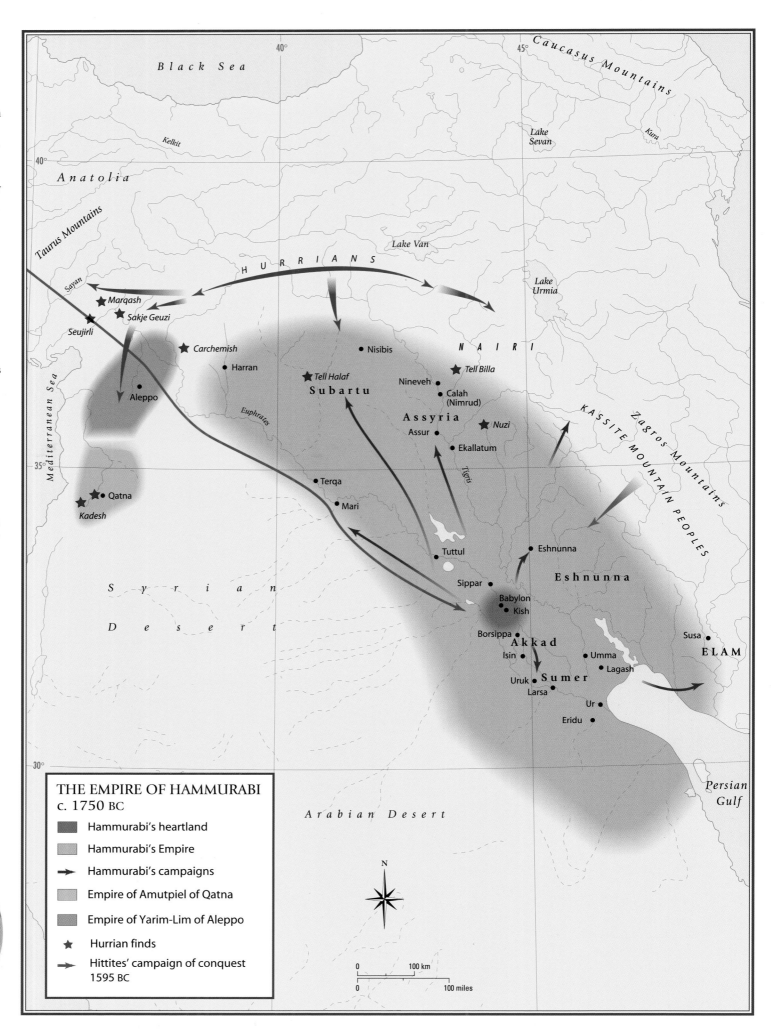

THE EMPIRE OF HAMMURABI
c. 1750 BC

- Hammurabi's heartland
- Hammurabi's Empire
- → Hammurabi's campaigns
- Empire of Amutpiel of Qatna
- Empire of Yarim-Lim of Aleppo
- ★ Hurrian finds
- → Hittites' campaign of conquest 1595 BC

THE DEFENSES OF EGYPT

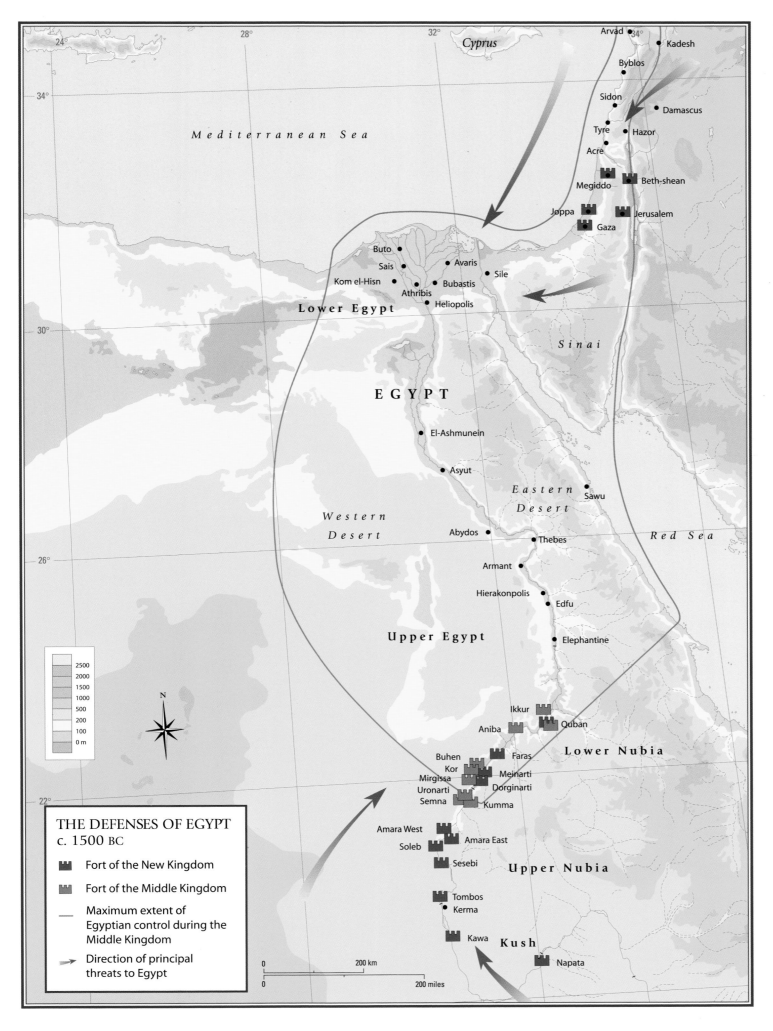

THE DEFENSES OF EGYPT
c. 1500 BC

🏰 Fort of the New Kingdom

🏰 Fort of the Middle Kingdom

── Maximum extent of Egyptian control during the Middle Kingdom

➤ Direction of principal threats to Egypt

THE DEFENSES OF EGYPT c. 1500 BC

The principle threats to Egypt came from Asia, where forces could cross the Sinai along the Levantine coast, and from Nubia in the south.

The Middle Kingdom began building a series of forts in lower Nubia, south of Elephantine to Kumma. This protected Egypt from any possible uprising in Upper Nubia and Kush while allowing a safe base for the continued Egyptianization of the region. The New Kingdom continued the policy of fortified defense. Eventually, however, Egypt fell prey to invaders. The Hyksos, an Asiatic people who themselves were descended from invaders, built their capital at Avaris. They rose to power in the 17th century BC and ruled Lower and Middle Egypt for over 100 years, forming the Fifteenth and possibly the Sixteenth Dynasties of Egypt. The Hyksos, in turn, were overthrown by a native Egyptian known as Ahmose in c. 550 BC, who set about defending Egypt through a fortification construction program and the development of an efficient standing army.

THE BATTLE OF KADESH

1274 *BC*

THE BATTLE OF KADESH 1274 BC

Ramesses II led an Egyptian army made up largely of Numidian mercenaries in an attack against a Hittite stronghold overlooking the Orontes River, Kadesh. The Hittites started as a loosely organized group of trading states, but had expanded their empire from their heartland of Anatolia, and by the reign of Ramesses II their empire bordered on the Egyptian sphere of influence, forcing Ramesses to act. Eager to capture the place before the main Hittite army could be bought into action, Ramesses rashly approached Kadesh without the precaution of careful reconnaissance. This had terrible consequences when he and his advanced guard were cut off by a surprise Hittite counterattack. Although Ramesses managed to hold out until reinforcements arrived, he could not capture Kadesh and was therefore forced into making peace with the Hittites. It is possible that the outcome of this battle was influenced by the Hittites' use of iron weapons against the Egyptians' bronze weapons. Although inconclusive, the battle is significant for being the largest chariot battle ever fought. Around 5,000 chariots were involved, as well as over 9,000 foot soldiers.

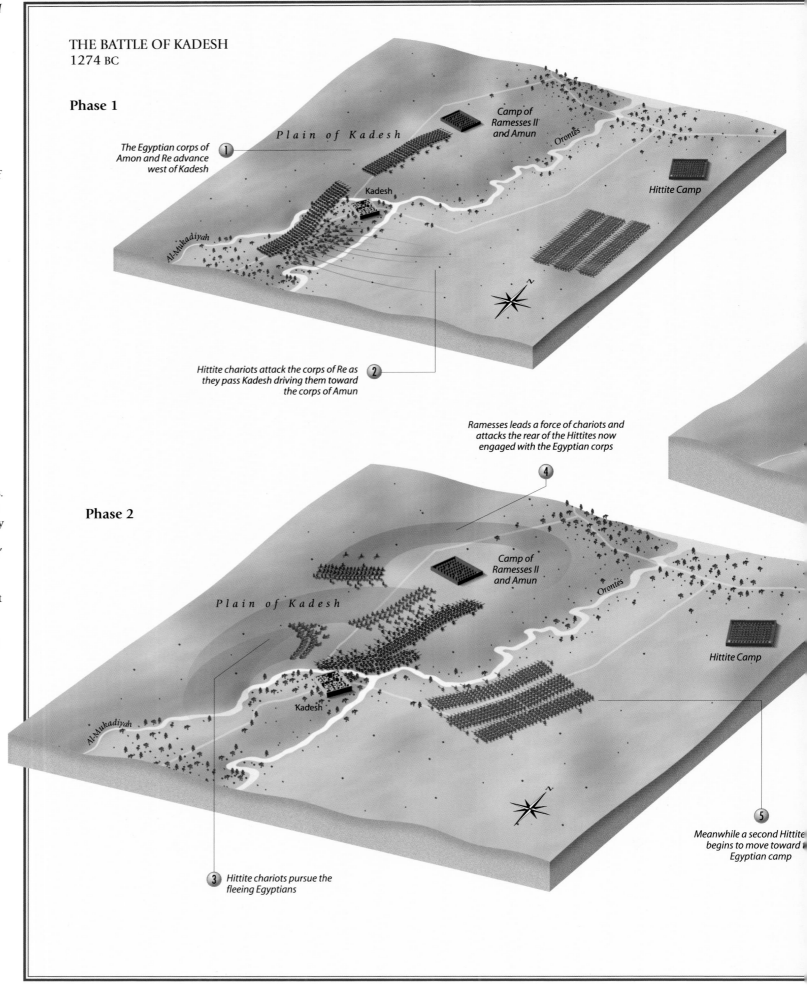

THE BATTLE OF KADESH
1274 BC

Phase 1

Plain of Kadesh

Camp of Ramesses II and Amun

Orontes

The Egyptian corps of Amon and Re advance west of Kadesh ①

Hittite Camp

Kadesh

Al-Mukadiyah

Hittite chariots attack the corps of Re as they pass Kadesh driving them toward the corps of Amun ②

Ramesses leads a force of chariots and attacks the rear of the Hittites now engaged with the Egyptian corps

④

Phase 2

Camp of Ramesses II and Amun

Orontes

Plain of Kadesh

Hittite Camp

Kadesh

Al-Mukadiyah

⑤

Meanwhile a second Hittite begins to move toward Egyptian camp

③ *Hittite chariots pursue the fleeing Egyptians*

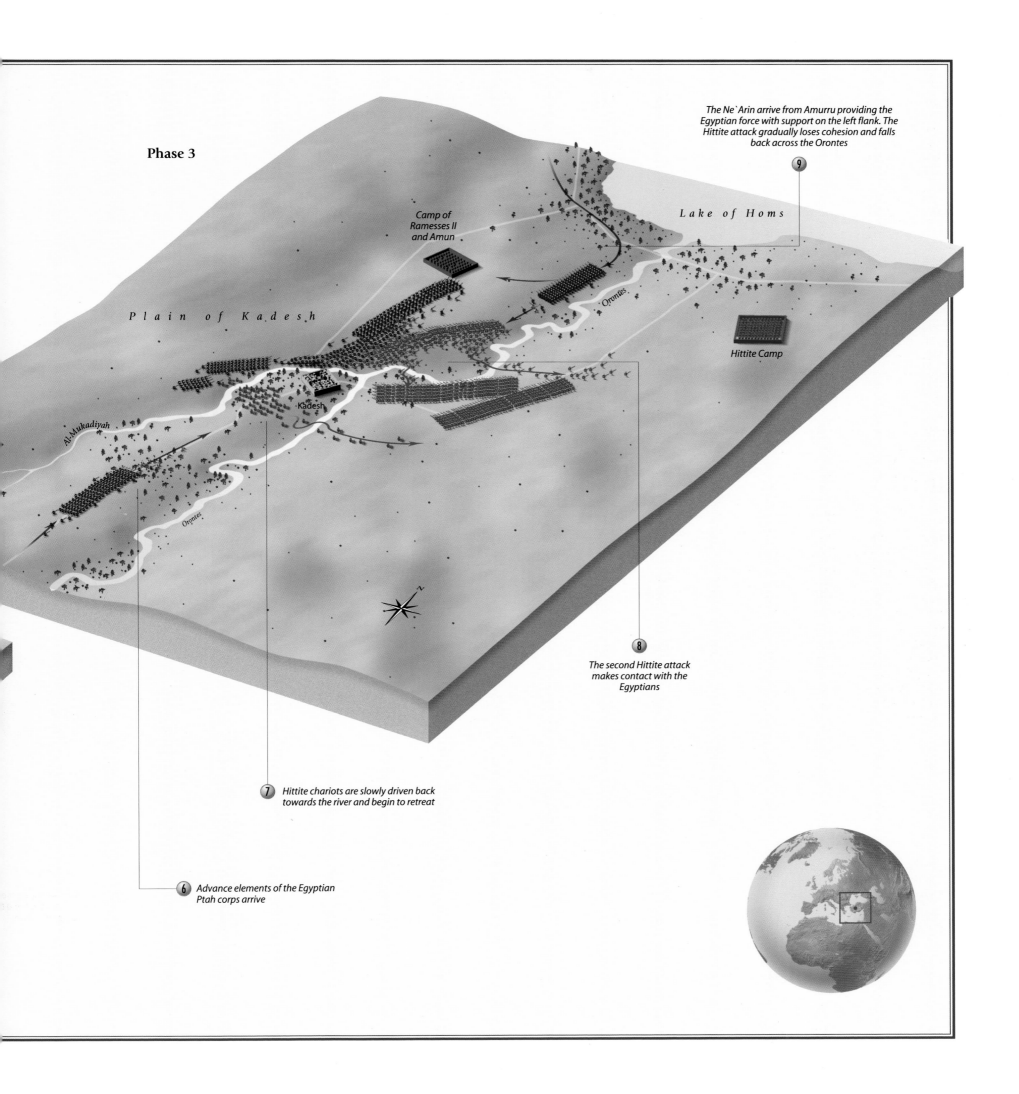

Phase 3

Plain of Kadesh

Al-Mukadiyah

Orontes

Kadesh

Camp of
Ramesses II
and Amun

Orontes

Lake of Homs

Hittite Camp

The Ne`Arin arrive from Amurru providing the
Egyptian force with support on the left flank. The
Hittite attack gradually loses cohesion and falls
back across the Orontes

9

8 The second Hittite attack
makes contact with the
Egyptians

7 Hittite chariots are slowly driven back
towards the river and begin to retreat

6 Advance elements of the Egyptian
Ptah corps arrive

C. 2000 BC –
C. 1200 BC

THE MIDDLE EAST

THE MIDDLE EAST c. 2000 BC
The beginning of the Bronze Age introduced the dagger, the first metallic weapon, into the art of warfare. This was followed by the sword, probably introduced by the Assyrians. Defensive armor, although still leather, was reinforced with metal. Around 1400 BC the desire to achieve greater mobility began to influence the composition of armies. The mass, still made up of large groups of infantry, were increasingly supported by chariots or armored carts, and from around 1000 BC cavalries were introduced, equipped with javelins, spears, or bows.

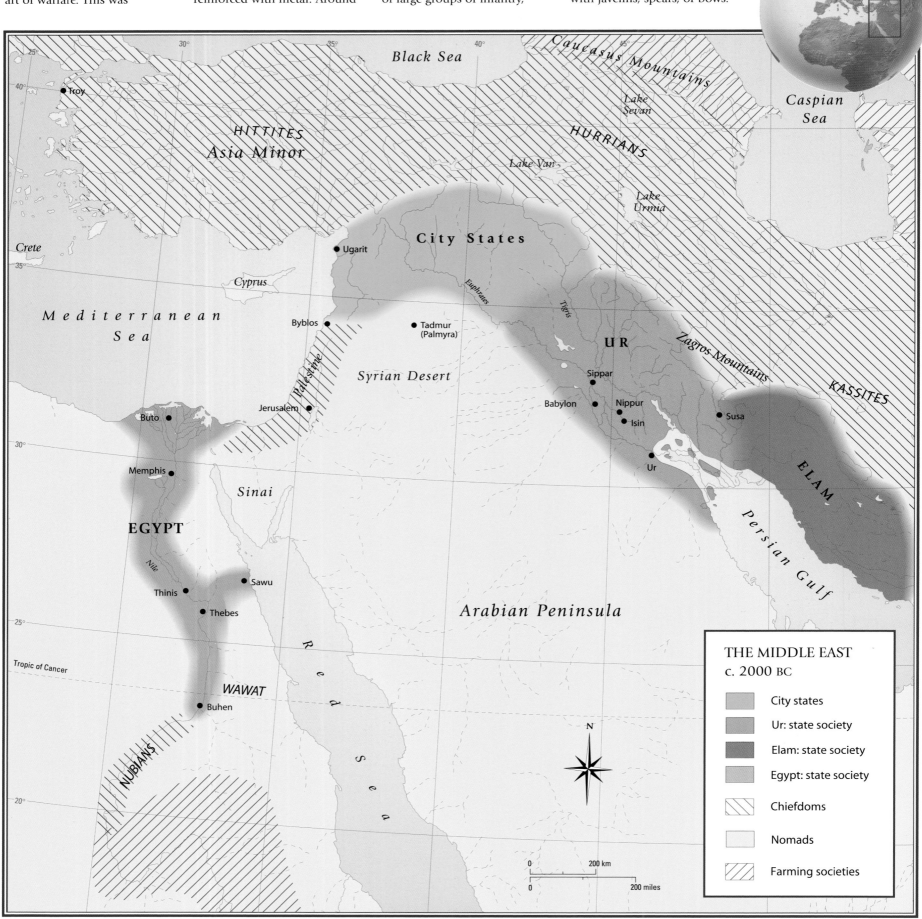

THE MIDDLE EAST
c. 2000 BC

	City states
	Ur: state society
	Elam: state society
	Egypt: state society
	Chiefdoms
	Nomads
	Farming societies

THE COLLAPSE OF MYCENAE

THE COLLAPSE OF MYCENAE c. 1200 BC
The Mycenaean civilization was a sophisticated and capable society, their military consisting of well-trained sailors and marines who were well able to defend their various interests. However, sometime around 1100 BC this civilization came to an end. Historians still disagree on why this should have occurred; it may have been famine or raiders from the sea, but the most likely explanation is that they succumbed to substantial invasions by Dorian Greeks, whose iron weapons overwhelmed the bronze weaponry used by the Mycenae.

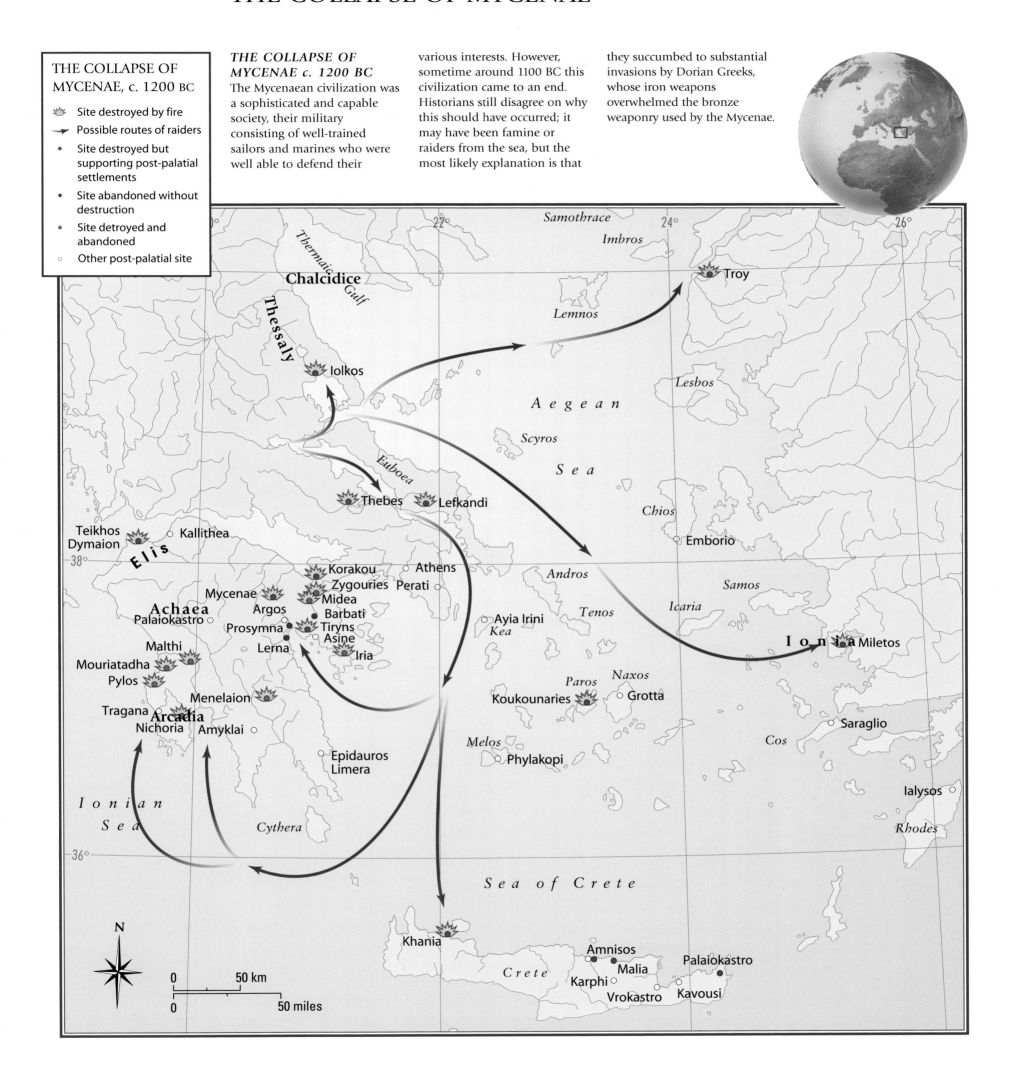

THE COLLAPSE OF MYCENAE, c. 1200 BC

- 🌸 Site destroyed by fire
- ⟶ Possible routes of raiders
- • Site destroyed but supporting post-palatial settlements
- • Site abandoned without destruction
- • Site detroyed and abandoned
- ○ Other post-palatial site

550 – 330 BC   THE PERSIAN EMPIRE

**THE PERSIAN EMPIRE
550 – 330 BC**
Cyrus extended the frontiers of
the Persian Empire westward
through Mesopotamia and
Asia Minor during the 6th
century BC, an expansion
given still greater impetus by
his successors, Cambyses II
and Darius I. The Persians
successfully incorporated the
various military capabilities of
their conquered peoples into
their own army, but were
decisively defeated by the
disciplined Greek phalanx on
the battlefield of Marathon in
490 BC. The Persians evetually
fell to Greece in the 4th
century BC. Alexander the
Great landed in Asia Minor in
334 BC, defeating Darius III at
Gaugamela in 331 BC and
capturing the capital at Susa.

THE PERSIAN EMPIRE
550–330 BC

- Extent of Empire
- Territorial boundaries
- ✕ Battle with date
- ← Cyrus the Great campaigns and battles
- ← Cambyses campaigns and battles
- ← Darius I campaigns and battles
- ← March of Cyrus the Younger against
  Artaxerxes and return route of the
  'Ten Thousand' Greek mercenaries

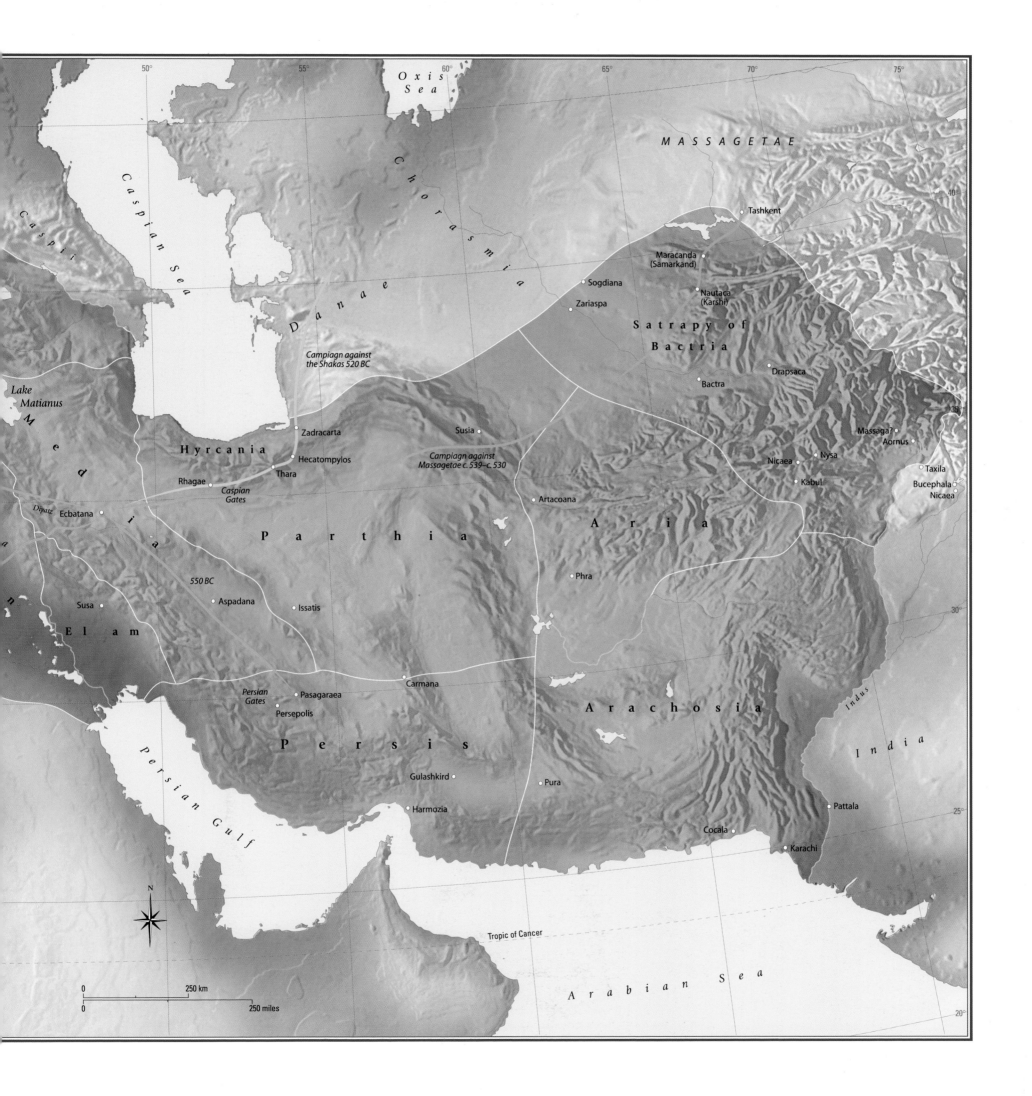

O x i s
S e a

C a s p i i

Caspian Sea

C h o r a s m i a

M A S S A G E T A E

Tashkent

Maracanda
(Samarkand)

Sogdiana

Nautaca
(Karshi)

Zariaspa

Lake
Matianus

D a n a e

Satrapy of
Bactria

M e d i a

Campiagn against
the Shakas 520 BC

Drapsaca

Bactra

Zadracarta

Susia

Massaga?

Hyrcania

Hecatompylos

Campiagn against
Massagetae c. 539–c. 530

Aornus

Nicaea

Nysa

Rhagae

Thara

*Caspian
Gates*

Kabul

Taxila

Diyatg

Ecbatana

Artacoana

A r i a

Bucephala
Nicaea

P a r t h i a

550 BC

Susa

Aspadana

Issatis

Phra

E l a m

*Persian
Gates*

Pasagaraea

Carmana

A r a c h o s i a

I n d u s

I n d i a

Persepolis

P e r s i s

Gulashkird

Pura

P e r s i a n   G u l f

Harmozia

Pattala

N

Cocala

Karachi

Tropic of Cancer

0   250 km
0   250 miles

A r a b i a n   S e a

THE BATTLE OF MARATHON

BATTLE OF MARATHON 490BC

The Battle of Marathon was the culmination of King Darius I of Persia's first full-scale attempt to conquer the remainder of Greece and incorporate it into the Persian Empire. After a year of military preparations, the Persians landed in Greek territory and set about their mission of conquest. Persian intelligence indicated that many Athenians were ready to surrender, and the Persians decided to land a force at Marathon to draw away Greek forces from the defense of Athens. Having accomplished this, the Persian plan was then to land the main force for a direct attack on the city.

The Greeks, nevertheless, guessed the Persian plan and urged an immediate attack on the Persian force at Marathon. The Greeks formed up their army opposite the Persian positions. They had too few men to maintain a full-depth phalanx formation for their whole line but were careful to maintain the full depth on each flank. The Greeks advanced across the narrow plain until within 600 feet of the Persians (bow shot distance), then charged so as to avoid damaging exposure to Persian bowmen. The Persians initially held the Greek center and almost broke it, but the Greek flanks pushed forward, defeating the Persian flanks and pushing the Persian ranks into a convex form. The Greek maneuver was the perfect envelopment. The Persians became increasingly disorganized, a sense of panic rising through their ranks, and they began to run for their ships, which were anchored along the beach.

Datis, the Persian commander, managed to organize a rearguard, allowing the majority of his troops to escape. In the battle and the final struggle on the beach, the Persians lost some 6400 men to the Greeks 192, once again showing the effectiveness of the phalanx. The Greeks immediately began a return

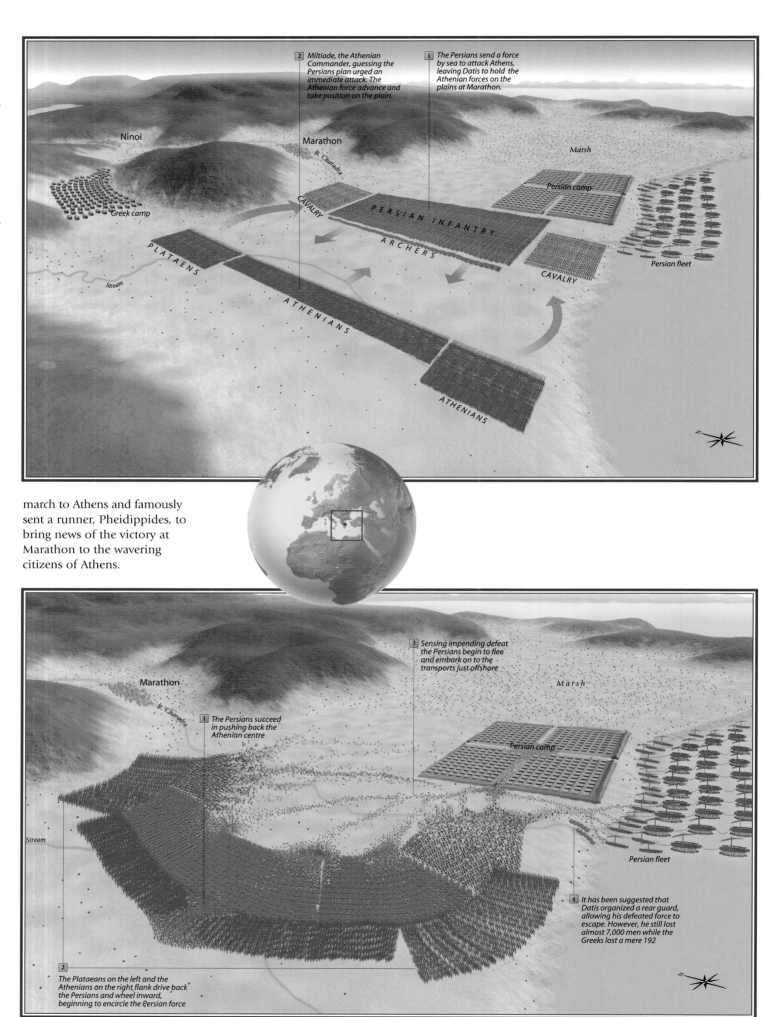

march to Athens and famously sent a runner, Pheidippides, to bring news of the victory at Marathon to the wavering citizens of Athens.

XERXES' INVASION OF GREECE

XERXES' INVASION 480 BC

The Greco-Persian Wars were a series of conflicts between a number of Greek city-states and the Persian Empire. Beginning in 499 BC, the conflict lasted for over 50 years. In 480 BC, the Persian King Xerxes led a huge army into Greece. The Greek attempt to hold northern Greece at the passes south of Mount Olympus was abandoned, as it required too many men to face the massive Persian force. The next point further south where a stand could hope to be made was the pass of Thermopylae. There the Greek King Leonidas, with 300 men of his personal contingent together with about 7000 other Greek hoplites and a few archers, deployed to block the pass. For three days the Persians, numbering around 200,000, vainly tried to batter their way through the pass by sheer weight of numbers. Even so, the disciplined Greeks held their ground. A Greek traitor, however, informed Xerxes of a narrow mountain track that would outflank the Greek position, and he immediately dispatched his "Immortals," the elite troops who acted as bodyguards to the Persian king, who overwhelmed the Greeks defending the narrow defile. Leonidas immediately sent reinforcements to face the new threat but they were quickly overrun, and few survived to surrender. Xerxes and his vast Persian army, now including some Greeks, continued the march on Athens. On reaching Athens, the Persians razed the city, but they were defeated a short time later in the naval Battle of Salamis, which marked a decisive turning point in the Greco-Persian war in favor of Greece.

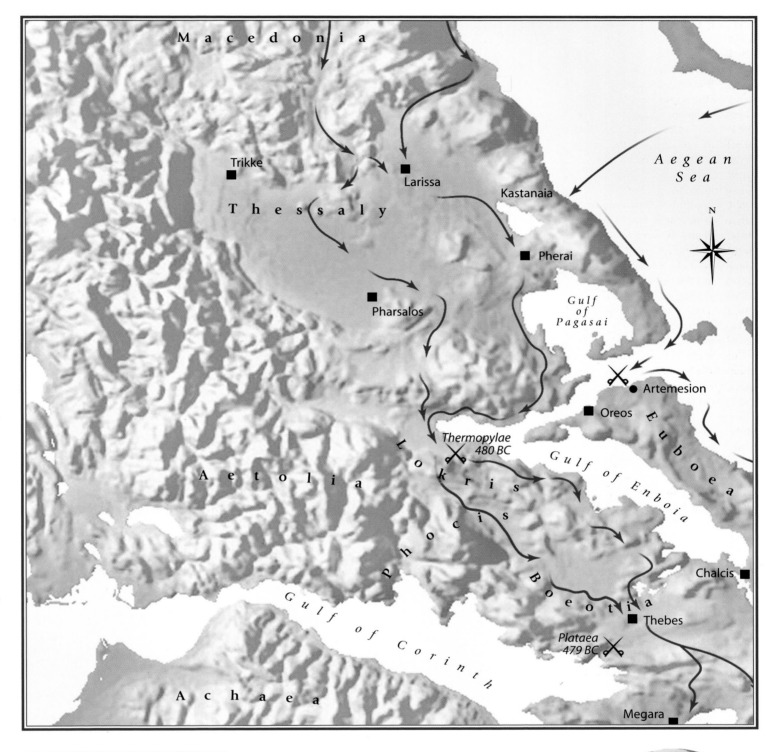

XERXES' INVASION, 480 BC

→ Route of Persian land forces

→ Route of Persian fleet

THE 1ST PELOPONNESIAN WAR; THE CAMPAIGN IN SICILY

431 – 336 BC

PELOPONNESIAN WAR 1 431–404 BC

- Athens and members of the Delian League, c. 431 BC
- Athens's allies
- → Athenian campaign
- ✕ Athenian victory
- Sparta and Spartan allies, c. 431 BC
- → Spartan campaign
- ✕ Spartan victory
- ✱ Revolt against Athens
- Persian Empire
- Neutral states

THE 1ST PELOPONNESIAN WAR 431 – 404 BC; THE CAMPAIGN IN SICILY

Athenian leader and orator Pericles realized that Athens didn't have the manpower to maintain a large standing army and a capable navy, and he concluded that future prosperity relied on colonization and trade. These ambitions aroused suspicion among other Greek cities, notably Corinth and Sparta. The war fought between 431 and 404 BC was waged across the Greek world and included expeditions by Athens against Syracuse in Sicily, which was an Athenian disaster; in its concluding phase the Spartans, led by Lysander, destroyed the Athenian fleet whilst at anchor, leaving Sparta the supreme force in Greece.

CAMPAIGN IN SICILY

- Athens and allied to Athens
- • Athenian ally in Sicily or Italy
- Sparta or allied to Sparta
- • Spartan ally in Sicily or Italy
- Greek settlement in Sicily and Southern Italy
- Neutral Greek states
- → Route of Athenian force under Alcibiades, 415
- ✕ Spartan victory

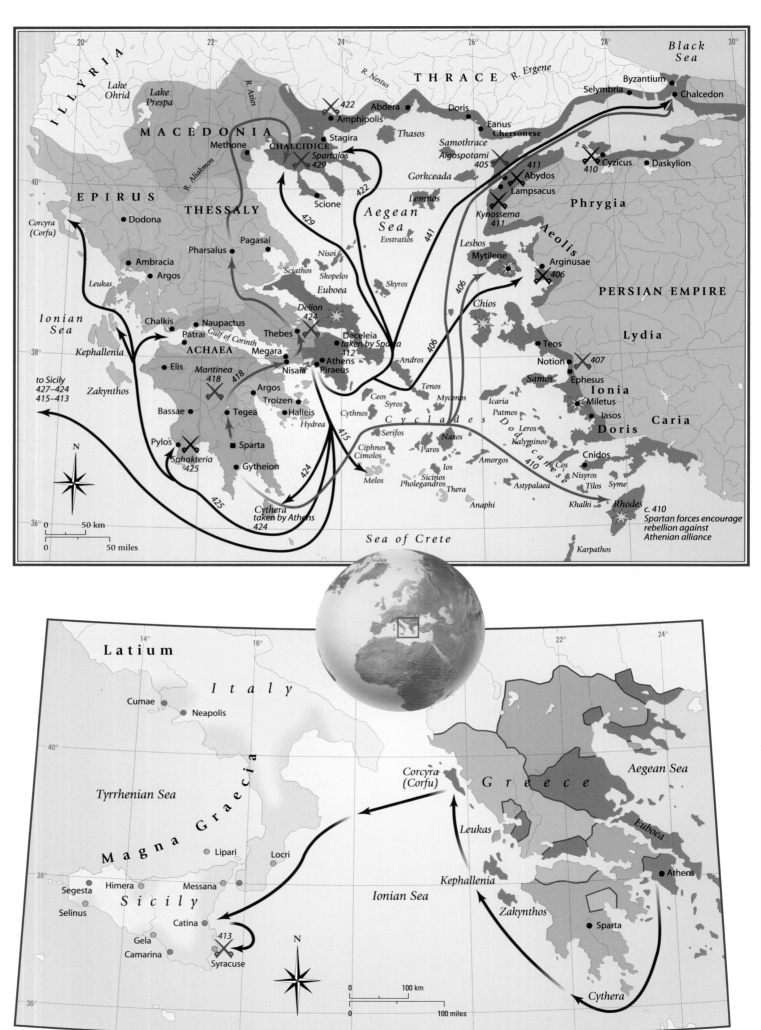

THE RISE OF MACEDONIA

THE RISE OF MACEDONIA

- Core area of Macedonian control, early 4th Century BC
- Added to Macedonia by 359 BC
- Added to or subdued by Macedonia by 336 BC
- Added to or subdued by Macedonia after 336 BC
- Probable extent of the Corinthian League from 337 BC
- Other Greek states

N

0   100 km

0   100 miles

River Danube

Istrus

Tomi

Callatis

Odessus

Black

Sea

Mesembria

Apollonia

Thrace

Philippopolis

Paeonia

Epidamnus

Byzantium

Chalcedon

Apollonia

Mt Pangaeus

Philippi

Perinthus

MACEDONIA

Pella

Aegae

Amphipolis

Stagira

Thasos

Thasos

Aenus

Cardia

Cyzicus

Methone

Chalcidice

Olynthus

Potidaea

Samothrace

Imbros

Phrygia

Parauaea

Thermaic Gulf

Lemnos

EPIRUS

(MOLOSSIAN KINGDOM)

Perrhaebia

Corcyra

(Corfu)

Thessaly

Larissa

Pherae

Pagasae

Crocotus

Campus

PERSIAN

Scyros

Mytilene

Lesbos

Pergamum

Mysina

Ambracia

Leukas

Acarnania

Thermopylae

Euboea

Phocis

Delphi

Chaeronea

338 BC

Thebes

Boeotia

Aegean

Sea

Chios

Lydia

EMPIRE

Kephallenia

Corinth

Andros

Samos

Ephesus

Tenos

Icaria

Caria

Peloponnese

Zakynthos

Naxos

Ionian

Sea

Sparta

Lycia

Melos

Cos

Cythera

Rhodes

Crete

Mediterranean   Sea

THE RISE OF MACEDONIA

When Philip II came to power in Macedonia his first act was to completely restructure and retrain the army. The bulk of Philip's army was made up of infantry; the Macedonian phalanx was sixteen men deep instead of the usual eight to twelve, and it added a small interval between the men instead of the more common shoulder to shoulder mass of the Greek phalanx. Each man carried a spear that was over 12 feet long, as well as a large shield, helmet, breastplate, greaves (shin-guards), and a short sword worn on the belt. The spears of the first five ranks were lowered so that they would protrude in front of the phalanx line in battle. Constant training made the Macedonian phalanx capable of maneuver while keeping to a perfect formation.

The cream of the Macedonian infantry was the Hypaspist. These soldiers were carefully selected for their physiques and strength of character. At 9 feet long, a Hypaspist's spear was shorter than those carried by the men of the phalanx, and their armour was lighter. As the elite group of the infantry, they received a greater degree of training than the men of the phalanx. The Hypaspists were usually stationed on the flank of the phalanx to provide a hinge between the phalanx and the fast-moving cavalry, creating the ability to perform highly coordinated maneuvers on the battlefield. With these innovations, Philip II had created the finest fighting force the world had yet seen.

336 – 323 BC THE EMPIRE OF ALEXANDER THE GREAT

THE EMPIRE OF ALEXANDER THE GREAT 336–323 BC

After campaigns of consolidation, punishing northern and northeastern tribes and bringing other Greek states into line, Alexander became captain general of the Hellenic League. He achieved this quickly due to his greatest inheritance, the Macedonian army, the finest fighting force of the Classical age, and his own unquestionable military skills. In 334 BC Alexander crossed the Hellespont Strait at the head of an army 35,000 strong. At the Granicus River Alexander quickly defeated a Persian army of 40,000. His first action was to seize the coastline of Asia Minor, nullifying the effect of the powerful Persian fleet. At the Battle of Issus he defeated a much larger Persian army than his own, inflicting over 50,000 casualties for the loss of less than 500 Macedonians. Once again Alexander resumed his advance, besieging and occupying cities along the Byzantine coast and on into Egypt, where he founded the city of Alexandria. In 331 BC, Alexander received information that Darius, the leader of the Persians, was assembling a vast new army in Mesopotamia. He rapidly marched and located the Persians and their allies. Darius had deployed a force of 200,000-strong on the Plain of Gaugemela.

THE EMPIRE OF ALEXANDER THE GREAT 336–323 BC

✗ Battle with date

▮ Extent of Empire

▮ Territorial boundaries

DARIUS'S ARMY
1. Armenian cavalry
2. Cappadocian cavalry
3. Parthian cavalry
4. Median cavalry
5. Indian and Carion cavalry
6. Chariots
7. Persian infantry
8. Greek mercenaries
9. Bactrian and Persian cavalry
10. Infantry levies from many areas
11. Fifteen war elephants

ALEXANDER'S ARMY
1. Alexander and Companion cavalry
2. Macedonian archers
3. Agrianian javelin men
4. Hypaspists
5. Macedonian phalanx
6. Thessalian cavalry
7. Cretan spearmen and archers
8. Left flank guard, cavalry
9. Right flank guard, cavalry, javelins and archers
10. Second line phalanx
11. Thracians

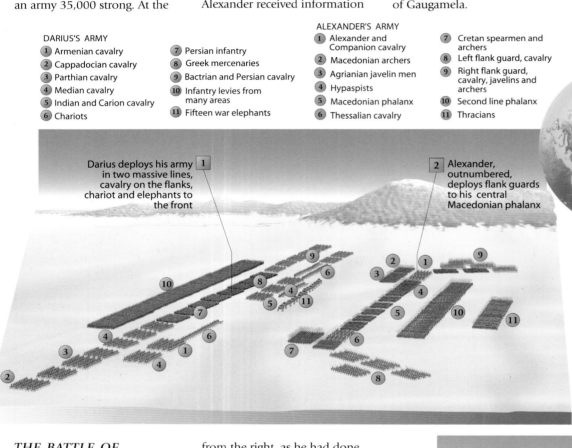

Darius deploys his army in two massive lines, cavalry on the flanks, chariot and elephants to the front **1**

Alexander, outnumbered, deploys flank guards to his central Macedonian phalanx **2**

THE BATTLE OF GAUGEMELA

Darius had lost his best infantry, butchered at the battle of Issus, and now had to rely mainly on cavalry, chariots, and elephants. Fearing a night attack he kept his tired army deployed on the battlefield. Alexander deployed an army of 50,000 opposite Darius, whose army front outflanked the Macedonians by almost a mile. Darius had also stationed crack units of Persian cavalry directly opposite Alexander and his cavalry.

The battle began with Alexander advancing on the Persians in echelon formation from the right, as he had done at the Battle of Issus. His Companion cavalry, covered by a screen of light infantry, were intended to strike a major blow. The Hypaspists, the cream of Macedonian infantry, marched with the main phalanx, and on each flank of the Macedonian line marched units of light cavalry and infantry whose job was to protect the Macedonians from envelopment by the massive Persian army. As the Macedonians advanced, they moved slightly towards their right, and the Persians attempted to mirror this by moving units to their left, but in

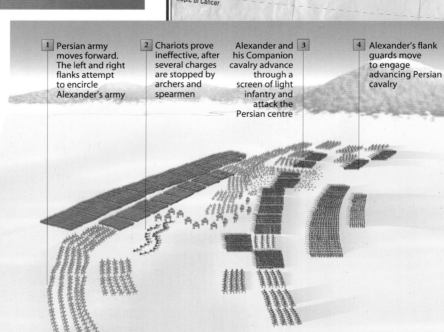

1 Persian army moves forward. The left and right flanks attempt to encircle Alexander's army

2 Chariots prove ineffective, after several charges are stopped by archers and spearmen

3 Alexander and his Companion cavalry advance through a screen of light infantry and attack the Persian centre

4 Alexander's flank guards move to engage advancing Persian cavalry

THE BATTLE OF GAUGEMELA

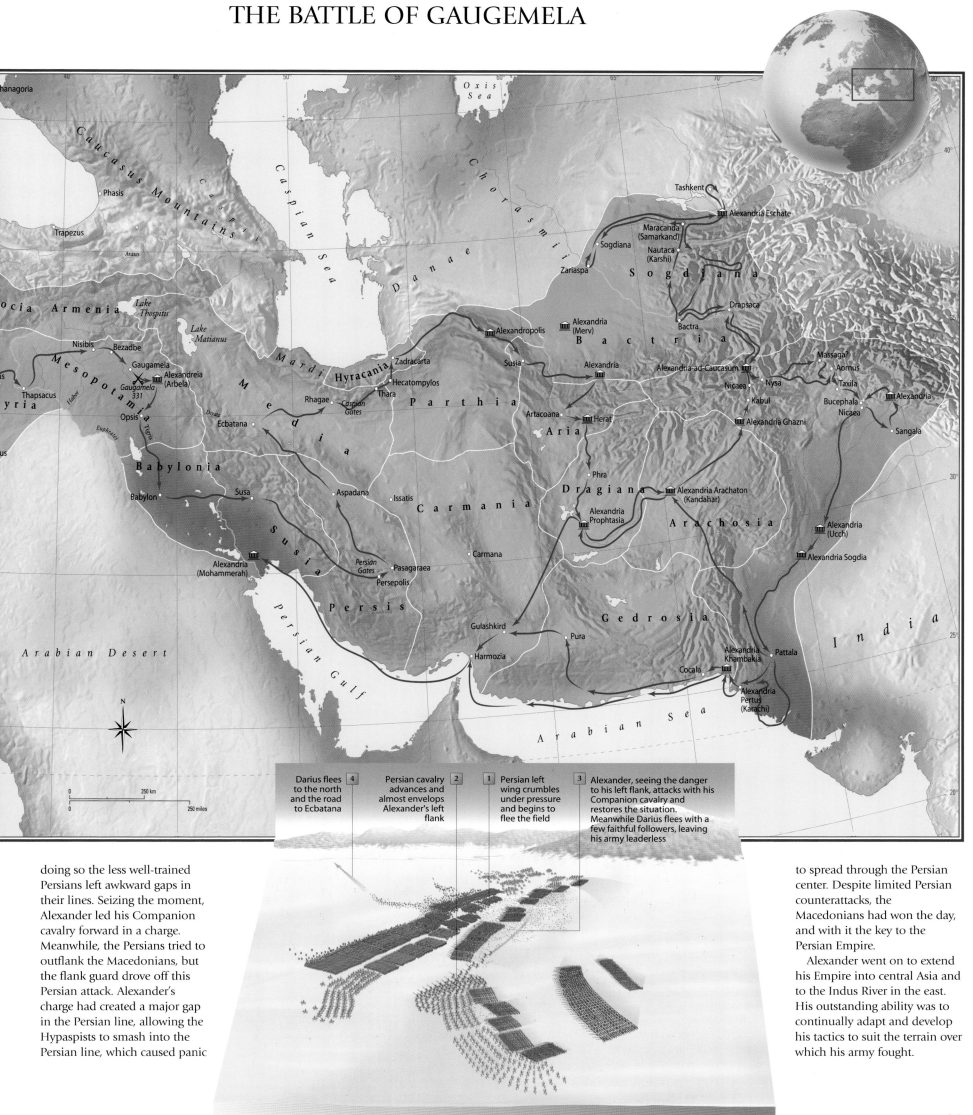

4 Darius flees to the north and the road to Ecbatana

2 Persian cavalry advances and almost envelops Alexander's left flank

1 Persian left wing crumbles under pressure and begins to flee the field

3 Alexander, seeing the danger to his left flank, attacks with his Companion cavalry and restores the situation. Meanwhile Darius flees with a few faithful followers, leaving his army leaderless

doing so the less well-trained Persians left awkward gaps in their lines. Seizing the moment, Alexander led his Companion cavalry forward in a charge. Meanwhile, the Persians tried to outflank the Macedonians, but the flank guard drove off this Persian attack. Alexander's charge had created a major gap in the Persian line, allowing the Hypaspists to smash into the Persian line, which caused panic

to spread through the Persian center. Despite limited Persian counterattacks, the Macedonians had won the day, and with it the key to the Persian Empire.

Alexander went on to extend his Empire into central Asia and to the Indus River in the east. His outstanding ability was to continually adapt and develop his tactics to suit the terrain over which his army fought.

700 – 225 BC   THE CELTS

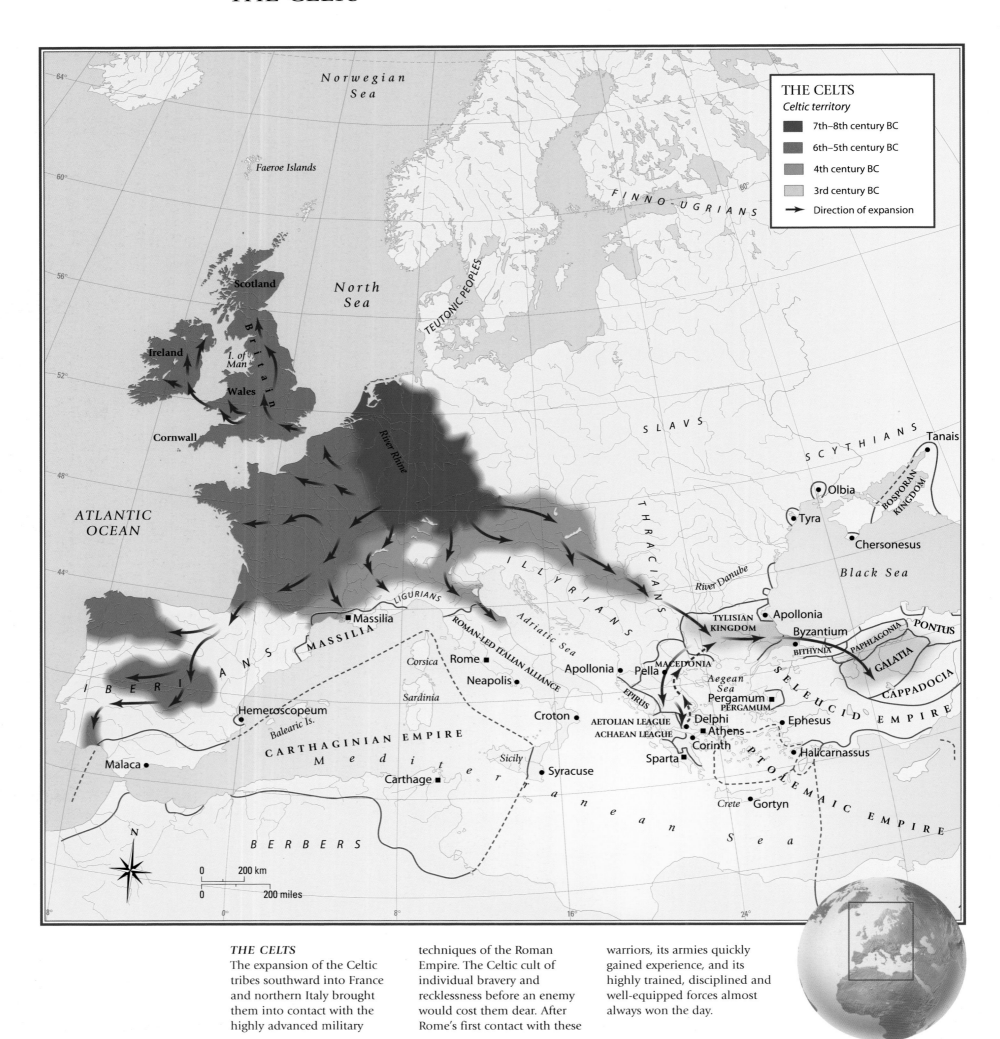

THE CELTS
The expansion of the Celtic tribes southward into France and northern Italy brought them into contact with the highly advanced military techniques of the Roman Empire. The Celtic cult of individual bravery and recklessness before an enemy would cost them dear. After Rome's first contact with these warriors, its armies quickly gained experience, and its highly trained, disciplined and well-equipped forces almost always won the day.

THE BATTLE OF TELAMON

BATTLE OF TELAMON 225 BC

In 225 BC an alliance of Celtic tribes and a number of mercenaries (Gaesatae) invaded Roman territory. The Romans immediately mobilized their forces and called on tribal enemies of the Celts to join the fight. They also signed a treaty with the Carthaginians ensuring their neutrality in this forthcoming campaign. The invading Celts won an initial victory at Faesulae and continued their advance through Roman territory. By now the Romans had mobilized two armies totalling over 75,000 men and succeeded in maneuvering the Celts into a position adjacent to the coastline of Tuscany at Telamon. Here the Celtic army awaited the Roman approach.

By this time, the Roman army had gained some experience in fighting Celtic warriors and were prepared to meet their headlong, frenzied rush at Roman ranks. The Romans, approaching from two directions, would force the Celtic army of around 55,000 to fight on two fronts. After several hours of vicious close-quarter fighting disciplined Roman tactics proved decisive against the warrior bravery of the Celts. By the end of fighting, 40,000 Celts had been slaughtered and another 10,000 taken into slavery. Few escaped to see their homes again.

After this battle, Rome decided on a policy to conquer the rest of northern Italy and to bring an end to any potential threat from that direction.

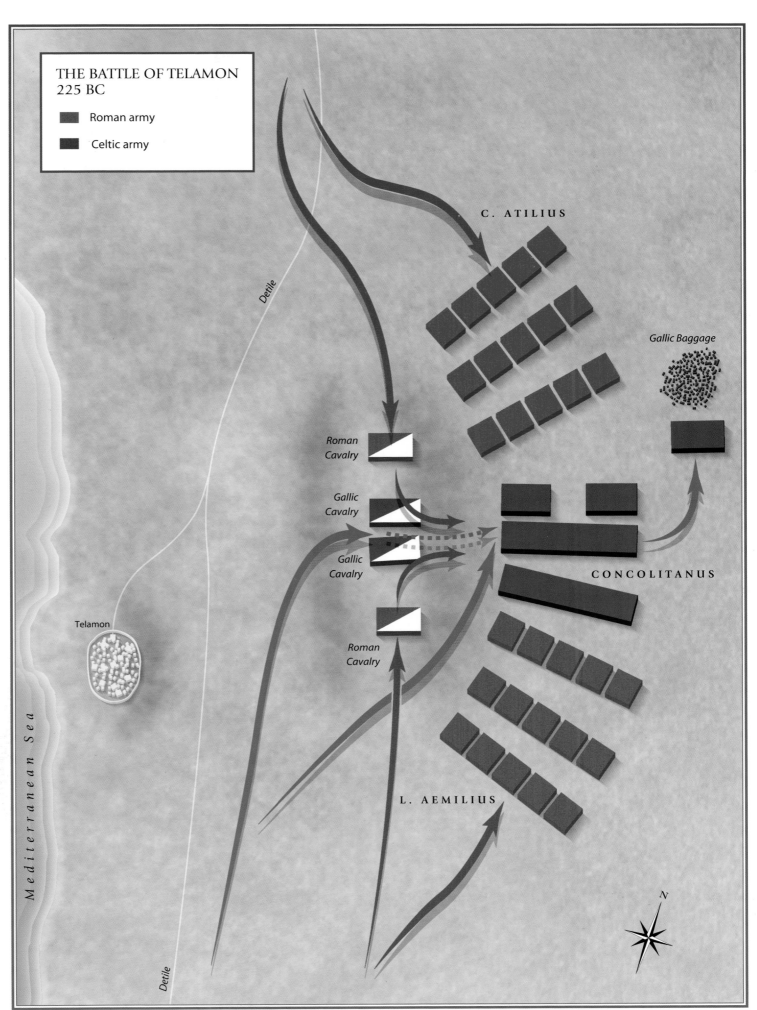

THE BATTLE OF TELAMON
225 BC

Roman army

Celtic army

C. ATILIUS

Gallic Baggage

Roman Cavalry

Gallic Cavalry

Gallic Cavalry

CONCOLITANUS

Telamon

Roman Cavalry

Mediterranean Sea

Detile

Detile

L. AEMILIUS

N

HANNIBAL'S CAMPAIGNS IN ITALY

HANNIBAL'S CAMPAIGNS IN ITALY 218–203 BC; BATTLE OF ZAMA

Hannibal, military commander of the Carthaginians, crossed the Alps into Italy in October 218 BC and began his legendary 16-year campaign against Rome. Despite his numerous victories he never succeeded in capturing Rome or destroying Rome's ability to field new armies and to recover from the disasters he inflicted on them.

By 204 BC the Romans were able to take an army of 30,000 men and attack Carthage, landing near Utica in north Africa. In desperation the Carthaginians sent for Hannibal, who met the Roman army, under the command of Scipio, at the Battle of Zama. The Roman army gained an overwhelming victory, killing 20,000 Carthaginians and taking 15,000 prisoners.

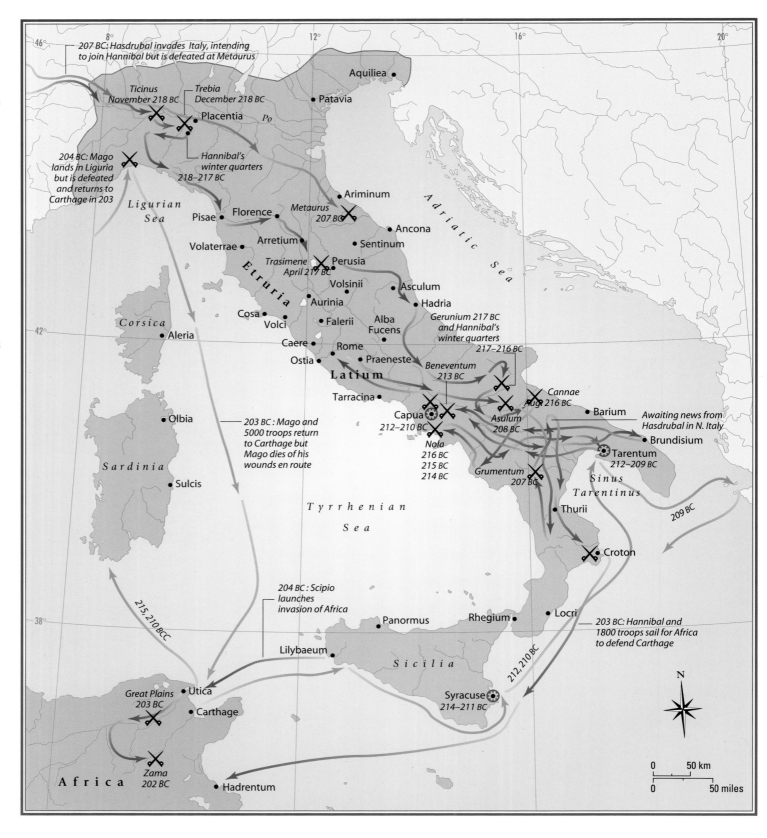

HANNIBAL'S CAMPAIGNS IN ITALY 218–203 BC

- → Hannibal's campaign
- → Hasdrubal's campaign
- → Mago's campaign
- → Major interventions of Carthaginian fleet
- → Scipio's campaign
- ✗ Site of battle
- ⊚ Siege
- ▨ Roman territory
- ▨ Carthaginian territory

THE PUNIC WARS (RIGHT)
The Punic Wars were a series of three wars fought between Rome and Carthage. The conflict started as a result of the increasing strength of Rome, which by the 3rd century BC was looking to expand its territory in the Mediterranean. This brought it into direct conflict with the Carthaginians, an extensive maritime empire who were the dominant power in the Mediterranean at this time. The Romans were initially interested in expansion via Sicily, part of which lay under Carthaginian control. The First Punic War ended in victory for Rome, who took Sicily and forced the defeated Carthaginians to pay a massive tribute. The Second Punic War ended with defeat for Hannibal's forces at the Battle of Zama. By the end of the Third Punic War, after the deaths of many hundreds of thousands of soldiers from both sides, Rome had conquered Carthage's empire and razed the city, and in so doing became the dominant force in the Mediterranean.

THE BATTLE OF ZAMA; THE PUNIC WARS

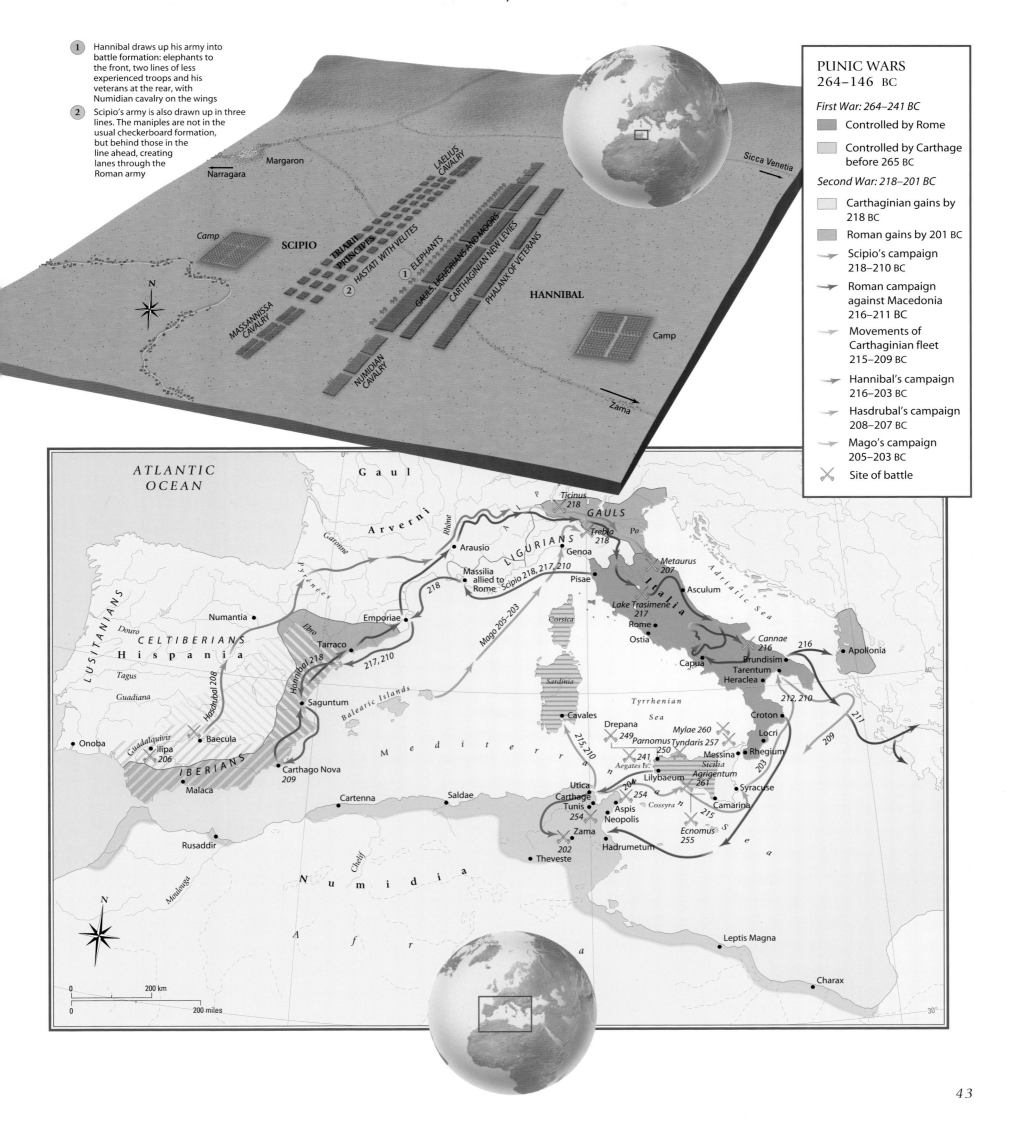

① Hannibal draws up his army into battle formation: elephants to the front, two lines of less experienced troops and his veterans at the rear, with Numidian cavalry on the wings

② Scipio's army is also drawn up in three lines. The maniples are not in the usual checkerboard formation, but behind those in the line ahead, creating lanes through the Roman army

Margaron

Narragara

Camp

SCIPIO

TRIARII

PRINCIPES

HASTATI WITH VELITES

① ELEPHANTS

②

GAULS, LIGURIANS AND MOORS

CARTHAGINIAN NEW LEVIES

PHALANX OF VETERANS

HANNIBAL

Camp

LAELIUS CAVALRY

MASSANNISSA CAVALRY

N

NUMIDIAN CAVALRY

Zama

Sicca Venetia

PUNIC WARS
264–146 BC

First War: 264–241 BC

Controlled by Rome

Controlled by Carthage before 265 BC

Second War: 218–201 BC

Carthaginian gains by 218 BC

Roman gains by 201 BC

→ Scipio's campaign 218–210 BC

→ Roman campaign against Macedonia 216–211 BC

→ Movements of Carthaginian fleet 215–209 BC

→ Hannibal's campaign 216–203 BC

→ Hasdrubal's campaign 208–207 BC

→ Mago's campaign 205–203 BC

✕ Site of battle

ATLANTIC OCEAN

Gaul

Arverni

Garonne

Rhône

LIGURIANS

GAULS

Po

Italia

Adriatic Sea

Ticinus 218

Trebia 218

Metaurus 207

Asculum

Arausio

Massilia allied to Rome

Scipio 218, 217, 210

Genoa

Pisae

Lake Trasimene 217

Rome

Ostia

Pyrenees

LUSITANIANS

Numantia

CELTIBERIANS

Hispania

Douro

Ebro

Emporiae

Tarraco

Hannibal 218

Corsica

Cannae 216

216

Apollonia

40°

Tagus

Hasdrubal 208

217, 210

Capua

Brundisim

Tarentum

Heraclea

212, 210

211

Guadiana

Saguntum

Balearic Islands

Sardinia

Tyrrhenian Sea

Croton

Locri

209

Onoba

Guadalquivir

Ilipa 206

Baecula

IBERIANS

Carthago Nova 209

Mediterranea

Cavales

Drepana 249

Parnomus 241

Mylae 260

Tyndaris 257

250

Messina

Sicilia

Agrigentum 261

Rhegium

203

Mago 205–203

215, 210

Aegates Is.

Lilybaeum

204

Cossyra

Camarina

Syracuse

Malaca

Cartenna

Saldae

Utica

Carthage

Tunis 254

Aspis

Neopolis

254

Ecnomus 255

Hadrumetum

215

Rusaddir

Chelif

Zama 202

Theveste

Numidia

Moulouga

Africa

Leptis Magna

Charax

N

0   200 km

0   200 miles

30°

THE BATTLE OF MAGNESIA

192 – 55 BC

THE BATTLE OF MAGNESIA 190 BC

Tensions between Antiochus III of Syria and Rome dissolved into open warfare in 192 BC. After campaigning in Greece and Asia Minor the contending armies met at the Battle of Magnesia in 190 BC. The Romans and their allies numbered around 40,000, while Antiochus III had a force of 75,000. Initially the Syrian cavalry units won some successes but the Romans eventually drove off the

Seleucid attack. Meanwhile, the Roman legions had repulsed a Syrian elephant attack, sending some of the wounded beasts back on their own lines. Suffering further blows, the Syrians broke and fled. The Romans quickly followed up their victory, gaining control over Syria and most of Asia Minor.

The Army of Scipio Africaines

1 Turmae cavalry
2 Latin ala
3 Roman legion
4 Roman legion
5 Latin ala
6 Peltasts, 3000
7 Cavalry, 3000

The Army of Antiochus

1 Dahae cavalry, 1200
2 Argyraspides infantry, 10000
3 Agema cavalry, 1000
4 Cataphracts cavalry, 3000
5 Galatians, 1500
6 Phalangites, 16000
7 Galatians, 1500
8 Light infantry, 4700
9 Cataphracts cavalry, 3000
10 Regia ala cavalry, 1000
11 Galatian cavalry, 2500
12 Tarentines cavalry, 500
13 Seleucid chariots

1 Antiochus attacks with agema and cataphracts and breaks through the Roman legion. He leads the cavalry on to the Roman camp but is checked by the Roman guards left outside the camp. A tribune, Lepidus, manages to reform enough of the routed legion to drive him back

2 The Seleucid chariots attack, but are driven off by missile fire. They retreat, causing some disorder to their own forces. The Roman cavalry advance and drive the Syrian cavalry to the rear

3 The Roman infantry closes with the phalanx and its supporting elephants, driving back the Seleucid skirmishes. Although under pressure, the phalanx stands firm

4 However, confusion is caused in the phalanx when some of the elephants panic and when the Roman cavalry return and attack its flanks and rear. This, combined with the pressure from the legions, is too much and Antiochus's centre dissolves into a rou

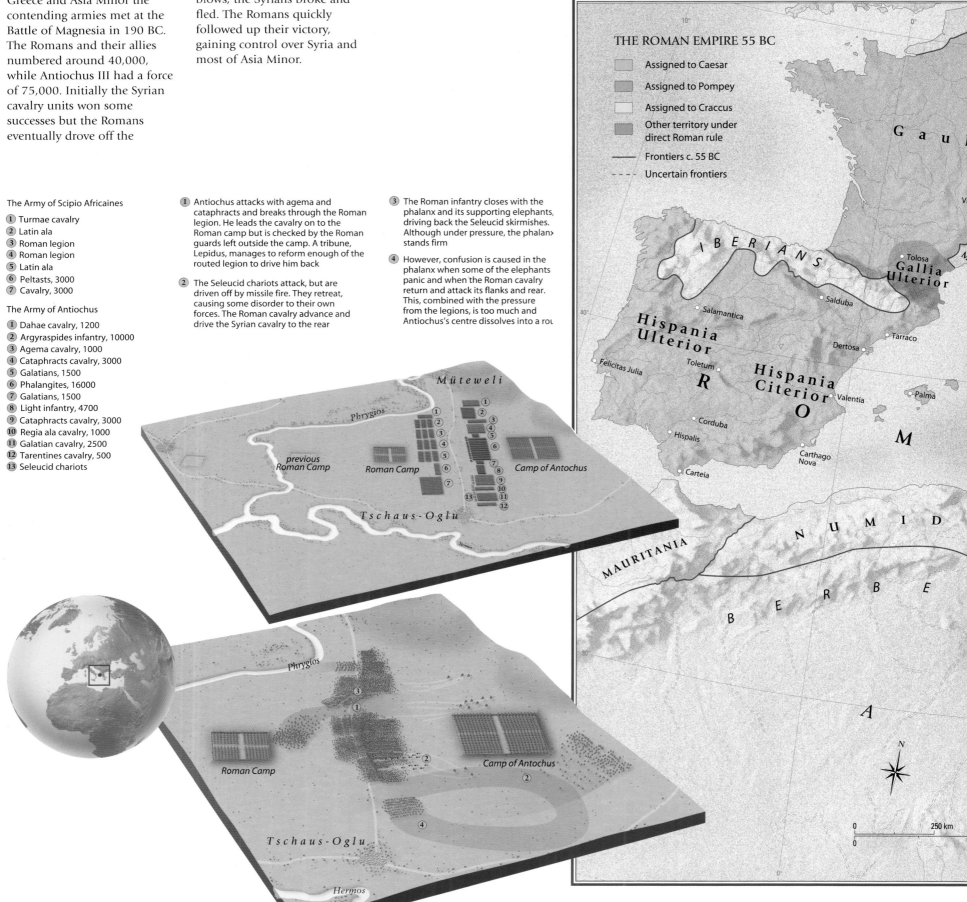

THE ROMAN EMPIRE 55 BC

Assigned to Caesar
Assigned to Pompey
Assigned to Craccus
Other territory under direct Roman rule
Frontiers c. 55 BC
Uncertain frontiers

THE ROMAN EMPIRE 55 BC

THE ROMAN EMPIRE 55 BC
By 55 BC, under the rule of the first triumvirate, the Roman Empire stretched from the North Sea to Egypt, its armies triumphant in Macedonia, Spain, and Gaul.

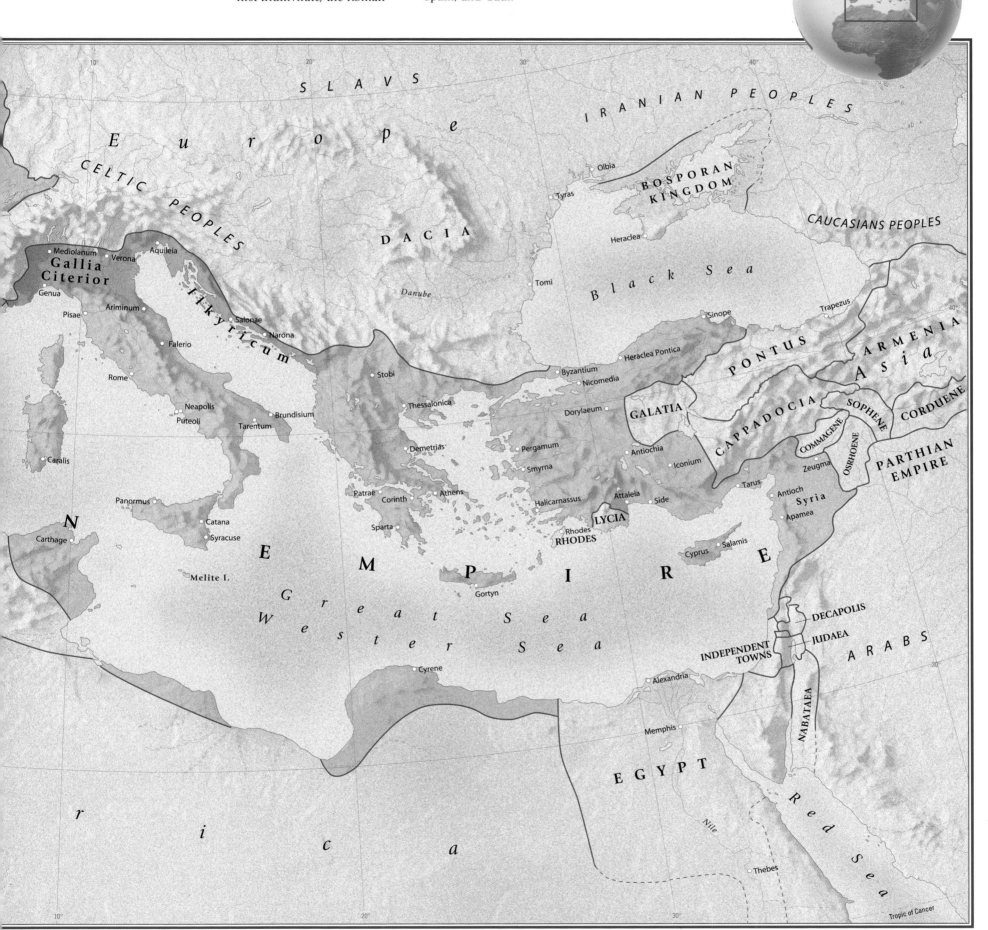

SLAVS

IRANIAN PEOPLES

E u r o p e

CELTIC PEOPLES

Mediolanum
Verona
Aquileia
Gallia Citerior
Genua
Pisae
Ariminum
Falerio
Rome
Neapolis
Puteoli
Tarentum
Brundisium
Caralis
Panormus
Catana
Syracuse
Carthage
N
Melite I.

Illyricum

Salonae
Narona

Stobi
Thessalonica
Demetrias
Patrae
Corinth
Athens
Sparta
Gortyn

DACIA

Danube

Olbia
Tyras

BOSPORAN KINGDOM

Heraclea

Tomi

Black Sea

CAUCASIANS PEOPLES

Sinope
Trapezus

Byzantium
Nicomedia
Heraclea Pontica

Dorylaeum

PONTUS
ARMENIA
Asia

GALATIA
CAPPADOCIA
SOPHENE
CORDUENE

Pergamum
Smyrna
Antiochia
Iconium

COMMAGENE
OSRHOENE
Zeugma

PARTHIAN EMPIRE

Halicarnassus
Attaleia
Side
Tarus
Antioch
Syria
Apamea

Rhodes
RHODES
LYCIA

Cyprus
Salamis

E M P I R E

G r e a t

W e s t e r n   S e a

Great Sea

Cyrene

Alexandria

DECAPOLIS
JUDAEA
INDEPENDENT TOWNS
NABATAEA
ARABS

Memphis

EGYPT

Nile

Red Sea

Thebes

Tropic of Cancer

A f r i c a

CAESAR'S CAMPAIGNS IN GAUL

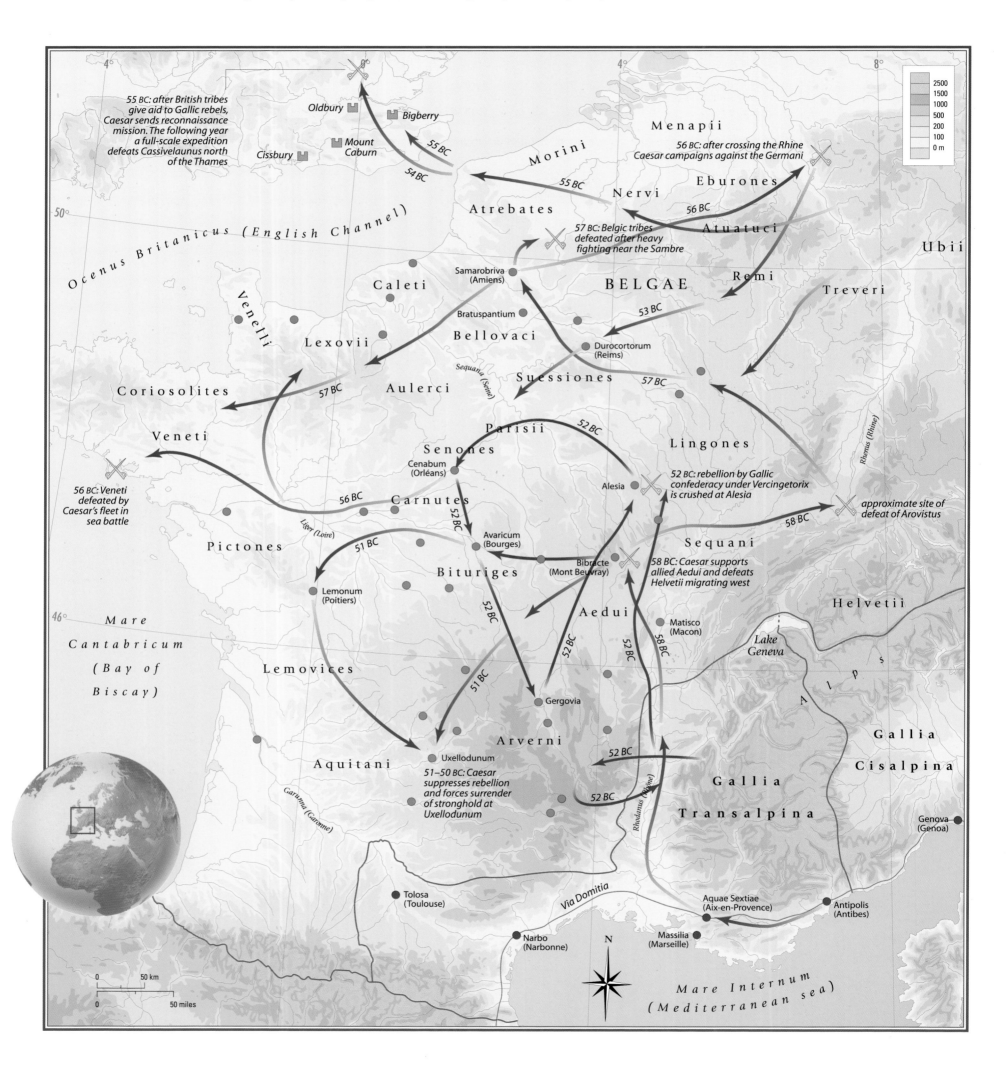

55 BC: after British tribes give aid to Gallic rebels, Caesar sends reconnaissance mission. The following year a full-scale expedition defeats Cassivelaunus north of the Thames

Oldbury

Bigberry

Cissbury

Mount Caburn

56 BC: after crossing the Rhine Caesar campaigns against the Germani

Menapii

Morini

Nervi

Eburones

Atrebates

Atuatuci

Ubii

57 BC: Belgic tribes defeated after heavy fighting near the Sambre

Remi

Treveri

BELGAE

Samarobriva (Amiens)

Caleti

Venelli

Bratuspantium

Bellovaci

Durocortorum (Reims)

Lexovii

Sequana (Seine)

Suessiones

Rhenus (Rhine)

Coriosolites

Aulerci

Parisii

Lingones

Veneti

Senones

Cenabum (Orléans)

Alesia

52 BC: rebellion by Gallic confederacy under Vercingetorix is crushed at Alesia

approximate site of defeat of Arovistus

56 BC: Veneti defeated by Caesar's fleet in sea battle

Carnutes

Ligar (Loire)

Avaricum (Bourges)

Sequani

Pictones

Bituriges

Bibracte (Mont Beuvray)

58 BC: Caesar supports allied Aedui and defeats Helvetii migrating west

Lemonum (Poitiers)

Helvetii

Mare Cantabricum (Bay of Biscay)

Aedui

Matisco (Macon)

Lake Geneva

Lemovices

Gergovia

A l p s

Aquitani

Uxellodunum

Arverni

Gallia Cisalpina

51–50 BC: Caesar suppresses rebellion and forces surrender of stronghold of Uxellodunum

Gallia

Garunna (Garonne)

Rhodanus (Rhône)

Transalpina

Genova (Genoa)

Tolosa (Toulouse)

Via Domitia

Aquae Sextiae (Aix-en-Provence)

Antipolis (Antibes)

Narbo (Narbonne)

N

Massilia (Marseille)

Mare Internum (Mediterranean sea)

Ocenus Britanicus (English Channel)

2500
1500
1000
500
200
100
0 m

0   50 km
0   50 miles

THE SIEGE OF ALESIA

CAESAR'S CAMPAIGNS IN GAUL 58–50 BC

→ Caesar's route (with date)

✕ Site of battle

● Major Gallic settlement

⬛ Major British hill fort

● Major Roman city

— Roman road

CAESAR'S CAMPAIGN IN GAUL 58–50 BC; THE SIEGE OF ALESIA 52 BC

Julius Caesar, by agreement of the Triumvirate, the ruling figures of the Roman Empire, was appointed governor of the two Gallic provinces, Gallia Transalpania and Gallia Cisalpania, together with Alesia. On taking up his new post he discovered that an entire people, the Helvetians, a Gallic tribe inhabiting an area approximating modern Switzerland, were on the move. Almost 400,000 people, of whom 100,000 were warriors, were heading for territory that was his responsibility.

Caesar moved into the northern part of the Rhone Valley, taking with him such troops that were available and raising allies from other Gallic tribes fearful of being overrun by the migrating Helvetians.

Finding their way blocked, the Helvetians continued eastward; Caesar attacked with 34,000 men at the Arar River, slaughtering some 30,000 Helvetian warriors caught on the east bank of the river. At the Battle of Bibracte (Mount Beuvray) the Helvetians turned and attacked Caesar with their remaining warriors. Caesar's 50,000-strong force succeeded in driving the Helvetians back toward their camp where they became intermingled with women and children. Pushing into this disorganized mass the Romans, in a vicious struggle, killed 130,000 people. The surviving Helvetians agreed to return to their homeland. A month later in August 58 BC Caesar launched a campaign against a marauding Germanic tribe under their chieftain Ariovistus. After careful maneuvering, Caesar attacked

Ariovistus, completely routing the Germans and driving them back across the Rhine. Most of south central Gaul now acknowledged Caesar as their ruler.

Caesar also stopped further Germanic incursions into Gallic territory in 55 BC, when two Germanic tribes, Usipetes and Tencteri, attempted to establish themselves in the area between the rivers Rhine and the Meuse. Caesar, anticipating a sneak attack during negotiations, struck first and completely annihilated the German force.

During 54 and 53 BC unrest seethed in Gaul. Hearing of various attacks on Roman detachments, Caesar marched with all the forces immediately available to him, only 7000 men, but still defeated 60,000 Gauls near Sabis, going on to join up with other Roman

units and consolidating his forces. By 53 BC Caesar now had ten legions under his command and went on to suppress the revolt in central Gaul. A further revolt broke out under the capable leadership of Vercingetorix. After a campaign through the spring and early summer of 52 BC Vercingetorix was cornered at Alesia. Here Caesar besieged the Gauls. Pleas from Vercingetorix brought a relief army of a quarter of a million men, which meant that the Romans themselves were now besieged. Caesar kept his head and repulsed attempts to relieve Vercingetorix. The Gauls trapped inside Alesia were now starving. In order to avoid further suffering, Vercingetorix surrendered. The Roman victory was complete—Gaul would be Roman for the next 450 years.

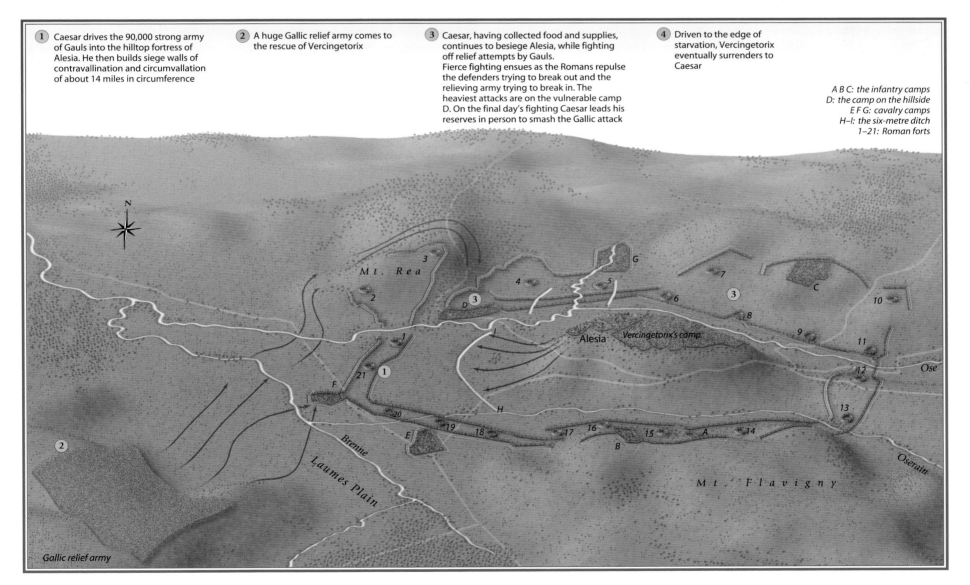

1 Caesar drives the 90,000 strong army of Gauls into the hilltop fortress of Alesia. He then builds siege walls of contravallation and circumvallation of about 14 miles in circumference

2 A huge Gallic relief army comes to the rescue of Vercingetorix

3 Caesar, having collected food and supplies, continues to besiege Alesia, while fighting off relief attempts by Gauls. Fierce fighting ensues as the Romans repulse the defenders trying to break out and the relieving army trying to break in. The heaviest attacks are on the vulnerable camp D. On the final day's fighting Caesar leads his reserves in person to smash the Gallic attack

4 Driven to the edge of starvation, Vercingetorix eventually surrenders to Caesar

A B C: the infantry camps
D: the camp on the hillside
E F G: cavalry camps
H–I: the six-metre ditch
1–21: Roman forts

Mt. Rea

Alesia

Vercingetorix's camp

Brenne

Laumes Plain

Mt. Flavigny

Ose

Oserain

Gallic relief army

THE BATTLE OF ACTIUM; ROMAN CIVIL WARS

THE BATTLE OF ACTIUM; ROMAN CIVIL WARS

In 50 BC Caesar was enjoying the benefits of his success, but was ordered to return to Rome by Pompey, who had been dubiously appointed sole Consul by the Senate. Pompey had urged the Senate to order Caesar to disband his legions and give up his provinces or face being declared a traitor. Caesar immediately marched on Rome, crossing the River Rubicon into Roman territory on the January 11 , 49 BC. Pompey, meanwhile, had failed to organize sufficient defenses and fled Italy with his government and a body of loyal troops.

Caesar immediately occupied Rome and set about securing Italy. With this achieved, Caesar turned his attention abroad during the next four years, with campaigns in Spain, southern France, Egypt, and Asia Minor. His charismatic leadership did much to ensure the devotion and loyalty of the troops under his command.

Caesar was murdered in a conspiracy by fellow members of the Senate on March 15 , 44 BC. Octavian, Caesar's nephew and heir, emerged to take Caesar's place; though no great soldier, Octavian was a capable politician. Initially as an ally of Brutus, a member of the conspiracy that had murdered his uncle, he fought a short campaign against the forces of Mark Antony. In August 43 BC he returned to Rome and forced the Senate to appoint him sole Consul, and by the end of the year he had reached an agreement with Mark Antony. Octavian then concentrated on punishing the assassins of Caesar. In the following ten years Octavian and Mark Antony consolidated power until, in 33 BC, Mark Antony rejected his marriage to Octavian's sister in favor of marriage to Cleopatra. Outraged, Octavian declared war against Cleopatra and stripped Antony of his titles. The Battle of Actium was a decisive victory for Octavian, allowing him to invade Egypt, and with the suicide, firstly of Mark Antony then Cleopatra, Octavian triumphed – Rome and the Empire was his.

CIVIL WARS 49–31 BC

- ■ Territory under Caesar
- ■ Territory under Pompey
- ■ Other Roman territory
- — Frontier of the Roman Empire c. 50 BC

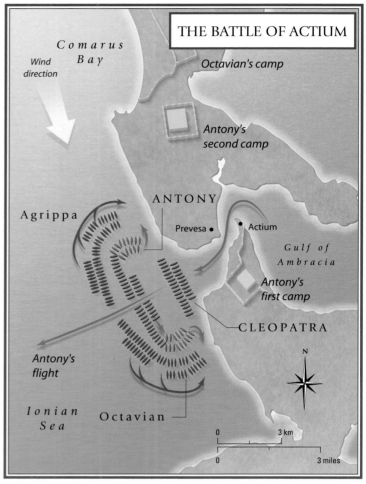

THE BATTLE OF ACTIUM

Comarus Bay

Wind direction

Octavian's camp

Antony's second camp

ANTONY

Agrippa

Prevesa • • Actium

Gulf of Ambracia

Antony's first camp

CLEOPATRA

Antony's flight

Ionian Sea

Octavian

0 — 3 km
0 — 3 miles

THE ROMAN EMPIRE AD 68; THE PARTHIAN WARS

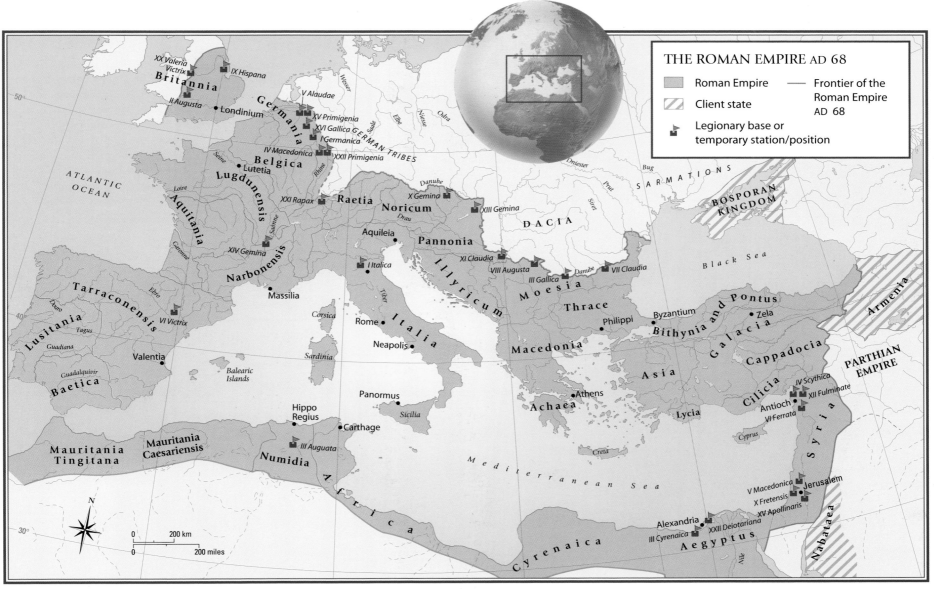

THE ROMAN EMPIRE AD 68

▨	Roman Empire
▨	Client state
⚑	Legionary base or temporary station/position
—	Frontier of the Roman Empire AD 68

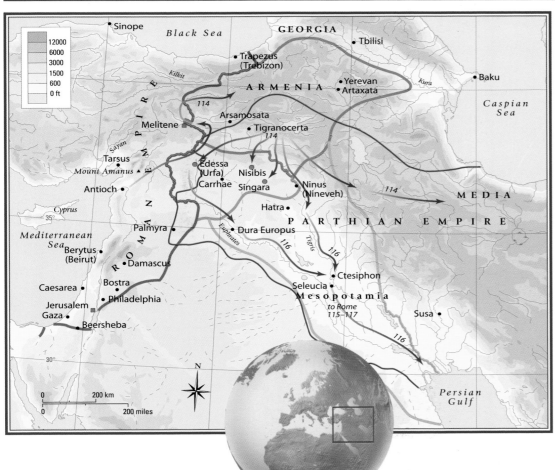

PARTHIAN WARS
AD 114–117

→	Trajan's campaigns (with date)
—	Frontier of Roman Empire
—	Annexed 114
—	Annexed 115
—	Temporary occupation by Rome in 116
—	Parthian Empire in 114
■	Roman provincial capital
■	Roman legionary base
●	Captured town

THE ROMAN EMPIRE AD 68

The Roman army numbered around 300,000 professional soldiers. Its highly trained, well-equipped troops ensured Roman domination of much of Europe and parts of the Near East. *Pax Romana*, the Peace of Rome, is usually considered to have begun in 29 BC under Octavian. It was a long period of relative peace and minimal expansion by military force. This golden age ended around AD 162 with the beginning of the eastern wars.

PARTHIAN WARS

In AD 113 Osroes of Parthia broke a long-standing treaty with Rome by installing a puppet regime on the throne of the valuable Kingdom of Armenia. The Emperor Trajan, who defeated the Parthians and captured the Persian capital at Ctesiphon, campaigned in the region until AD 116. He returned to subdue the Judian revolt in AD 117. The Peace of Rome was finally expunged in AD 162 with another Parthian invasion, this time led by Vologases III. After a three-year campaign the Parthians sued for peace.

THE ROMAN EMPIRE AD 214

THE ROMAN EMPIRE
AD 214
The defense of the Empire rested on the professionalism of its army, both in its ability to field mobile armies to meet threats along any point of its thousands of miles of frontiers and its ability to construct defenses at vulnerable points. Political instability at the center of the empire inevitably had some effect on the quality of Rome's armies. Two other trends began to influence Roman military policy. The first of these was a slow move from a highly trained infantry force toward a more mobile

cavalry force. The second was an increasing reliance on mercenaries recruited from neighboring tribes who lacked the professionalism and training of the Roman legion. There may have also been a subtle change in emphasis by the Roman leadership, from from one of offense to defense.

THE ROMAN EMPIRE
AD 395 (RIGHT)
The Roman requirement for increasing mobility to meet growing threats, especially in the east European steppe, involved a greater and greater deployment of cavalry. The Romans, copying their Persian opponents, covered the cavalryman and his steed with coats of chain mail, which gave a real degree of protection from lighter weapons. Despite

the increasing role for the cavalry, the Roman army still maintained garrisons and mobile armies at various bases around their Empire. The typical legion now stood at 6000 men composed of ten cohorts, two of which were 1000 strong, the other eight 500 in strength. By the end of the 4th century, the army could deploy a force of around 300,000 men.

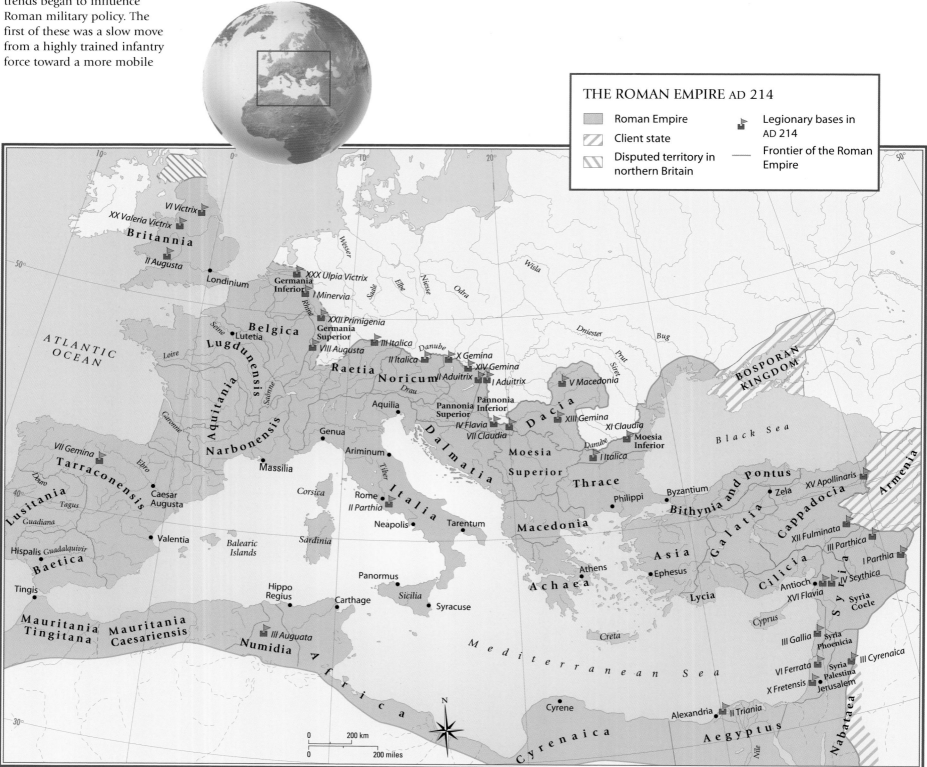

THE ROMAN EMPIRE AD 214

- ▨ Roman Empire
- ▨ Client state
- ▨ Disputed territory in northern Britain
- ⚑ Legionary bases in AD 214
- — Frontier of the Roman Empire

THE ROMAN EMPIRE AD 395

WESTERN DIVISION

Britanniae
1. Valentia
2. Britannia II
3. Flavia Caesariensis
4. Britannia
5. Maxima Caesariensis

Galliae
1. Ludgunensis III
2. Ludgunensis II
3. Belgica II
4. Germania II
5. Ludgunensis Senonia
6. Ludgunensis I
7. Belgica I
8. Germania I
9. Maxima Sequanorum

Septum Provinciae
1. Aquitanica II
2. Aquitanica I
3. Novem Populi

4. Narbonensis I
5. Viennensis
6. Narbonensis II
7. Alpes Maritimae

Hispaniae
1. Gallaecia
2. Carthaginiensis
3. Tarraconensis
4. Lusitania
5. Baetica
6. Insulae Balearum
7. Tingitania

Africa
1. Mauretania Caesariensis
2. Mauretania Sitifensis
3. Numidia
4. Africa
5. Byzacena
6. Tripolitania

Italia
1. Alpes Cottiae
2. Aemilia
3. Raetia I
4. Raetia II
5. Liguria
6. Venetia et Histria
7. Flaminia et Picenum

Suburbicaria
1. Corsica
2. Sardinia
3. Tuscia et Umbria
4. Valeria
5. Picenum Suburbicarium
6. Roma
7. Campania
8. Samnium
9. Bruttii et Lucania
10. Apulia et Calabria
11. Sicilia

Pannonia (to ca.400); Illyricum (after ca. 400)
1. Noricum Ripense
2. Noricum Meditterraneum
3. Pannonia I
4. Valeria
5. Savia
6. Pannonia II
7. Dalmatia

EASTERN DIVISION

Dacia
1. Moesia I
2. Dacia Ripensis
3. Praevalitana
4. Dardania
5. Dacia Mediterranea

Macedonia
1. Epirus Nova
2. Macedonia
3. Epirus Vetus

4. Thessalia
5. Achaea
6. Creta

Thraciae
1. Moesia II
2. Scythia
3. Thracia
4. Haemimontus
5. Rhodope
6. Europa

Asiana
1. Hellespontus
2. Phrygia Pacatiana
3. Phrygia Salutaris
4. Asia
5. Lydia
6. Pisidia
7. Lycaonia
8. Caria

9. Pamphylia
10. Insulae
11. Lycia

Pontica
1. Bithynia
2. Honorias
3. Paphlagonia
4. Helenopontus
5. Pontus Polemoniacus
6. Galatia
7. Armenia I
8. Galatia Salutaris
9. Cappadocia II
10. Cappadocia I
11. Armenia II

Oriens
1. Isauria
2. Cilicia I
3. Cilicia II

4. Euphratensis
5. Mesopotamia
6. Syria
7. Osrhoene
8. Cyprus
9. Syria Salutaris
10. Phoenice
11. Phoenice Libanensis
12. Palaestina II
13. Arabia
14. Palestina I
15. Palestina Salutaris

Aegyptus
1. Libya Superior
2. Libya Inferior
3. Aegyptus
4. Augustamnica
5. Arcadia
6. Thebais

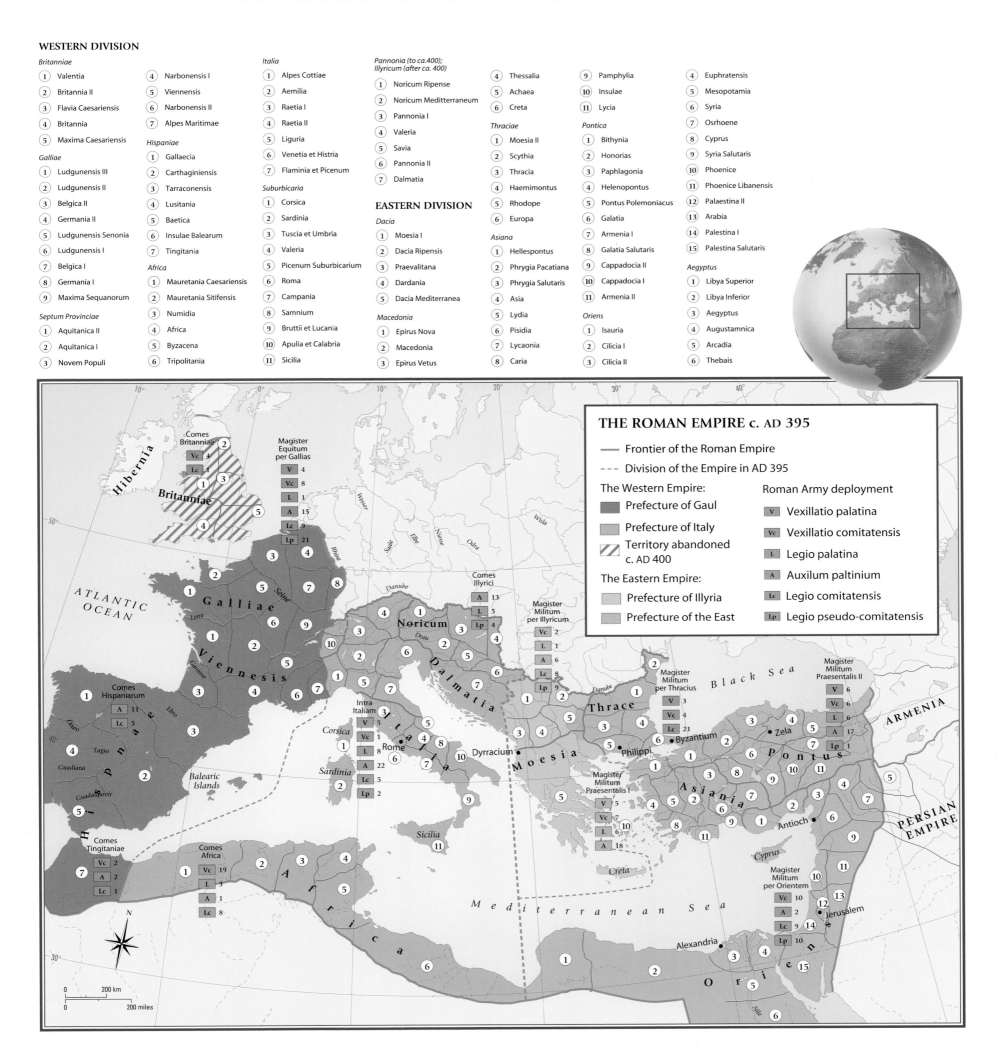

THE ROMAN EMPIRE c. AD 395

— Frontier of the Roman Empire

– – – Division of the Empire in AD 395

The Western Empire:
- Prefecture of Gaul
- Prefecture of Italy
- Territory abandoned c. AD 400

The Eastern Empire:
- Prefecture of Illyria
- Prefecture of the East

Roman Army deployment
- **V** Vexillatio palatina
- **Vc** Vexillatio comitatensis
- **L** Legio palatina
- **A** Auxilium paltinium
- **Lc** Legio comitatensis
- **Lp** Legio pseudo-comitatensis

AD 357 – 475 ENEMY AT THE GATES

ENEMY AT THE GATES
By AD 300 the Goths had arrived on the lower Danube, while the Franks occupied the middle and lower Rhine. These, along with other wandering Germanic tribes, posed the greatest potential threat to the Roman Empire. By now the Roman Empire itself had been reorganised into the Eastern and Western Empires. In AD 375 war-like Huns from central Asia attacked the Ostrogoths, forcing them to head for the protection of Rome, where they

were allowed to settle.

Further west, other Germanic groups continued to migrate into the Empire. They were absorbed and granted federate status in return for defending imperial interests against some of their fellow Germanic tribes. But in reality the settlers formed power centers in their own right.

During the 4th and 5th centuries Rome's taxation income fell, together with its ability to control its new Germanic allies.

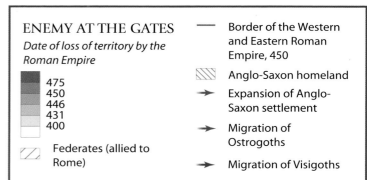

ENEMY AT THE GATES
Date of loss of territory by the Roman Empire

- 475
- 450
- 446
- 431
- 400

Federates (allied to Rome)

— Border of the Western and Eastern Roman Empire, 450

Anglo-Saxon homeland

→ Expansion of Anglo-Saxon settlement

→ Migration of Ostrogoths

→ Migration of Visigoths

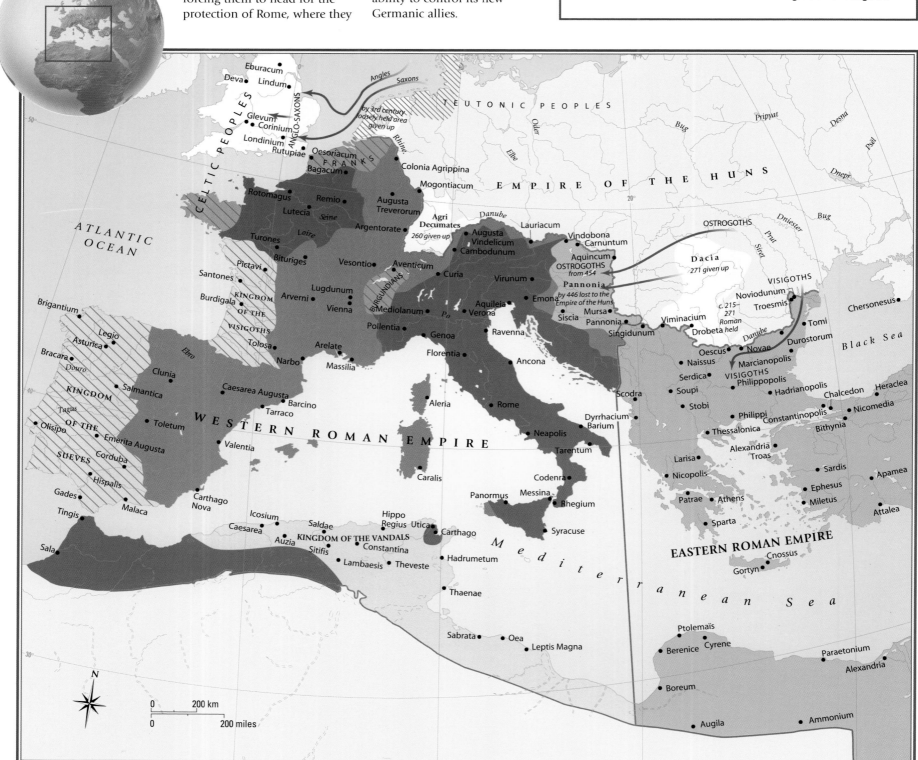

THE BATTLE OF STRASBOURG

THE BATTLE OF STRASBOURG AD 357

In AD 357 the Roman army faced a Germanic force—from the Alamanni alliance of tribes —of around 35,000 men. However, although the Roman Empire was by this time showing signs of weakness, the army's professionalism and training still prevailed in a hard-fought battle.

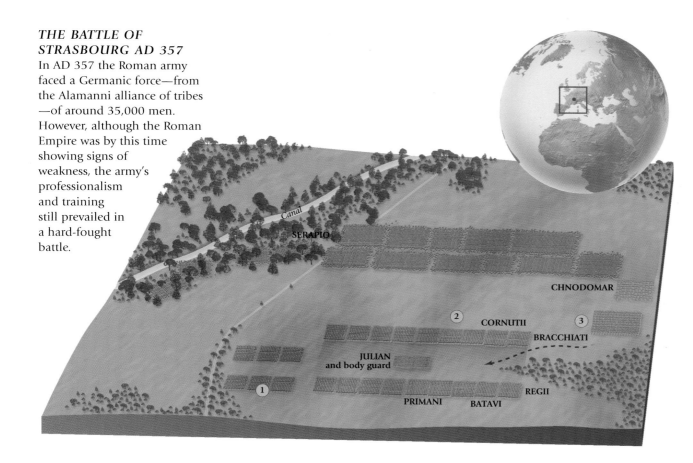

1. Romans suspicious of ambush in the broken ground. The Roman left flank commanded by Seveus halts

2. Remainder of Roman line advances and Germans advance to meet them

3. Roman cavalry and German cavalry engage heavily. Fight sways one way then the other. Roman cavalry panic while reforming and flee towards the second line of the Roman infantry

4. The infantry remain steady in the face of this panic. The cavalry begin to rally behind the formed infantry. The process is aided by Julian who arrives, presumably with his 200 bodyguard cavalry

5. Continued German pressure on the first Roman line. The Batavi and the Regii are sent forward to reinforce the veteran Cornuti and Bracchiati in the front ranks

6. A group of Germans led by several of their kings surge forward to break the stalemate in the center. They penetrate the Roman first line and advance against the Primani in the center of the second line. This legion remains firm

7. Gradual Roman pressure along the whole line causes the Alamanni to collapse. They suffer heavy losses in the pursuit. 243 Romans are killed

8. Defeated Roman cavalry reforming

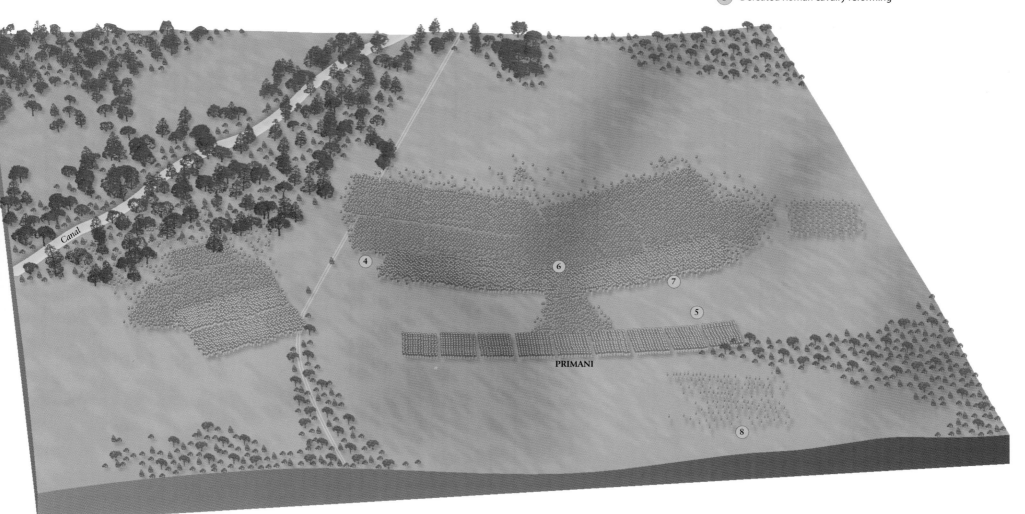

FRONTIERS OF NORTHERN BRITAIN

AD 122 – C. 500

FRONTIERS OF NORTHERN BRITAIN

The far borders of the Roman Empire were always vulnerable and the risk of invasion by marauding tribes was ever present. When Emperor Hadrian visited Britain in AD 122 he ordered a wall to be built along the northern border to prevent military raids by Pictish tribes. After his death in 138 the new emperor, Antonius Pius decided that these northern tribes would be more easily conquered if another wall was built 100 miles further north. The tribes remained unconquered and Antonius's successor, Marcus Arelius abandoned the Antonine Wall and in 164 the Legions reoccupied Hadrian's Wall where they remained until the Roman withdrawal in around 407.

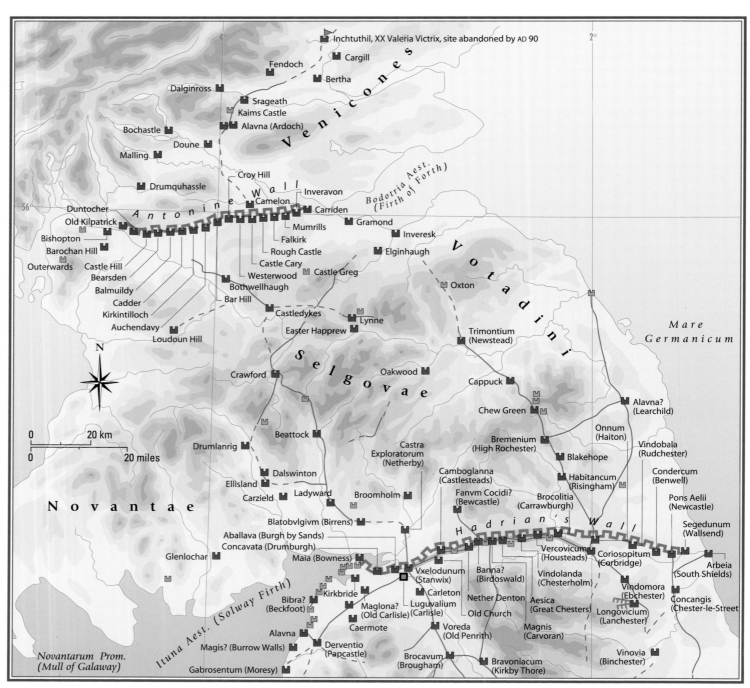

FRONTIERS OF NORTHERN BRITAIN 1st–4th CENTURY AD

— Stanegate

⊓⊔ Roman wall

Legionary fortress

Fort

Fortlet

Walled town

Aquaduct

? Roman name doubtful

THE GERMANIC KINGDOMS

THE GERMANIC KINGDOMS C. 500

In AD 395 the Visigoths renounced their allegiance to Rome, invaded Greece, then moved through Italy into Spain. Many other Germanic tribes were also on the move around this time; the Angle and Saxon tribes were intent on seizing the eastern part of the British Isles, while the Vandals were moving through Spain and into north Africa, where they seized Carthage and made it their capital.

The Roman world dissolved under this onslaught. However, the Roman world did not disappear completely. Elements of Roman administration continued under Theoderic's Ostrogothic rule, and somehow Christianity survived. This would create a continuing link with Rome and a new form of Christian civilization.

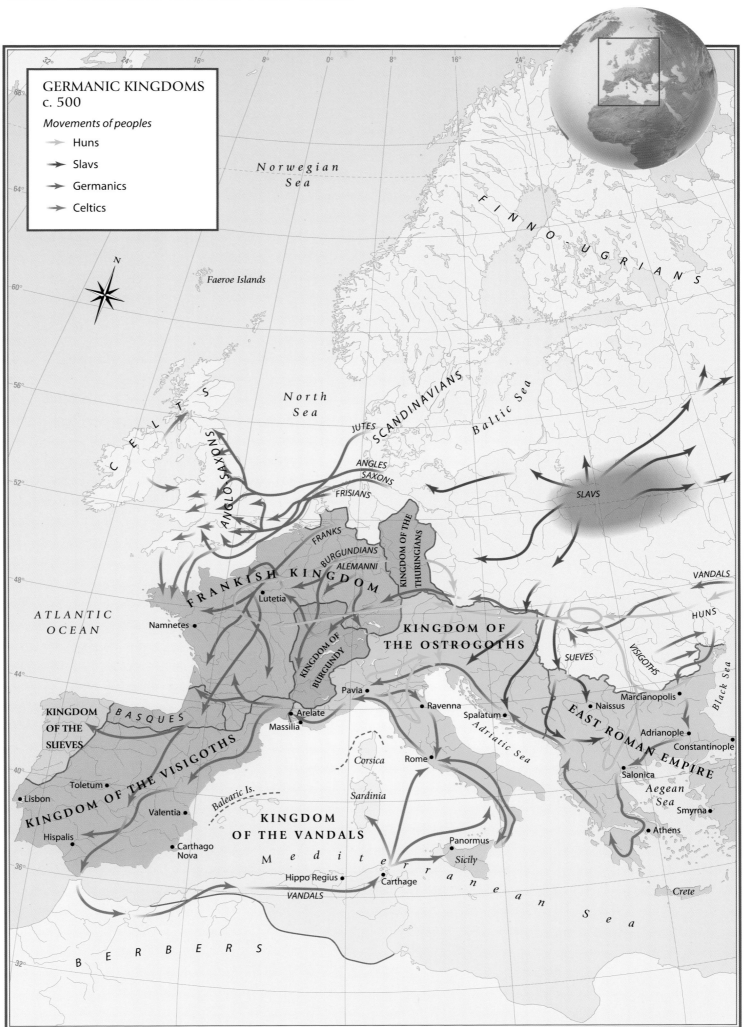

GERMANIC KINGDOMS
c. 500

Movements of peoples

→ Huns
→ Slavs
→ Germanics
→ Celtics

THE EMPIRE IN THE EAST

THE EMPIRE IN THE EAST

During the 4th and 5th centuries the Roman Empire split in two, with the eastern part centered around Constantinople and the west around Rome. The East Roman Empire, under the rule of Justinian I in the 6th century, was inspired by the idea of a Christian Roman Empire that might be restored to its old boundaries, especially in the west. The vision was for Rome to once again dominate the Mediterranean world. In a series of successful military campaigns, Justinian I brought Italy, Dalmatia, north Africa, and southern Spain under Roman control. However, Justinian's ambition to restore the Roman Empire to its former glory was only partly realized. In the west, the brilliant early military successes of the 530s were followed by years of stagnation. The dragging war with the Goths was a disaster for Italy, and large parts of Italy, Spain, and Africa were lost to Roman control shortly after Justinian's death. In short, the victories under Justinian were successful in boosting Roman prestige, but unsuccessful in providing a platform for long-term expansion. Justinian had overstretched the resources of the Eastern Empire, and in so doing may have contributed to its subsequent decline.

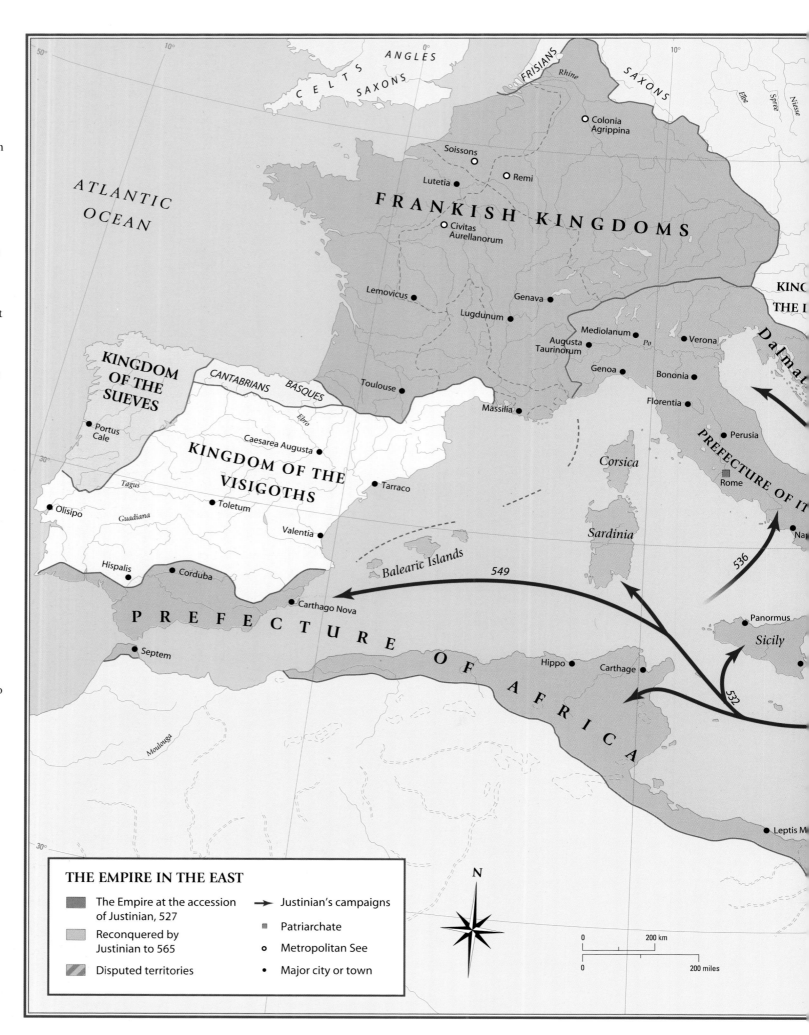

THE EMPIRE IN THE EAST

■ The Empire at the accession of Justinian, 527	→ Justinian's campaigns
■ Reconquered by Justinian to 565	■ Patriarchate
▨ Disputed territories	○ Metropolitan See
	● Major city or town

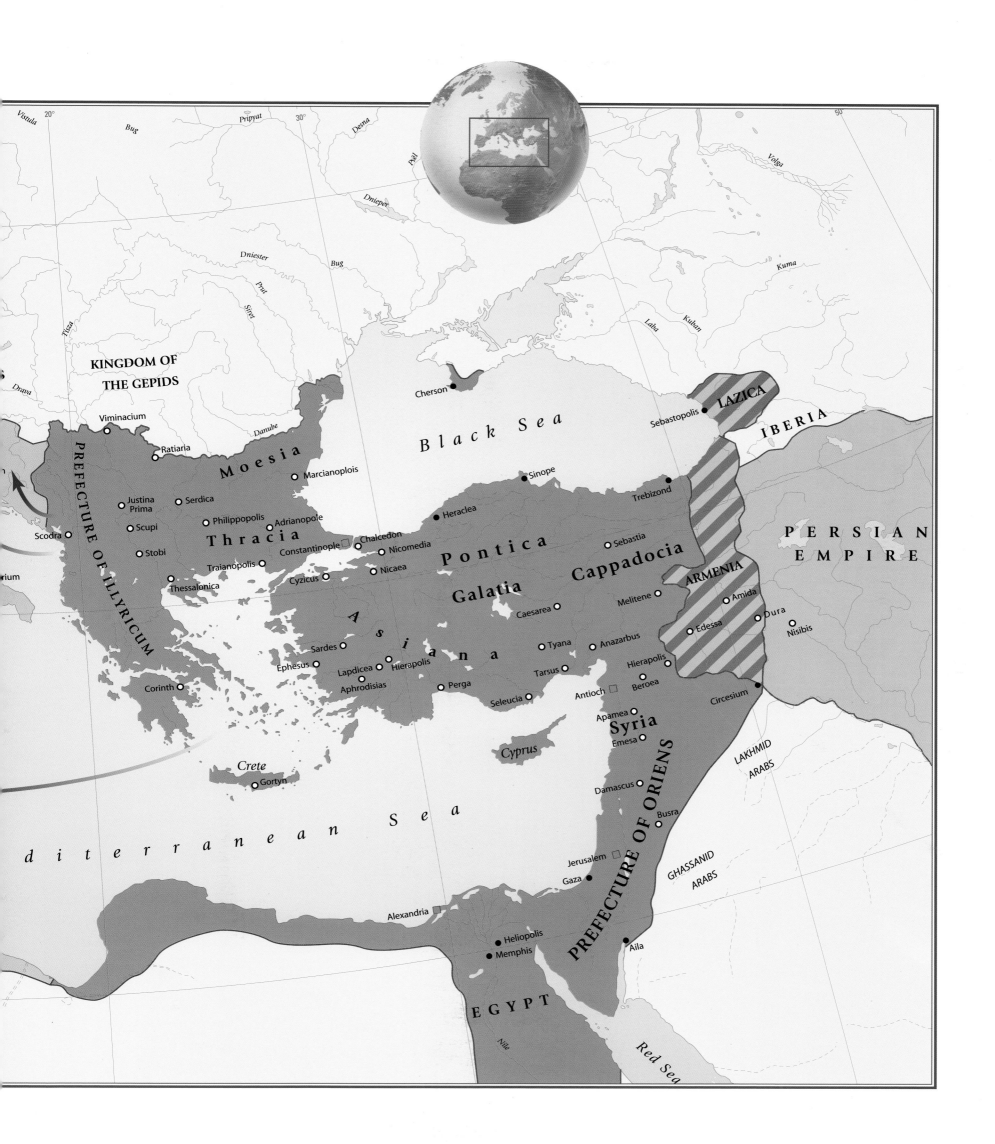

KINGDOM OF
THE GEPIDS

Vistula 20° *Bug* *Pripyat* 30° *Desna*

Dniester *Bug*

Prut *Siret* *Danube*

Drava

Tisza

Dnieper

Volga

Kuma

Laba *Kuban*

Black Sea

LAZICA

IBERIA

Sebastopolis ● LAZICA

PREFECTURE OF ILLYRICUM

Viminacium

Ratiaria

Moesia

● Marcianoplis

Sinope ●

Trebizond ●

P E R S I A N
E M P I R E

Justina
Prima

Serdica

Philippopolis

Scupi Adrianopole

Thracia

Stobi

Traianopolis

Thessalonica

Scodra

rium

Heraclea ●

Cherson ●

Sebastia ●

ARMENIA

Melitene ● Amida ●

Dura ●

Nisibis ●

Chalcedon
Constantinople □ Nicomedia
Nicaea

Cyzicus

Pontica

Galatia *Cappadocia*

Caesarea ●

Edessa ●

A s i a n a

Sardes ●

Tyana ● Anazarbus ●

Ephesus ●

Lapdicea ● Hierapolis ●

Aphrodisias ●

Perga ●

Tarsus ●

Hierapolis ●

Beroea ●

Seleucia ●

Antioch □

Circesium ●

Corinth ○

Apamea ●
Emesa ●

Syria

LAKHMID
ARABS

Cyprus

Crete

● Gortyn

diterranean Sea

Damascus ●

Busra ●

PREFECTURE OF ORIENS

Jerusalem □

Gaza ●

GHASSANID
ARABS

Alexandria □

Heliopolis ●

Memphis ●

Aila ●

Nile

Red Sea

EGYPT

THE EMERGENCE OF HUNGARY; THE BATTLE OF LECHFELD

C. 895 – 1000

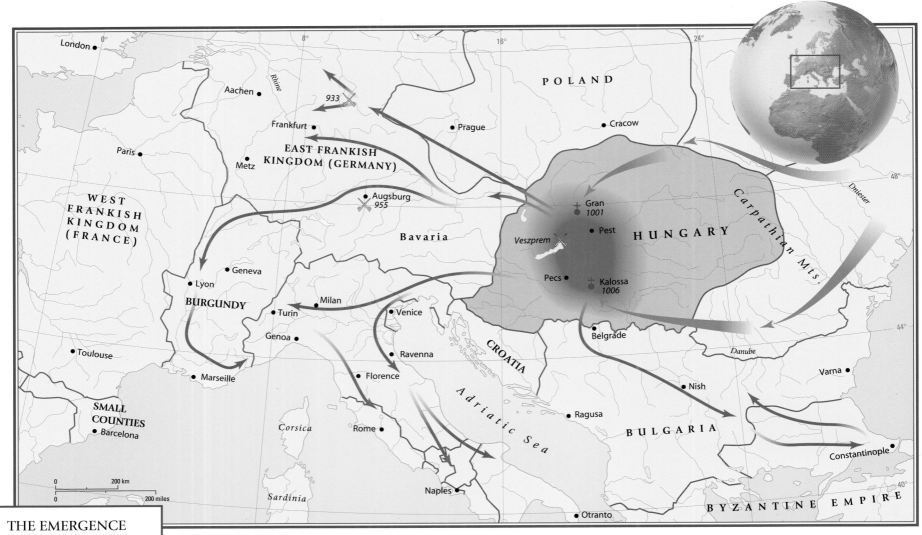

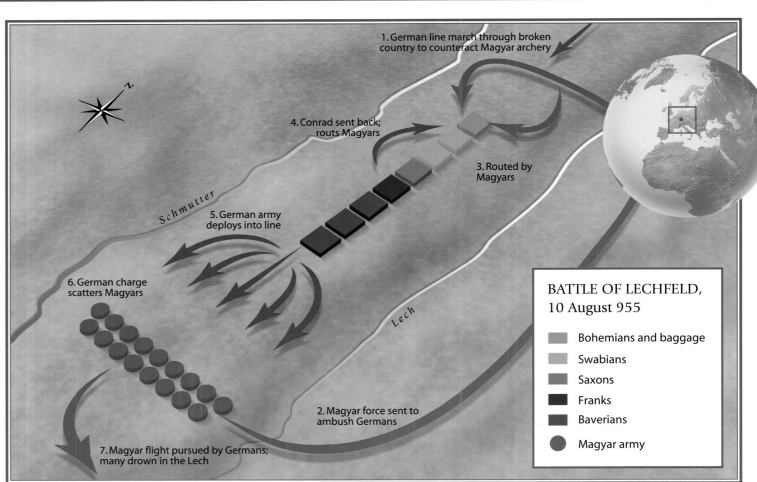

THE EMERGENCE OF HUNGARY

→ Magyar migration into central Europe, c. 895

■ Area of settlement by 900

→ Major Magyar raid, 900–55

Hungary by 1000

☦ Archbishopric, with date of foundation

THE EMERGENCE OF HUNGARY; THE BATTLE OF LECHFELD 10 AUGUST, 955

The Magyars, an ethnic group from Hungary, were light un-armoured horsemen who relied on manoeuvrability and delivery of their missile weapon, the bow, to achieve success. They would if at all possible avoid hand-to-hand combat with the heavily armed west Europeans. In 955, at the Battle of Lechfeld, their usual tactics fell apart when the Magyar main body was successfully charged by German heavy cavalry.

BATTLE OF LECHFELD, 10 August 955

■ Bohemians and baggage

■ Swabians

■ Saxons

■ Franks

■ Baverians

● Magyar army

1. German line march through broken country to counteract Magyar archery

4. Conrad sent back; routs Magyars

3. Routed by Magyars

5. German army deploys into line

6. German charge scatters Magyars

2. Magyar force sent to ambush Germans

7. Magyar flight pursued by Germans; many drown in the Lech

PART 2

DARK AGES TO THE RISE OF ISLAM

*T*HIS PERIOD SAW THE DISAPPEARANCE of the classical infantry phalanx in favor of the mounted warrior. The major weapon on the battlefield, whether used by the mounted or the foot soldier, was the bow. This dictated a tactic of fire and movement; the impact of cavalry or infantry in any engagement was secondary to the effect of missile attack. However, the Byzantines retained distinct elements of the classical tradition, and they required their army to attain a high state of discipline and control which involved a great degree of cooperation between cavalry and infantry. The Byzantines also utilized intelligence and disinformation operations against any potential enemy.

After AD 634 Islamic armies, converted into a formidable ideological as well as military force, broke out of the Arabian peninsula and defeated the greatest military forces of the age: Sassanian Persia and Byzantium. They captured Jerusalem in 638, and by 644 they had conquered Egypt and Libya. By 700 they had advanced into central Asia, conquered Spain, and were capable of raiding deep into central France.

VIKING, MAGYAR, AND ABBASID INVASIONS

C. 800 – 913

VIKING, MAGYAR, AND ABBASID INVASIONS OF C. 910

Between the 8th and 10th centuries Europe was subject to Viking raids from the north and Magyar and Muslim raids from the south. By the 10th century the Muslims occupied Spain, the Balearic Islands, Sardinia, Sicily, and Corsica. The Magyars had arrived along the shores of the Danube in the 890s. These nomadic cavalrymen raided across Germany, France, and northern Italy, using speed and mobility. They later settled under King Stephan I in an area that became Hungary and which also became Christian.

The Vikings were natural sailors and used their nautical skills in their raids. They were able to appear without warning at any point along thousands of miles of coastline. They sailed the coasts of western Europe into the Mediterranean and also along the river systems of eastern Europe, reaching the Black and Caspian Seas. In the Atlantic, they settled Iceland and Greenland and were the first Europeans to visit north America. Aside from raiding substantial population movements they created new political entities, with Dane Law introduced in England and in Normandy, France.

INVASIONS OF c. 910

→ Viking invasions

→ Magyar invasions

→ Abbasid invasions

▨ Permanent Scandinavian settlement

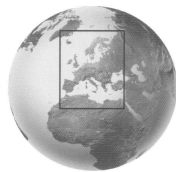

THE SWEDES IN THE EAST

THE SWEDES IN THE EAST 800–913
While Vikings from Norway and Denmark looked southwards and westwards, Swedish Vikings looked to the east. They used the rivers Dvina and Dnieper to navigate across eastern Europe, establishing colonies at Novgorod and Kiev and on to the Black Sea. Here they challenged the Khazars for control of the lucrative Black Sea trade. Eventually they would found the Kievan Rus state and were, in time, absorbed into the Slav population and the eastern orthodox Christian culture. By the year 1000 the scourge of the Viking raider had to all intents and purposes come to an end. Their descendants, the Normans, now picked up the sword.

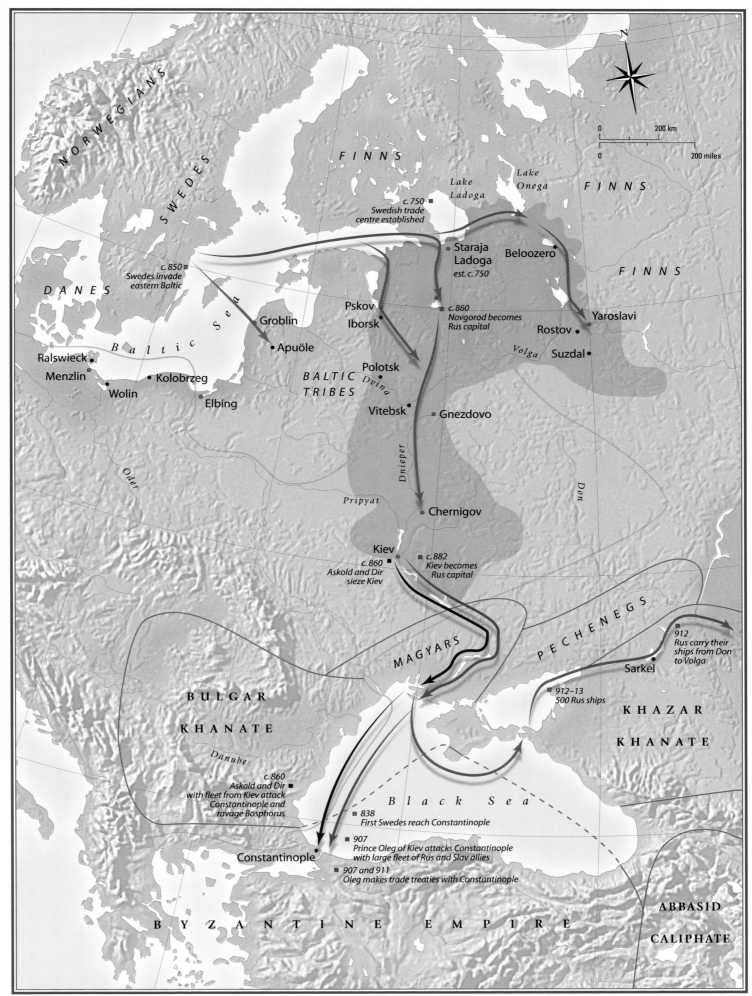

THE SWEDES IN
THE EAST, 800–913

— Slavs, c. 800

▨ Area under Rus control
  by 912

• Center of significant
  Swedish population

→ Main lines of Swedish
  penetration

➤ Askold and Dir, c. 860

➤ Oleg 907

➤ Rus fleet, 912–13

1035 – 1092

NORMANDY AND THE BRITISH ISLES; THE BATTLE OF HASTINGS

NORMANDY AND THE BRITISH ISLES 1035–1092; BATTLE OF HASTINGS 1066

When Rollo, a Viking leader, was made Count of Normandy by the King of France in an attempt to make peace with the Viking raiders, he inadvertently created a new society. An amalgam of Viking settlers and the local population forged a military society that left a lasting mark on European history.

King Edward the Confessor's death, in 1066, left England without an heir to the throne. Duke William of Normandy claimed that the English King had promised him the Kingdom in 1051 and that Harold Godwinson had sworn to be William's vassal and to help him acquire the English throne. However, Edward gave the Kingdom to Harold on his deathbed.

Claimants to the English throne began mobilizing their armies. As well as William of Normandy, Harold Hardrada of Norway set out to claim England for his own.

In September 1066 King Harold of England defeated the Norwegian invasion at Stamford Bridge, 7 miles East of York in the north of England, but he then learned that William of Normandy had landed at Pevensey on the south coast. Harold rushed south to meet this new threat, but was defeated at the Battle of Hastings.

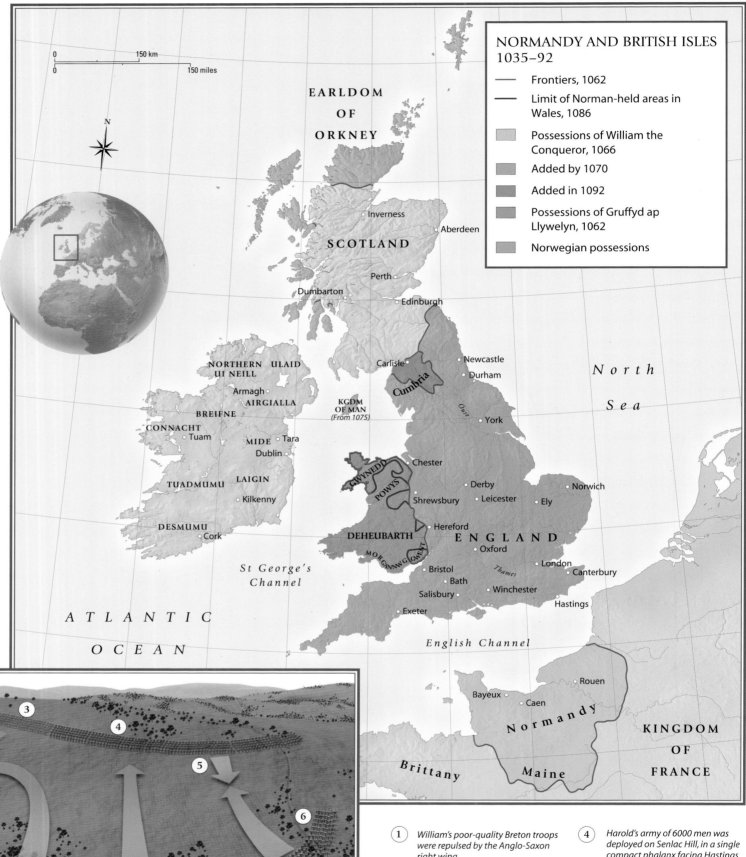

NORMANDY AND BRITISH ISLES 1035–92

- —— Frontiers, 1062
- —— Limit of Norman-held areas in Wales, 1086
- Possessions of William the Conqueror, 1066
- Added by 1070
- Added in 1092
- Possessions of Gruffyd ap Llywelyn, 1062
- Norwegian possessions

① William's poor-quality Breton troops were repulsed by the Anglo-Saxon right wing

② The Anglo-Saxon right wing then pursued the fleeing Bretons but were hit in the rear by Norman knights

③ Harold's left and right wings were staffed by unarmoured fyrdmen (local militia), with housecarls in the centre

④ Harold's army of 6000 men was deployed on Senlac Hill, in a single compact phalanx facing Hastings

⑤ A feint attack by William's right wing drew more of the Anglo-Saxons out from the daunting shield wall

⑥ William's centre and right faltered after the loss of the left wing but William rallied them successfully

CONQUEST OF ENGLAND

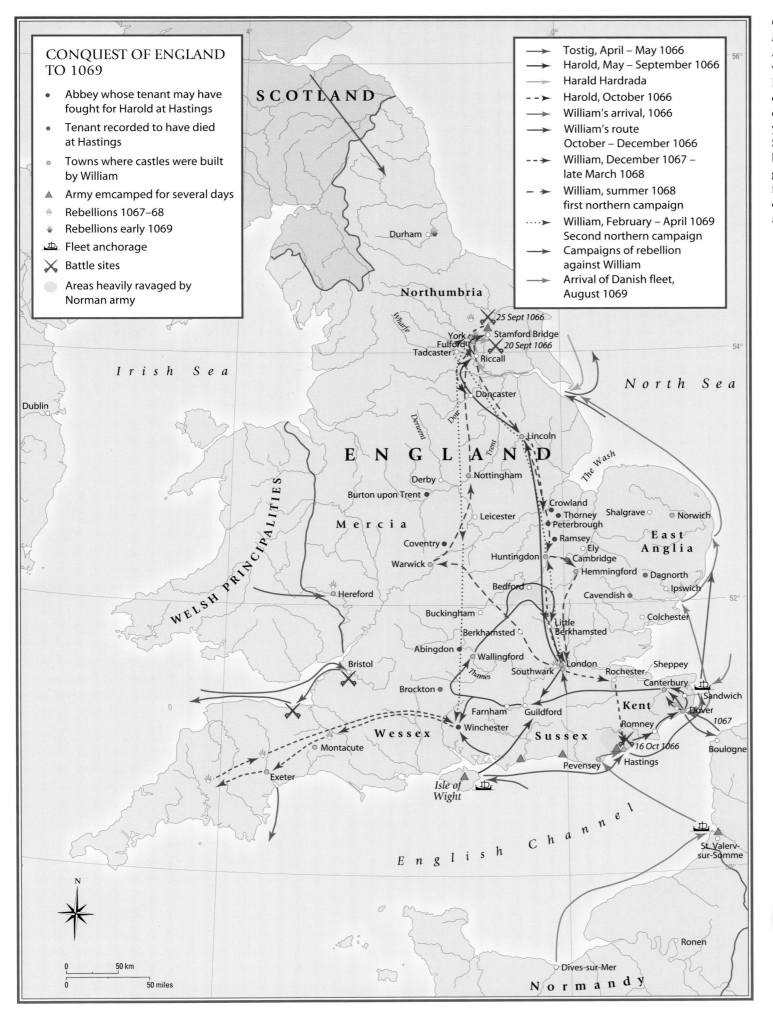

CONQUEST OF ENGLAND TO 1069

- • Abbey whose tenant may have fought for Harold at Hastings
- • Tenant recorded to have died at Hastings
- ○ Towns where castles were built by William
- ▲ Army emcamped for several days
- ⚜ Rebellions 1067–68
- ⚜ Rebellions early 1069
- ⚓ Fleet anchorage
- ✕ Battle sites
- ⬤ Areas heavily ravaged by Norman army

→	Tostig, April – May 1066
→	Harold, May – September 1066
→	Harald Hardrada
⇢	Harold, October 1066
→	William's arrival, 1066
→	William's route October – December 1066
⇢	William, December 1067 – late March 1068
⇢	William, summer 1068 first northern campaign
⋯⋯→	William, February – April 1069 Second northern campaign
→	Campaigns of rebellion against William
→	Arrival of Danish fleet, August 1069

CONQUEST OF ENGLAND TO 1069

After William's hard-fought victory at the Battle of Hastings, he set about claiming his new kingdom, campaigning for almost three years. Bit by bit the Anglo-Saxon aristocracy was replaced by loyal followers who were granted the right to build fortifications from which they could control the districts allotted to them.

636 – 750   THE BATTLE OF YARMUK

***THE BATTLE OF
YARMUK 636***
This battle was fought between
the Muslim Arabs and the
Byzantine Roman Empire and
took place northeast of the Sea
of Galilee. Many historians
regard it as being one of the
most significant battles in
history, because it marked the
first great wave of Muslim
conquest outside the Arabian
Peninsular. It also heralded the
rapid advance of Islam into
Christian Palestine, Syria, and
Mesopotamia. The battle lasted
for six days and at the end the
exhausted Byzantine army were
surrounded so that they were
unable to use their weapons.
Most were killed or captured.

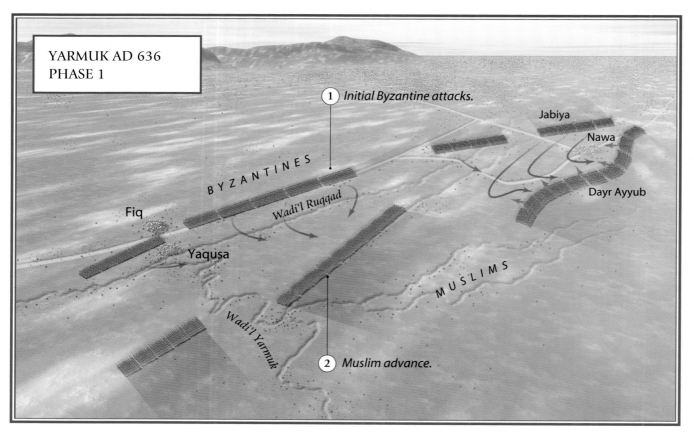

YARMUK AD 636
PHASE 1

1 *Initial Byzantine attacks.*

2 *Muslim advance.*

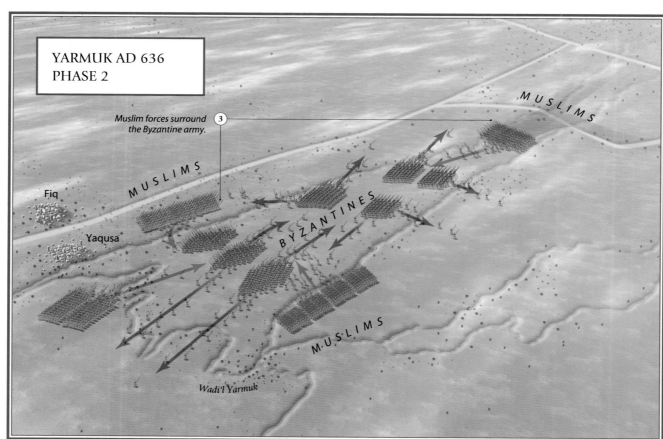

YARMUK AD 636
PHASE 2

*Muslim forces surround
the Byzantine army.* 3

***THE EXPANSION
OF ISLAM TO 750*** (RIGHT)
Islam is a religion based on
the teachings of the prophet
Muhammad. Muhammad was
born in Mecca, but local
hostility forced him to move
to Medina in 615. Within five
years he had united the Arab
tribes over a large area, but in
632 he died. For the next 29
years Islamic expansion was
overseen by four Islamic
leaders, known as Caliphs. The
first of these was Abu Bakr, and
within two years the faith had
spread throughout the Arabian
Peninsula and beyond. Within
little more than 100 years
Islam had spread throughout
the Middle East and included
territory from Central Asia to
the Atlantic.

THE EXPANSION OF ISLAM

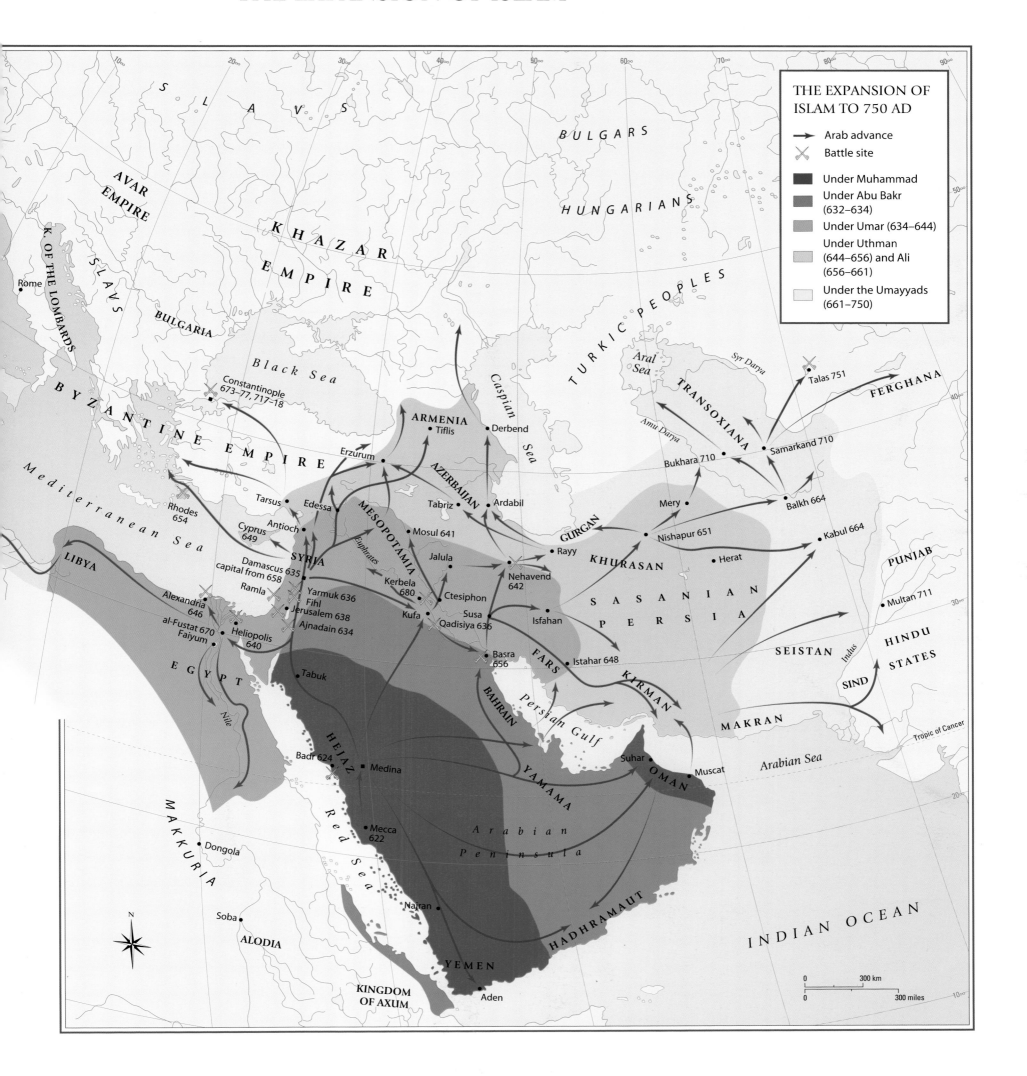

THE EXPANSION OF
ISLAM TO 750 AD

→ Arab advance

✕ Battle site

Under Muhammad

Under Abu Bakr
(632–634)

Under Umar (634–644)

Under Uthman
(644–656) and Ali
(656–661)

Under the Umayyads
(661–750)

SLAVS

AVAR
EMPIRE

K. OF THE LOMBARDS

SLAVS

Rome

BULGARIA

BYZANTINE EMPIRE

KHAZAR
EMPIRE

BULGARS

HUNGARIANS

TURKIC PEOPLES

Black Sea

Constantinople
673–77, 717–18

Aral
Sea

Syr Darya

Talas 751

TRANSOXIANA

FERGHANA

ARMENIA
Tiflis
Derbend

Caspian
Sea

Amu Darya

Bukhara 710

Samarkand 710

Erzurum

AZERBAIJAN

Tabriz
Ardabil

Mery

Balkh 664

Mediterranean Sea

Tarsus
Edessa

MESOPOTAMIA

GURGAN

Nishapur 651

Rhodes
654

Antioch

Cyprus
649

SYRIA

Euphrates

Mosul 641

Jalula

Rayy

KHURASAN

Herat

Kabul 664

PUNJAB

LIBYA

Damascus 635
capital from 658

Ramla

Kerbela
680

Nehavend
642

Ctesiphon

SASANIAN PERSIA

Multan 711

Alexandria
646

Yarmuk 636
Fihl
Jerusalem 638
Ajnadain 634

Kufa

Susa
Qadisiya 636

Isfahan

SEISTAN

HINDU
STATES

al-Fustat 670
Faiyum

Heliopolis
640

Istahar 648

KIRMAN

SIND

EGYPT

Tabuk

Basra
656

FARS

Nile

BAHRAIN

Persian Gulf

MAKRAN

Tropic of Cancer

MAKKURIA

HEJAZ

Badr 624

Medina

Red Sea

YAMAMA

Suhar

OMAN

Muscat

Arabian Sea

Dongola

Mecca
622

Arabian
Peninsula

Najran

Soba

ALODIA

HADHRAMAUT

INDIAN OCEAN

YEMEN

Aden

KINGDOM
OF AXUM

0   300 km
0   300 miles

1071 – 1220 THE SELJUK ERA

THE SELJUQ ERA

→ Major Seljuq campaign

▢ Seljuq sultinate at its
maximum extent,
c. 1090

▢ Byzantine Empire,
c. 1095

▢ Territory lost to
Byzantine Empire and
crusader states,
1097–99

◯ Extent of the Khwarizm
Shahdom, c. 1220

THE SELJUK ERA
The Seljuks were a Turkic Sunni
Muslim dynasty that ruled
major parts of the Middle East
and central Asia from the 11th
to 12th centuries. At its
greatest extent the Great Seljuk
Empire stretched from Anatolia to the
Punjab. In the 1090s the
Empire suffered a period of
great internal discord. When
the First Crusade arrived in
1095 the fractured states of the
empire were more concerned
with consolidating their own
territories and gaining control
of their neighbours than with

co-operating against the
invading crusaders. As a result
the First Crusade succeeded in
capturing the Holy land and
setting up the Crusader States.

BATTLE OF MANZIKERT
This battle was fought between
the Byzantine Empire and the
Seljuk Turkish forces, led by
Seljuk Sultan Alp Arslan. It
resulted in the defeat of the
Byzantines and the capture of
Emperor Romanos IV. The
slow-moving Byzantine
infantry were no real match
against the fast-moving Turkish
cavalry, who used the classic
hit and run tactics of the
steppe warriors. The Byzantines
were confused by this form of
attack and the Seljuks seized
the advantage, repeatedly

attacking and eventually
routing the Byzantines.
Romanos was taken prisoner,
and on his release he was
deposed by his own people. He
was brutally blinded and died
from a subsequent infection.

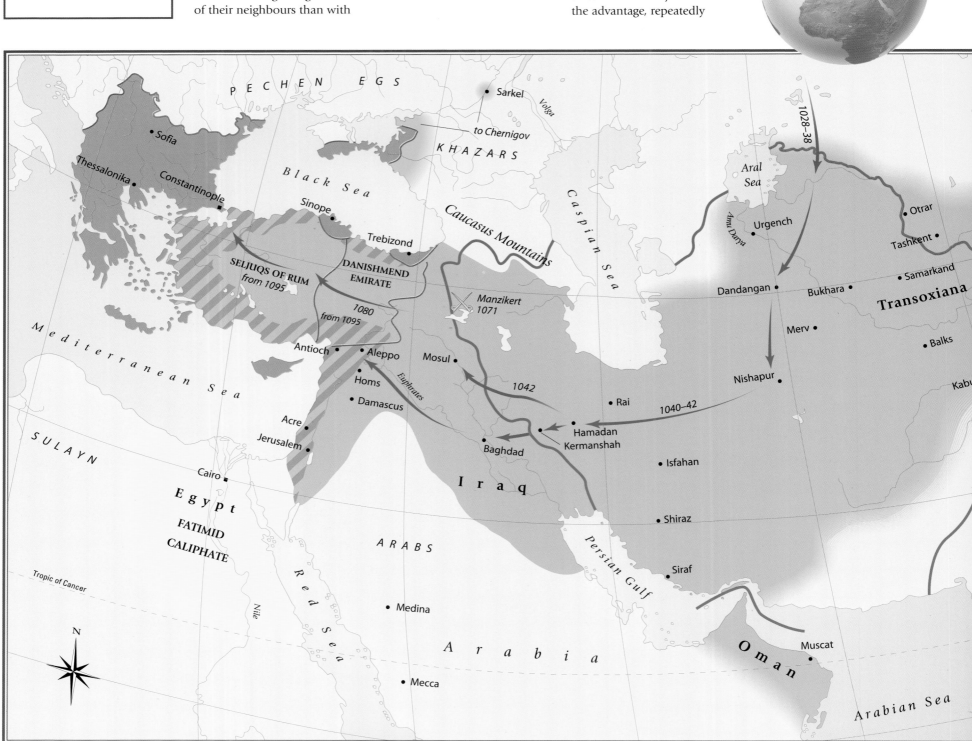

BATTLE OF MANZIKERT

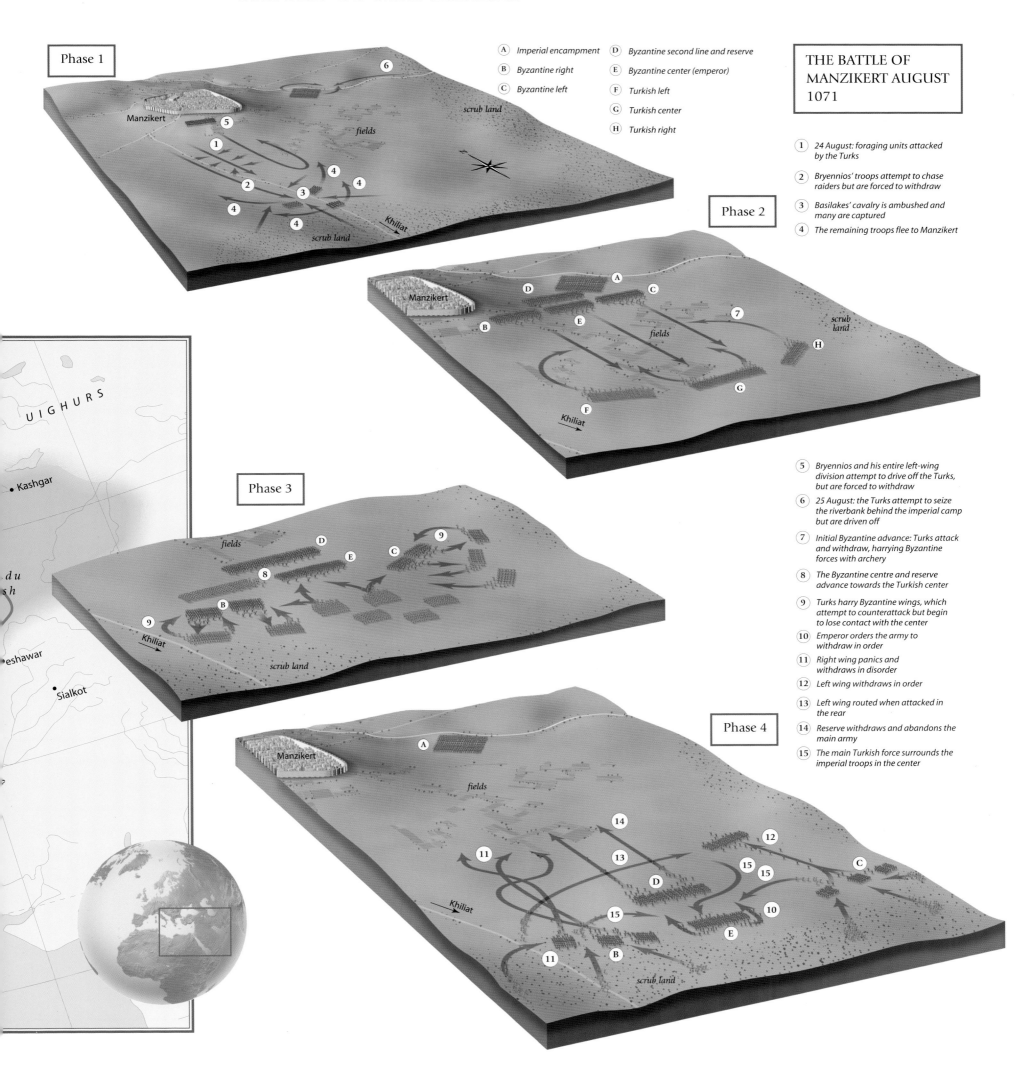

Phase 1

Manzikert

scrub land

fields

5

1

2

4

3

4

4

4

4

Khiliat

scrub land

6

Ⓐ Imperial encampment
Ⓑ Byzantine right
Ⓒ Byzantine left

Ⓓ Byzantine second line and reserve
Ⓔ Byzantine center (emperor)
Ⓕ Turkish left
Ⓖ Turkish center
Ⓗ Turkish right

THE BATTLE OF
MANZIKERT AUGUST
1071

① 24 August: foraging units attacked
by the Turks

② Bryennios' troops attempt to chase
raiders but are forced to withdraw

③ Basilakes' cavalry is ambushed and
many are captured

④ The remaining troops flee to Manzikert

Phase 2

Manzikert

D

A

C

B

E

fields

7

scrub
land

H

G

F

Khiliat

⑤ Bryennios and his entire left-wing
division attempt to drive off the Turks,
but are forced to withdraw

⑥ 25 August: the Turks attempt to seize
the riverbank behind the imperial camp
but are driven off

⑦ Initial Byzantine advance: Turks attack
and withdraw, harrying Byzantine
forces with archery

⑧ The Byzantine centre and reserve
advance towards the Turkish center

⑨ Turks harry Byzantine wings, which
attempt to counterattack but begin
to lose contact with the center

⑩ Emperor orders the army to
withdraw in order

⑪ Right wing panics and
withdraws in disorder

⑫ Left wing withdraws in order

⑬ Left wing routed when attacked in
the rear

⑭ Reserve withdraws and abandons the
main army

⑮ The main Turkish force surrounds the
imperial troops in the center

Phase 3

fields

D

E

C

9

8

B

9

Khiliat

scrub land

UIGHURS

Kashgar

du
sh

eshawar

Sialkot

Phase 4

Manzikert

A

fields

14

11

13

12

D

15

15

C

Khiliat

15

10

B

E

11

scrub land

1096 – 1204   THE CRUSADES; THE SIEGE OF JERUSALEM

THE CRUSADES

It has been suggested that the Crusades began as a Papal ploy to unite the squabbling states of Central Europe by giving them a common sense of purpose. It is true that most of the Crusades were sanctioned by the Pope in the name of Christendom. The "official" reason for the launch of the Crusades was in response to a call from the Eastern Orthodox Byzantine Empire for help against the expansion of the Muslim Seljuk dynasty into Anatolia. The avowed goal of a Crusader was the recapture of Jerusalem and the sacred Holy Land from Muslim rule.

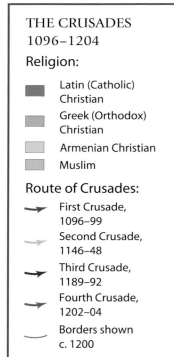

THE CRUSADES
1096–1204
Religion:

- Latin (Catholic) Christian
- Greek (Orthodox) Christian
- Armenian Christian
- Muslim

Route of Crusades:

- First Crusade, 1096–99
- Second Crusade, 1146–48
- Third Crusade, 1189–92
- Fourth Crusade, 1202–04
- Borders shown c. 1200

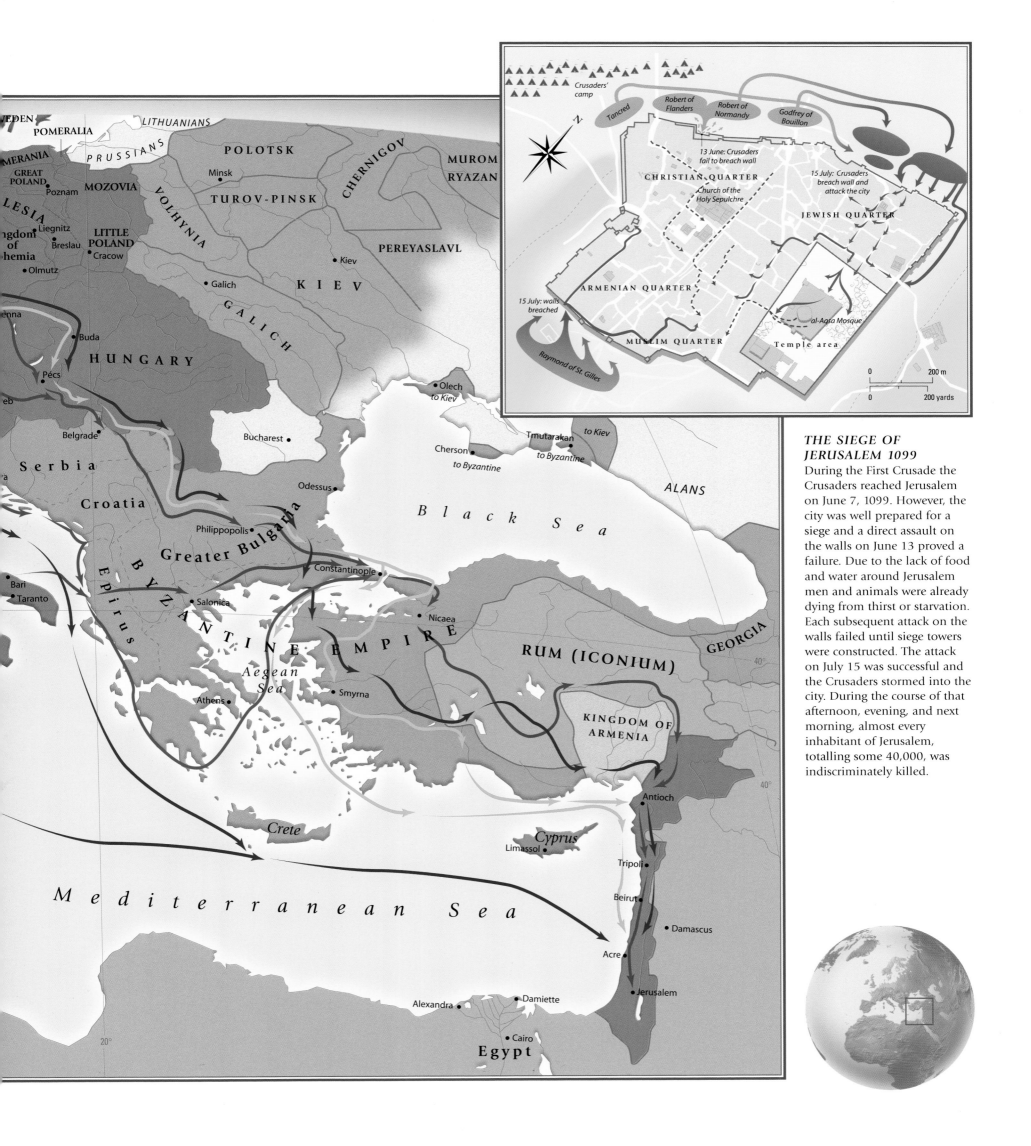

Crusaders' camp

Tancred

Robert of Flanders

Robert of Normandy

Godfrey of Bouillon

13 June: Crusaders fail to breach wall

CHRISTIAN QUARTER

Church of the Holy Sepulchre

15 July: Crusaders breach wall and attack the city

JEWISH QUARTER

ARMENIAN QUARTER

15 July: walls breached

al-Aqsa Mosque

MUSLIM QUARTER

Temple area

Raymond of St. Gilles

| 0 | | 200 m |
| 0 | | 200 yards |

SWEDEN

POMERALIA

LITHUANIANS

POMERANIA

PRUSSIANS

GREAT POLAND

Poznam

MOZOVIA

POLOTSK

Minsk

CHERNIGOV

MUROM

RYAZAN

SILESIA

Liegnitz

Breslau

LITTLE POLAND

TUROV-PINSK

Kingdom of Bohemia

Olmutz

Cracow

VOLHYNIA

Galich

KIEV

Kiev

PEREYASLAVL

Vienna

Buda

GALICH

Pécs

HUNGARY

Zeb

Belgrade

Bucharest

Olech to Kiev

Serbia

Cherson to Byzantine

Tmutarakan to Kiev

to Kiev

Croatia

Odessus

to Byzantine

ALANS

GEORGIA

Black Sea

Philippopolis

Greater Bulgaria

Constantinople

BYZANTINE EMPIRE

Epirus

Salonica

Nicaea

RUM (ICONIUM)

Bari

Taranto

Aegean Sea

Smyrna

40°

Athens

KINGDOM OF ARMENIA

40°

Crete

Cyprus

Limassol

Antioch

Tripoli

Mediterranean Sea

Beirut

Damascus

Acre

Jerusalem

Alexandra

Damiette

Cairo

Egypt

20°

THE SIEGE OF JERUSALEM 1099

During the First Crusade the Crusaders reached Jerusalem on June 7, 1099. However, the city was well prepared for a siege and a direct assault on the walls on June 13 proved a failure. Due to the lack of food and water around Jerusalem men and animals were already dying from thirst or starvation. Each subsequent attack on the walls failed until siege towers were constructed. The attack on July 15 was successful and the Crusaders stormed into the city. During the course of that afternoon, evening, and next morning, almost every inhabitant of Jerusalem, totalling some 40,000, was indiscriminately killed.

THE EMPIRE AND CAMPAIGNS OF SALADIN

THE EMPIRE & CAMPAIGNS OF SALADIN 1173–1185

Saladin was an illustrious Kurdish Muslim general and warrior born in 1138. After studying in Damascus, he became Sultan of Egypt in 1174. Later, he also became Sultan of Syria. Although he tended to leave the Crusaders alone, he was generally victorious when they met in battle. One exception was the Battle of Montgisard in November 1177. Defeated by Raynald of Chatillon and the Knights Templar, only a tenth of his army made it back to Egypt. Further tit-for-tat battles continued, culminating in Saladin's attack on Raynald's fortress at Kerak. Raynald responded by looting Muslim pilgrim caravans. One of Saladin's greatest victories over Crusader forces was at the Battle of Hattin in 1187, in which he beat the combined forces of Guy of Lusignan, King consort of Jerusalem, and Raymond III of Tripoli. The Crusader army was largely annihilated by the motivated army of Saladin, and many see this as a decisive turning point in the history of the Crusades.

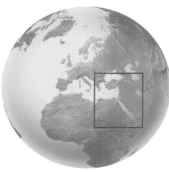

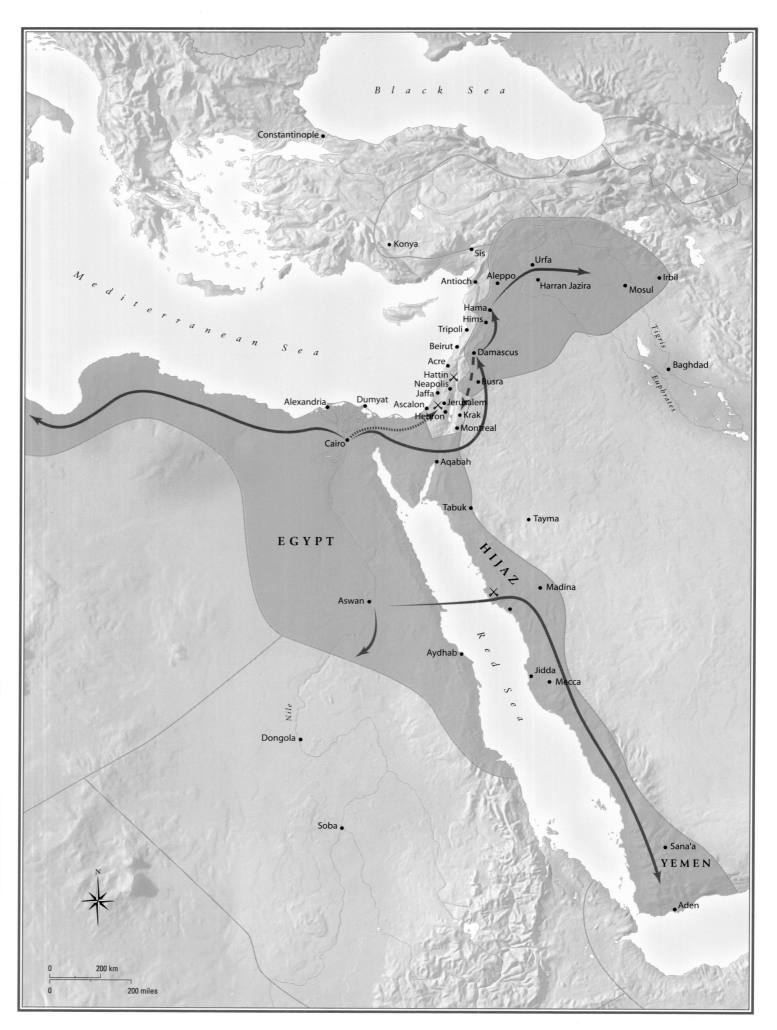

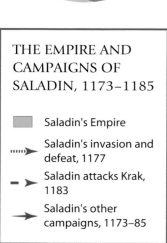

THE EMPIRE AND
CAMPAIGNS OF
SALADIN, 1173–1185

- Saladin's Empire
- Saladin's invasion and defeat, 1177
- Saladin attacks Krak, 1183
- Saladin's other campaigns, 1173–85

PART 3

MEDIEVAL TO RENAISSANCE WARFARE

*I*N THE 13TH CENTURY THE Mongols reigned supreme. Genghis Khan founded his Empire in 1206 and within 50 years it had expanded to include most of Asia and a large part of Europe. His secret was the effective use of horse-mounted archers, coupled with highly trained infantry.

By the 1400s heavy cavalry had become the major force in battle. These were the traditional knights of history, on large horses and heavy armour. The traditional weapon was the lance, but weapons such as the mace and chain would often be used in close contact. At the Battle of Tannenberg in 1410, where a combined Polish-Lithuanian alliance defeated the army of the Teutonic Knights, there were thousands of heavy cavalry on both sides.

By now gunpowder had been invented and new weapons were being introduced. These early weapons were very cumbersome, very heavy, dangerous to use, difficult to load and not very accurate, but all this improved with the advance of technology.

Gunpowder was also used in siege fighting. Tunnels were dug under walls and explosives were used to destroy them.

Cannons were developed. Early cannons were as dangerous for the attacker as they were for the defender. Metal technology needed to advance in order to make a canon that was strong enough not to explode when fired, and light enough for relatively easy transportation.

These lighter guns and cannons brought about a significant change to warfare on land and sea.

MONGOL CONQUESTS

***MONGOL CONQUESTS
1206–1259***
Founded by Genghis Khan in
1206, the Mongol Empire grew
over the next fifty years to
become the largest contiguous
land empire in history. The
empire started as an alliance of

central Asian tribes, but
following a number of
conquests it expanded to
include most of Asia and large
parts of Europe. The Mongol
conquests were built on a
highly effective military set-up.
This included the famous horse-

mounted archers, but also a
very well-trained infantry. What
set their armies apart from their
rivals was their discipline and
their mobility. By the middle
decades of the 13th century the
Mongols threatened to advance
into western Europe.

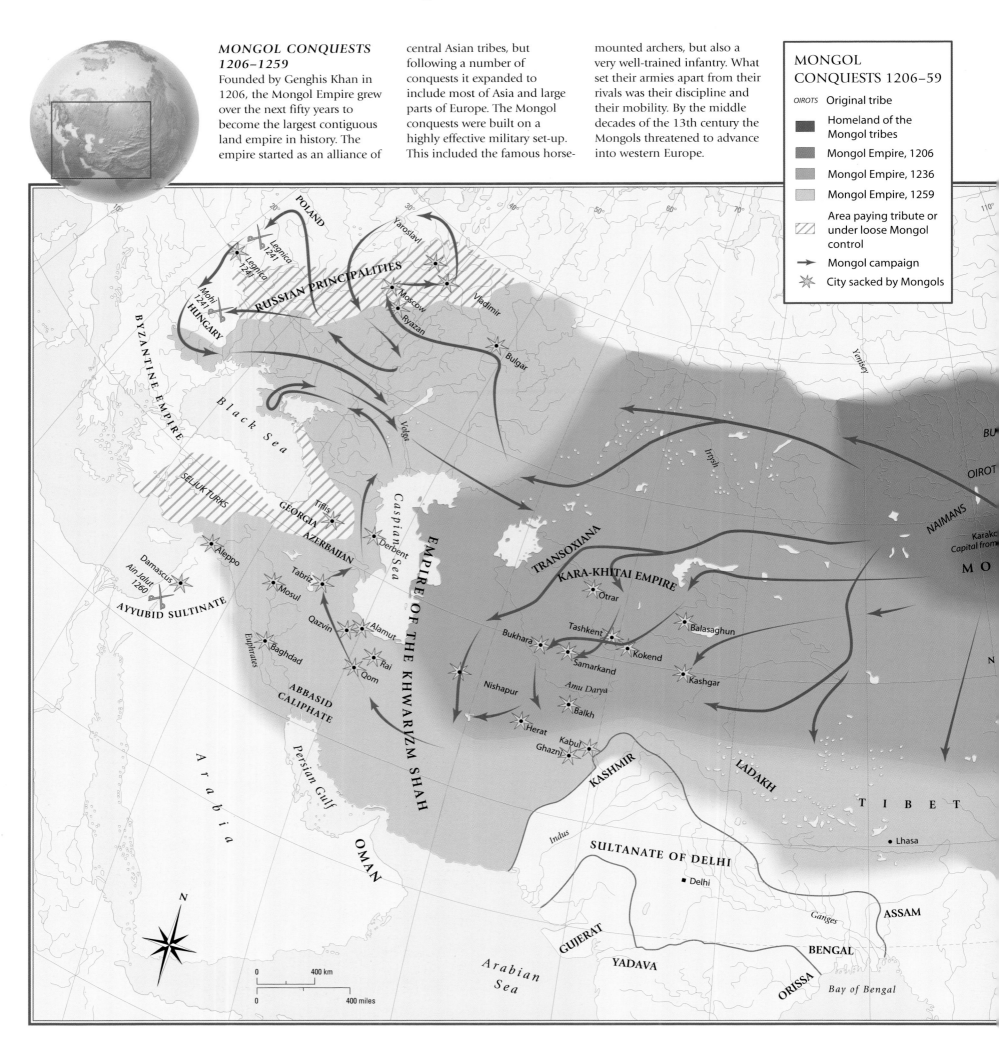

MONGOL
CONQUESTS 1206–59

OIROTS Original tribe

Homeland of the
Mongol tribes

Mongol Empire, 1206

Mongol Empire, 1236

Mongol Empire, 1259

Area paying tribute or
under loose Mongol
control

→ Mongol campaign

✳ City sacked by Mongols

THE BATTLE OF LIEGNITZ 1241

THE BATTLE OF LIEGNITZ 1241
This battle took place near the Silesian town of Liegnitz (Legnica). There was great concern that a Mongol invasion would completely overrun Europe. A combined force of Poles and Germans under the command of Henry II the Pious, Duke of Silesia, supported by feudal nobility and knightly military orders sent by the Pope, set out to halt this invasion. The Mongols employed a tactic of fake retreats and when the European knights with their heavy armour gave chase, their horses were shot from under them and they were then killed with lances. Henry was killed in the battle and his army was effectively destroyed.

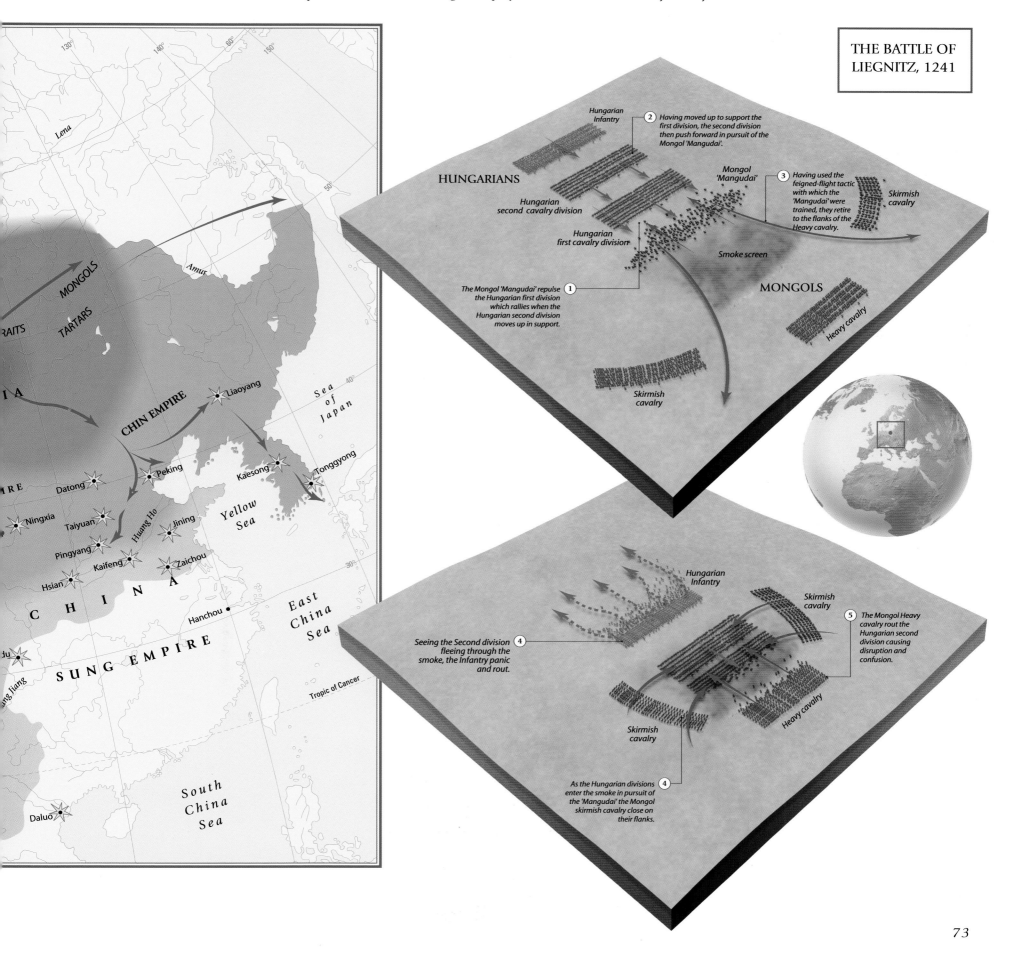

THE BATTLE OF LIEGNITZ, 1241

Hungarian Infantry

2 Having moved up to support the first division, the second division then push forward in pursuit of the Mongol 'Mangudai'.

HUNGARIANS

Mongol 'Mangudai'

3 Having used the feigned-flight tactic with which the 'Mangudai' were trained, they retire to the flanks of the Heavy cavalry.

Skirmish cavalry

Hungarian second cavalry division

Hungarian first cavalry division

Smoke screen

MONGOLS

1 The Mongol 'Mangudai' repulse the Hungarian first division which rallies when the Hungarian second division moves up in support.

Heavy cavalry

Skirmish cavalry

Hungarian Infantry

Skirmish cavalry

5 The Mongol Heavy cavalry rout the Hungarian second division causing disruption and confusion.

4 Seeing the Second division fleeing through the smoke, the Infantry panic and rout.

Skirmish cavalry

Heavy cavalry

4 As the Hungarian divisions enter the smoke in pursuit of the 'Mangudai' the Mongol skirmish cavalry close on their flanks.

1240 – 1245   MONGOL CAMPAIGNS IN EUROPE

MONGOL CAMPAIGNS IN EUROPE, 1240–45

→ Main attack

→ Flank attack

→ Reconnaissance and minor raids

✗ Battle site

MONGOL CAMPAIGNS IN EUROPE 1240–1245

The Mongol invasions of Europe were centered on their destruction of the Slavic states and principalities, especially Kiev. They were planned by Subatai, a Mongol general and skilled military tactician, but the nominal commander was Batu Khan, a Mongol ruler and grandson of Genghis. In 1241 the Mongols invaded the Kingdom of Hungary and a fragmented Poland, winning important battles in both cases. Following this, they extended their control into Austria and Dalmatia. It has been speculated that had the Mongol leader Ögedei Khan not died, necessitating the return of all the Mongol leaders ("Princes of the Blood") in 1241, all of Europe might have fallen as easily as Poland and Hungary, but in the event there was no further Mongolian advance.

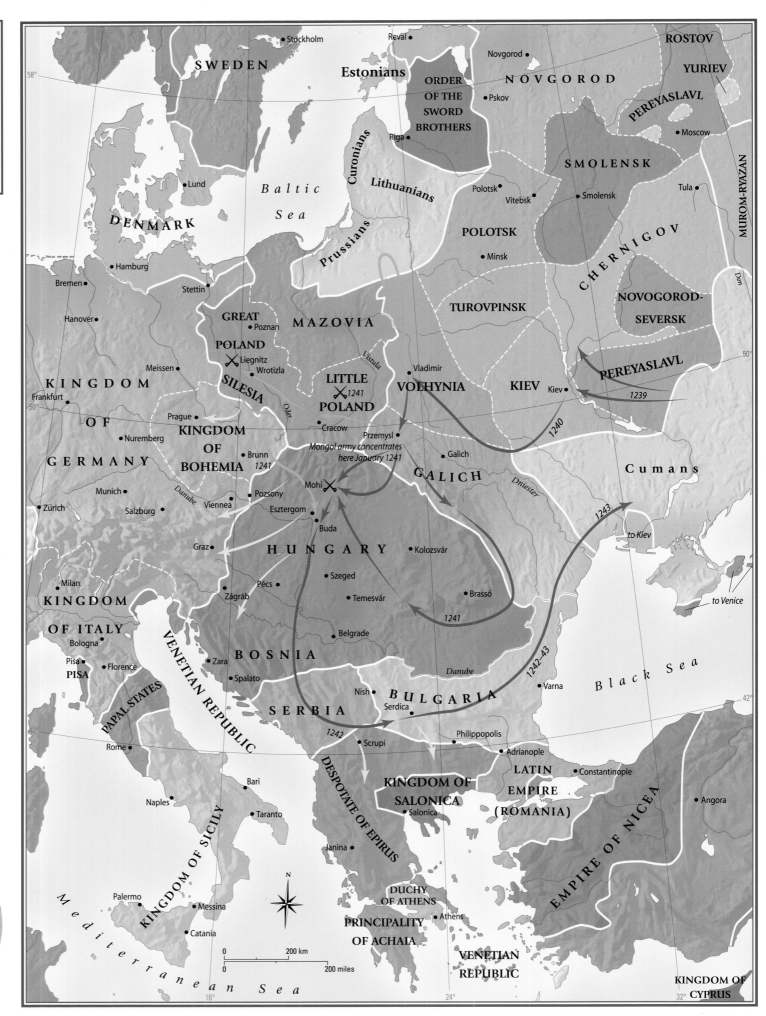

THE BATTLE OF MOHI 1241

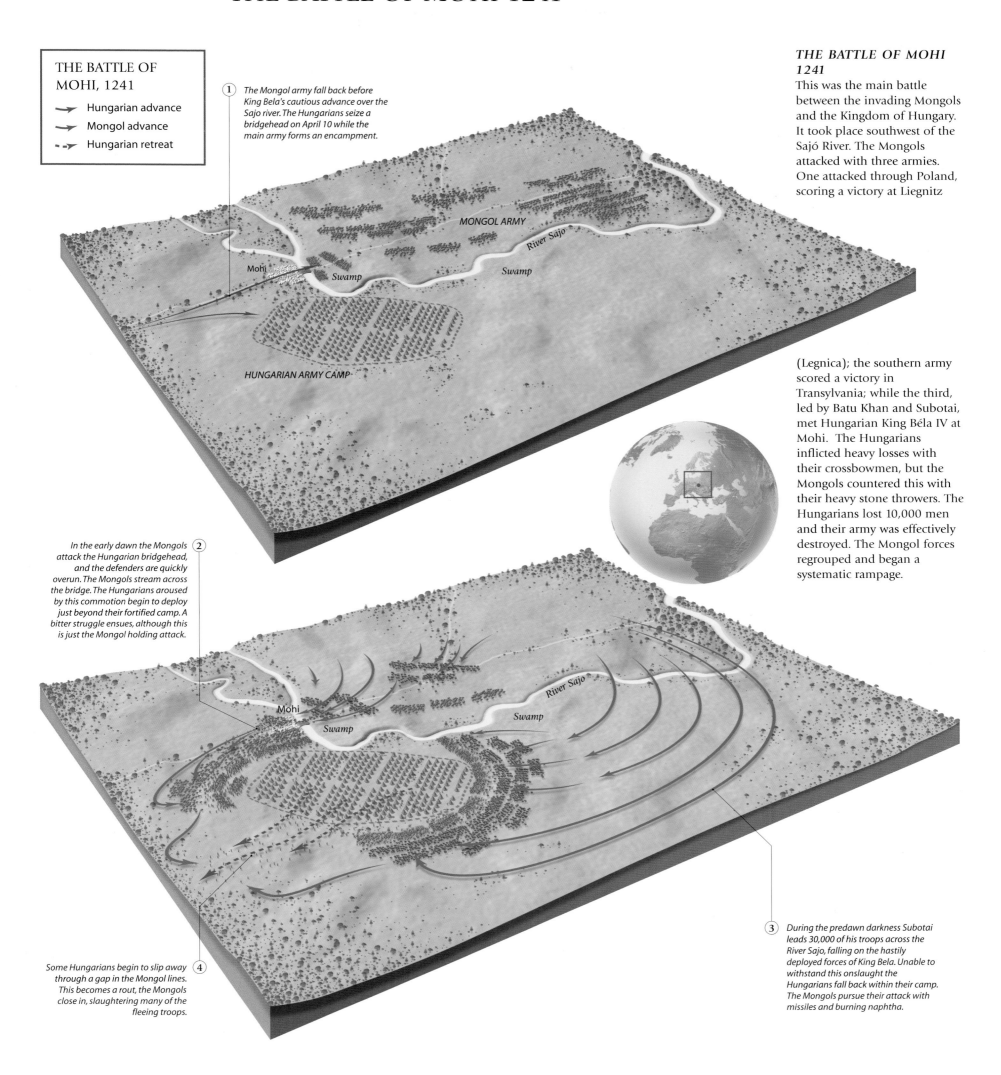

THE BATTLE OF
MOHI, 1241

→ Hungarian advance

→ Mongol advance

⇢ Hungarian retreat

① *The Mongol army fall back before King Bela's cautious advance over the Sajo river. The Hungarians seize a bridgehead on April 10 while the main army forms an encampment.*

MONGOL ARMY

River Sajo

Mohi

Swamp

Swamp

HUNGARIAN ARMY CAMP

② *In the early dawn the Mongols attack the Hungarian bridgehead, and the defenders are quickly overrun. The Mongols stream across the bridge. The Hungarians aroused by this commotion begin to deploy just beyond their fortified camp. A bitter struggle ensues, although this is just the Mongol holding attack.*

Mohi

Swamp

River Sajo

Swamp

④ *Some Hungarians begin to slip away through a gap in the Mongol lines. This becomes a rout, the Mongols close in, slaughtering many of the fleeing troops.*

③ *During the predawn darkness Subotai leads 30,000 of his troops across the River Sajo, falling on the hastily deployed forces of King Bela. Unable to withstand this onslaught the Hungarians fall back within their camp. The Mongols pursue their attack with missiles and burning naphtha.*

THE BATTLE OF MOHI 1241
This was the main battle between the invading Mongols and the Kingdom of Hungary. It took place southwest of the Sajó River. The Mongols attacked with three armies. One attacked through Poland, scoring a victory at Liegnitz (Legnica); the southern army scored a victory in Transylvania; while the third, led by Batu Khan and Subotai, met Hungarian King Béla IV at Mohi. The Hungarians inflicted heavy losses with their crossbowmen, but the Mongols countered this with their heavy stone throwers. The Hungarians lost 10,000 men and their army was effectively destroyed. The Mongol forces regrouped and began a systematic rampage.

1200 – 1420 THE BALTIC

THE BALTIC
1200–1400

→ Major crusade with
date where known

THE BALTIC 1200–1400
During the 12th and 13th
centuries, there was
considerable effort made by
bishops, their vassals,
merchants, the Livonian
Knights, and many visiting
crusaders to work together to
defeat the native pagan tribes
and drive away Orthodox
Christian and pagan
competitors to create a large
superficially Roman Christian
state with reasonably
defensible borders. Throughout
the 13th century the Teutonic
Knights came to personify this
crusade. With a combination of
pious and crass motives they
attracted support from all Latin
Christian states along the Baltic
Sea, and this became known as
the Baltic Crusade. This
Teutonic State became a
formidable power in the region.

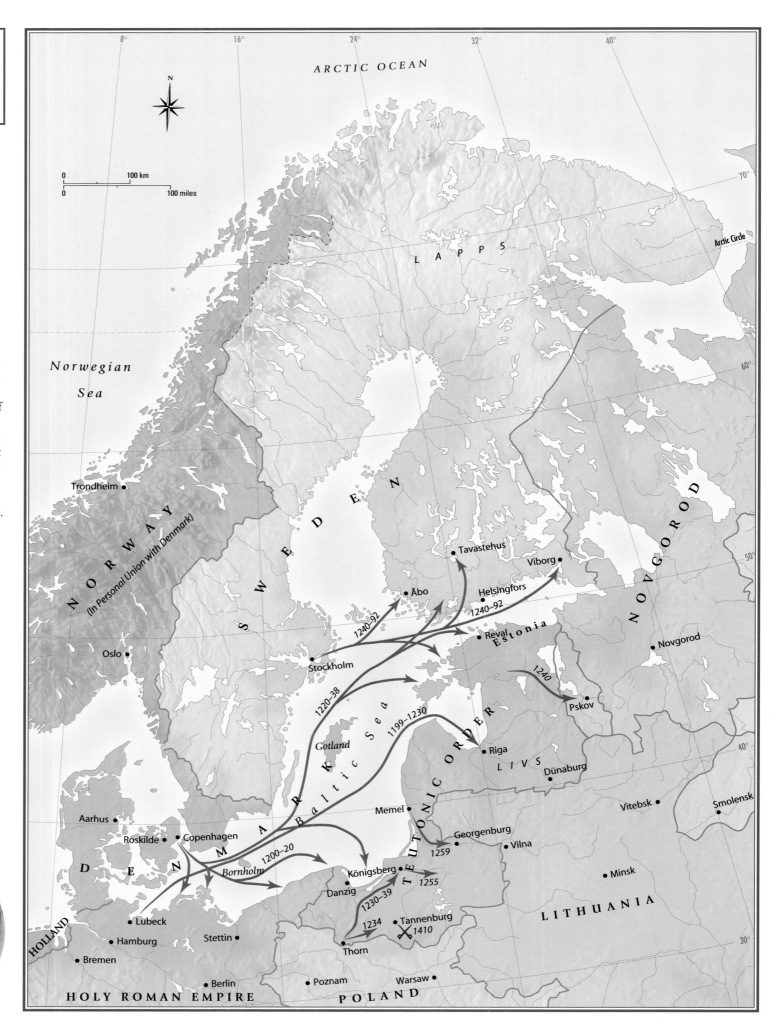

THE BATTLE OF TANNENBERG

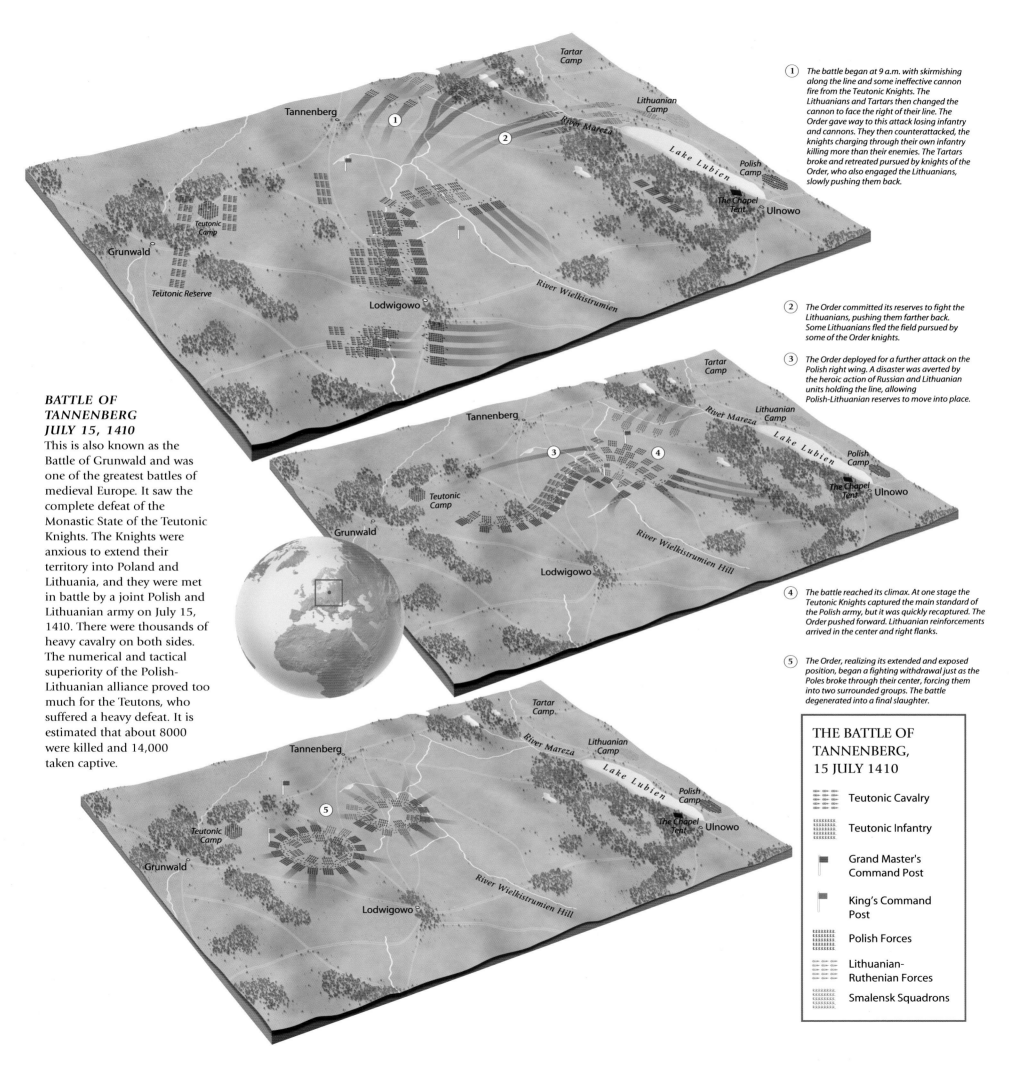

1 The battle began at 9 a.m. with skirmishing along the line and some ineffective cannon fire from the Teutonic Knights. The Lithuanians and Tartars then changed the cannon to face the right of their line. The Order gave way to this attack losing infantry and cannons. They then counterattacked, the knights charging through their own infantry killing more than their enemies. The Tartars broke and retreated pursued by knights of the Order, who also engaged the Lithuanians, slowly pushing them back.

2 The Order committed its reserves to fight the Lithuanians, pushing them farther back. Some Lithuanians fled the field pursued by some of the Order knights.

3 The Order deployed for a further attack on the Polish right wing. A disaster was averted by the heroic action of Russian and Lithuanian units holding the line, allowing Polish-Lithuanian reserves to move into place.

4 The battle reached its climax. At one stage the Teutonic Knights captured the main standard of the Polish army, but it was quickly recaptured. The Order pushed forward. Lithuanian reinforcements arrived in the center and right flanks.

5 The Order, realizing its extended and exposed position, began a fighting withdrawal just as the Poles broke through their center, forcing them into two surrounded groups. The battle degenerated into a final slaughter.

BATTLE OF TANNENBERG JULY 15, 1410

This is also known as the Battle of Grunwald and was one of the greatest battles of medieval Europe. It saw the complete defeat of the Monastic State of the Teutonic Knights. The Knights were anxious to extend their territory into Poland and Lithuania, and they were met in battle by a joint Polish and Lithuanian army on July 15, 1410. There were thousands of heavy cavalry on both sides. The numerical and tactical superiority of the Polish-Lithuanian alliance proved too much for the Teutons, who suffered a heavy defeat. It is estimated that about 8000 were killed and 14,000 taken captive.

THE BATTLE OF TANNENBERG, 15 JULY 1410

	Teutonic Cavalry
	Teutonic Infantry
	Grand Master's Command Post
	King's Command Post
	Polish Forces
	Lithuanian-Ruthenian Forces
	Smalensk Squadrons

1420 – c. 1460   THE HUSSITE CRUSADES

THE HUSSITE CRUSADES, 1420–1431

Lands of the Bohemian crown

Border of the Holy Roman empire

Catholic forces

First crusade 1420–21

Second crusade 1421–22

Third crusade 1426

Fourth crusade 1427

Fifth crusade 1431

Hussites

1420–22

1424

1427

1431

The Great Raids

1428

1429–30

X Hussite victory

X Hussite defeat

THE HUSSITE CRUSADES 1420–1431

The Hussites were followers of Jan Hus, a Bohemian Protestant reformer. Many knights and nobles in Bohemia and Moravia favored church reform, and after the execution of Hus, the Hussite movement took on a revolutionary character. Emperor Sigismund persuaded the Pope to proclaim a crusade to destroy the Hussites and other heretics.

At the head of a vast army of crusaders he marched on Prague and laid siege to the city. Other crusades followed. A Hussite victory at Domalice in 1431 was followed by a defeat at Lipany in 1434. These were the first wars in which weapons such as muskets made an important contribution.

BRANDENBURG

Oder

POLAND

Lower Lusatia

Upper Lusatia

Elbe

SILESIA

Wurzen

Lipsko

Lützen

Naumburg

MEISSEN

Bautzen

Görlitz

Luban

Legnica (Liegnitz)

Wroclaw (Breslau)

Olava

Breh

FRANCONIA

Dresden

Löbau

Zittau

Sudeten Highlands

Molvice

Nysa

Voigland

Usti

Litomerice

Horice X 1422

1420

Glatz

Most

Louny

Slany

Cesky Brod

Lipany X 1434

Kalan

1422

1421

1427

Bayreuth

Zatec

B

O

H

E

M

I

A

Hradec Kralove

Cheb

Zlutice

Nymburg

Kolin

Kutna Hora X 1421

Opova

Tetschen

Prague X 1420

Kourim

Caslav

Malesov X 1424

Habry

Upper

1422

Stribro

1427

Tachov

1431

Plzen (Pilsen)

1421

Sudomer 1420

Niemczi Brod

Pribyslav

Moravian Heights

Nuremburg

Palatinate

Waldmünchen

Domazlice 1431 X

X 1433

Rabi

Tabor

Budejovice

MORAVIA

Brno (Brünn)

Tyrnau

Regensburg

Danube

BAVARIA

Bohemian Forest

Karlstein

Vltava

Morava

White mountains

1421–22

HUNGARY

Passau

Waidhofen X 1431

Lower Austria

N

0   50 km

0   50 miles

14°

18°

52°

50°

EASTERN EUROPE

EASTERN EUROPE
c.1460

— Holy Roman Empire
Lithuania-Poland
Ottoman Empire

NOVGOROD

• Abo
• Helsingfors
• Reval

MUSCOVY

• Kazan

KHANATE OF KAZAN

• Novgorod

ROSTOV

TVER

• Pskov

• Nizhniy Novgorod

Volga

• Riga

• Moscow

• Ryazan

TEUTONIC ORDER

• Dünaburg

DENMARK

• Malmo

• Königsberg

• Gdarisk

• Wilno

• Vitebsk

• Smolensk

• Tula

RYAZAN

• Stettin

• Berlin

• Poznan

Vistula

• Minsk

SMALL PRINCIP-ALITIES

Don

• Warsaw

LITHUANIA

• Kursk

GREAT KHANATE (GOLDEN HORDE)

• Breslau

LANDS OF THE BOHEMIAN CROWN

POLAND

• Prague

• Cracow

• Kharkov

• Brünn

• Lwow

• Kiev

Dnieper

• Kassa

Dniester

AUSTRIA

• Pozsony

• Vienna

• Buda

• Debrecen

• Suceava

KHANATE OF CRIMEA

• Graz

STYRIA

HUNGARY

• Kolozsvar

MOLDAVIA

• Jassy

(to Genoa)

• Zagrab

• Pecs

• Szeged

• Temesvar

• Brasso

(to Genoa)

• Caffa

Danube

• Belgrade

WALLACHIA

• Tergovist

• Zara

• Bucharest

• Bosna Seray

HERZEGOVINA

• Ruschuk

• Mostar

• Nish

Black Sea

REPUBLIC OF RAGUSA

• Sofia

• Varna

GEORGIA

VENETIAN REPUBLIC

OTTOMAN

• Uskub

• Philippopolis

• Adrianople

• Trebizond

NAPLES

• Bari

Local rulers

• Salonica

• Constantinople

• Taranto

• Janina

EMPIRE

• Angora

DULKADIR

KARA KOYUNLU

(to Genoa)

• Smyrna

RAMAZAN

• Athens

KNIGHTS OF ST JOHN

Morea

Mediterranean Sea

MAMELUKES

EASTERN EUROPE
c.1460

Eastern Europe in the 1460s was a very unsettled region. To the north, Poland and Lithuania were fighting the Thirteen Years War against the Teutonic Order. This war was fought after a number of towns had revolted against the Order to form the Prussian Union, with Poland agreeing to incorporate them. This war lasted until 1466. To the east the Khanates of the Mongol Empire were quiet, but an invasion of Lithuania would take place in less than 50 years. To the south, the Ottomans were already beginning to cast their eyes northward toward the other side of the River Danube.

THE BATTLE OF PAVIA

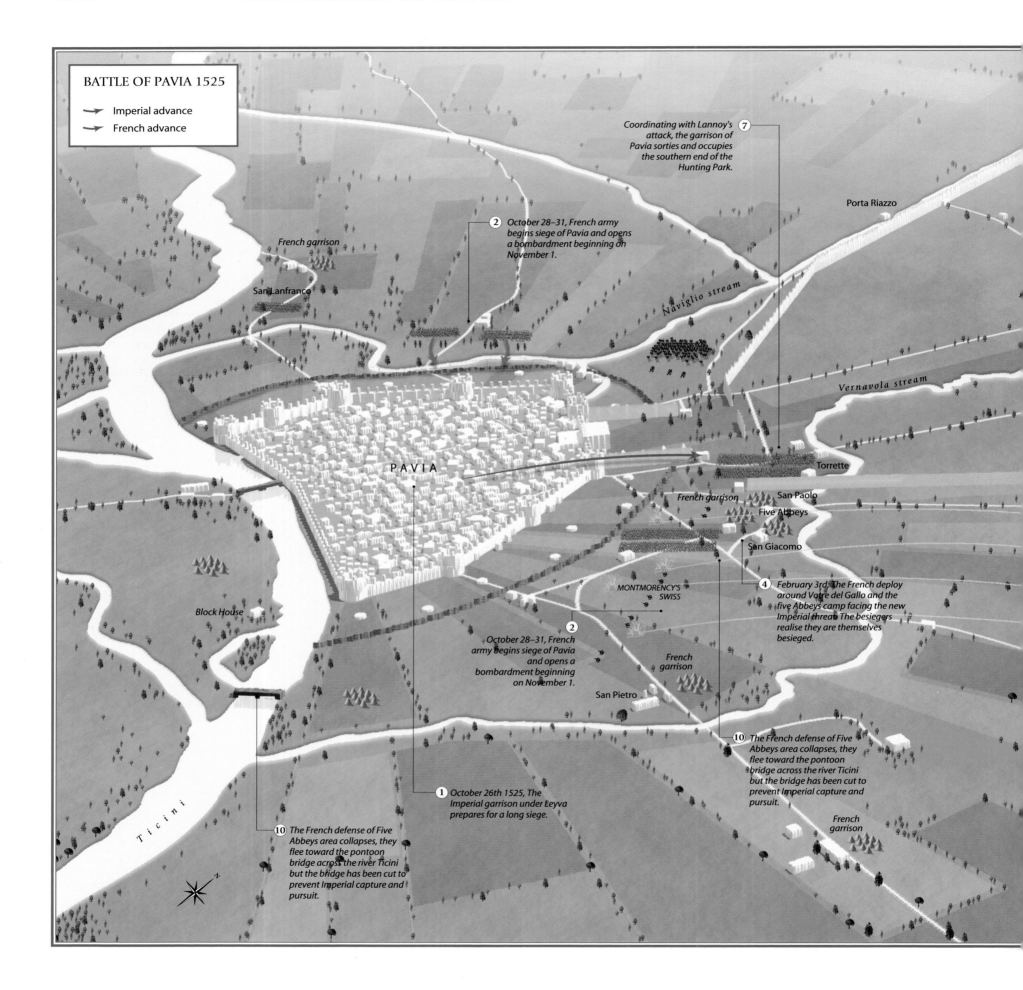

BATTLE OF PAVIA 1525

→ Imperial advance
→ French advance

Coordinating with Lannoy's attack, the garrison of Pavia sorties and occupies the southern end of the Hunting Park. **7**

Porta Riazzo

October 28–31, French army begins siege of Pavia and opens a bombardment beginning on November 1. **2**

Naviglio stream

French garrison

Vernavola stream

San Lanfranco

PAVIA

Torrette

French garrison

San Paolo

Five Abbeys

San Giacomo

4 *February 3rd, The French deploy around Votre del Gallo and the five Abbeys camp facing the new Imperial threat. The besiegers realise they are themselves besieged.*

MONTMORENCY'S SWISS

Block House

October 28–31, French army begins siege of Pavia and opens a bombardment beginning on November 1. **2**

French garrison

10 *The French defense of Five Abbeys area collapses, they flee toward the pontoon bridge across the river Ticini but the bridge has been cut to prevent Imperial capture and pursuit.*

San Pietro

1 *October 26th 1525, The Imperial garrison under Leyva prepares for a long siege.*

Ticini

10 *The French defense of Five Abbeys area collapses, they flee toward the pontoon bridge across the river Ticini but the bridge has been cut to prevent Imperial capture and pursuit.*

French garrison

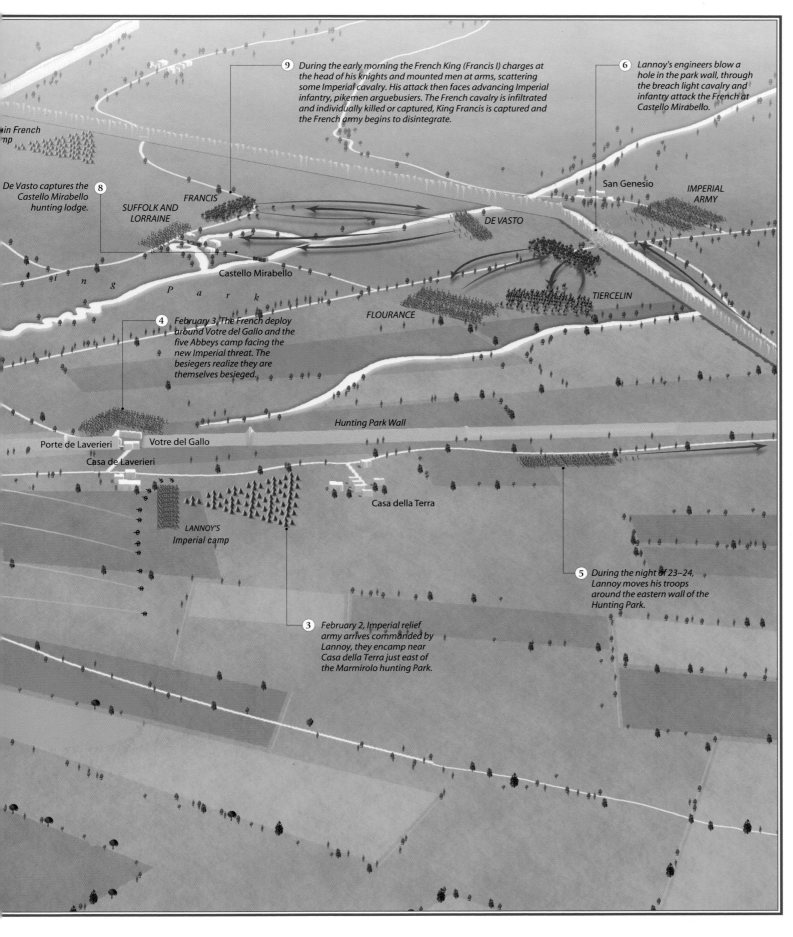

During the early morning the French King (Francis I) charges at the head of his knights and mounted men at arms, scattering some Imperial cavalry. His attack then faces advancing Imperial infantry, pikemen arguebusiers. The French cavalry is infiltrated and individually killed or captured, King Francis is captured and the French army begins to disintegrate. **9**

6 Lannoy's engineers blow a hole in the park wall, through the breach light cavalry and infantry attack the French at Castello Mirabello.

De Vasto captures the Castello Mirabello hunting lodge. **8**

FRANCIS

SUFFOLK AND LORRAINE

San Genesio

IMPERIAL ARMY

DE VASTO

Castello Mirabello

TIERCELIN

4 February 3, The French deploy around Votre del Gallo and the five Abbeys camp facing the new Imperial threat. The besiegers realize they are themselves besieged.

FLOURANCE

Hunting Park Wall

Porte de Laverieri

Votre del Gallo

Casa de Laverieri

Casa della Terra

LANNOY'S Imperial camp

5 During the night of 23–24, Lannoy moves his troops around the eastern wall of the Hunting Park.

3 February 2, Imperial relief army arrives commanded by Lannoy, they encamp near Casa della Terra just east of the Marmirolo hunting Park.

THE BATTLE OF PAVIA 1525

This was the decisive engagement of the Italian War that began in 1521. In the great park of Mirabello outside the city of Pavia a Habsburg army attacked King Francis I's French army. The battle lasted for four hours and resulted in a massive defeat for the French force. French casualties were estimated at 12,000 dead or wounded, against approximately 500 on the Habsburg side. Further humiliation came when King Francis was captured by Spanish troops. Following a period of imprisonment, he was forced to sign the Treaty of Madrid, surrendering significant territory to his captor.

1328 – 1585   EXPANSION OF THE OTTOMAN EMPIRE

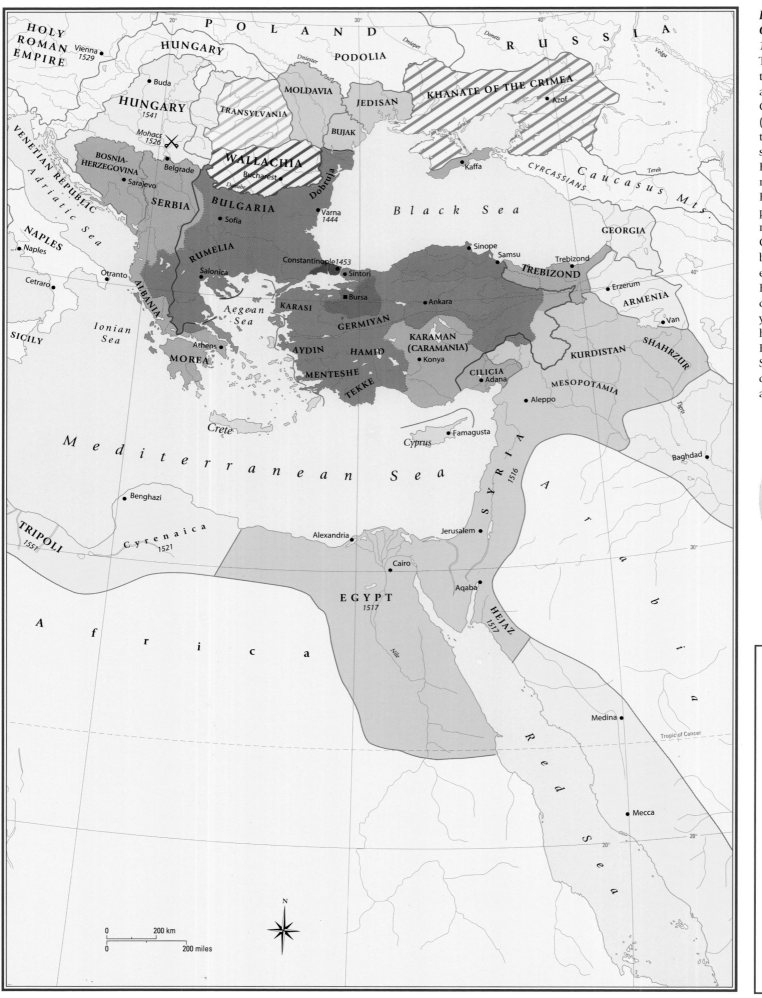

EXPANSION OF THE OTTOMAN EMPIRE 1328–1566

The period up to 1566 was the time of territorial, economic and cultural growth in the Ottoman Empire. Osman I (1258–1326) had extended the frontiers of Ottoman settlement to the edge of the Byzantine Empire. He had moved the Ottoman capital to Bursa and shaped the early political development of the nation. In the century after Osman's death, Ottoman rule began to extend over the eastern Mediterranean and the Balkans. Constantinople was captured in 1453 by the 21-year-old Mohammed II. Before he was killed in 1481 his Empire included Corsica, Sardinia, and Sicily. Expansion continued under Selim and Suleiman.

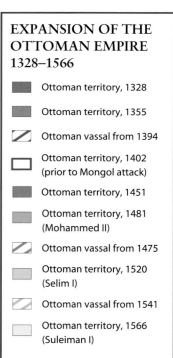

EXPANSION OF THE OTTOMAN EMPIRE 1328–1566

- Ottoman territory, 1328
- Ottoman territory, 1355
- Ottoman vassal from 1394
- Ottoman territory, 1402 (prior to Mongol attack)
- Ottoman territory, 1451
- Ottoman territory, 1481 (Mohammed II)
- Ottoman vassal from 1475
- Ottoman territory, 1520 (Selim I)
- Ottoman vassal from 1541
- Ottoman territory, 1566 (Suleiman I)

THE SIEGE OF ANTWERP

THE SIEGE OF ANTWERP SEPTEMBER 1584 – AUGUST 1585

1. September 1584: Parma encircles Antwerp with a ring of forts and begins construction of a massive pontoon bridge across the Scheldt to cut off river traffic. The blockade has begun

2. September 1584: In response to Parma's encirclement, Antwerp's defenders open the flood gates and drown the surrounding country. Fighting and fort building will be restricted to high ground and the tops of dikes, while boats with small cannon serve as mobile artillery

3. 22 December 1584: Boat attack fails to break Parma's bridge, still under construction

4. 25 February 1585: Bridge is complete. This masterpiece of Renaissance military engineering is 2400 feet long, anchored at each end by a great earthwork fort, and protected by more than 200 cannon

5. 5 April 1585: The first bomb ship sent down river to destroy the bridge grounds upstream and bursts harmlessly. Parma's soldiers flock to watch the firework show

6. 5 April 1585: The second bomb ship explodes against the bridge, swamping the nearest shore fort, killing hundreds, and showering the countryside with debris. The bridge is ruptured but the extensive damage is promptly repaired, and the blockade continues without interruption

7. 17 August 1585: An exhausted Antwerp surrenders: not a single shot had been fired against its walls. Ten days later, Parma enters the city in triumph

THE SIEGE OF ANTWERP 1584–1585
The Siege of Antwerp took place during the Eighty Years' War between the Netherlands and Spain. In the late 1500s Antwerp was the largest Dutch city and the cultural, economic, and financial center of the Seventeen Provinces and of northwestern Europe. In 1576 Spanish soldiery had plundered the city, massacred thousands of people, and burnt down hundreds of houses. What had begun as a Protestant rebellion was now a revolt of all Dutch provinces. Philip II of Spain sent the Duke of Parma to restore order. The city finally surrendered and the majority of the city's population fled north. The golden century of Antwerp had come to an end.

1571 – 1588   THE BATTLE OF LEPANTO

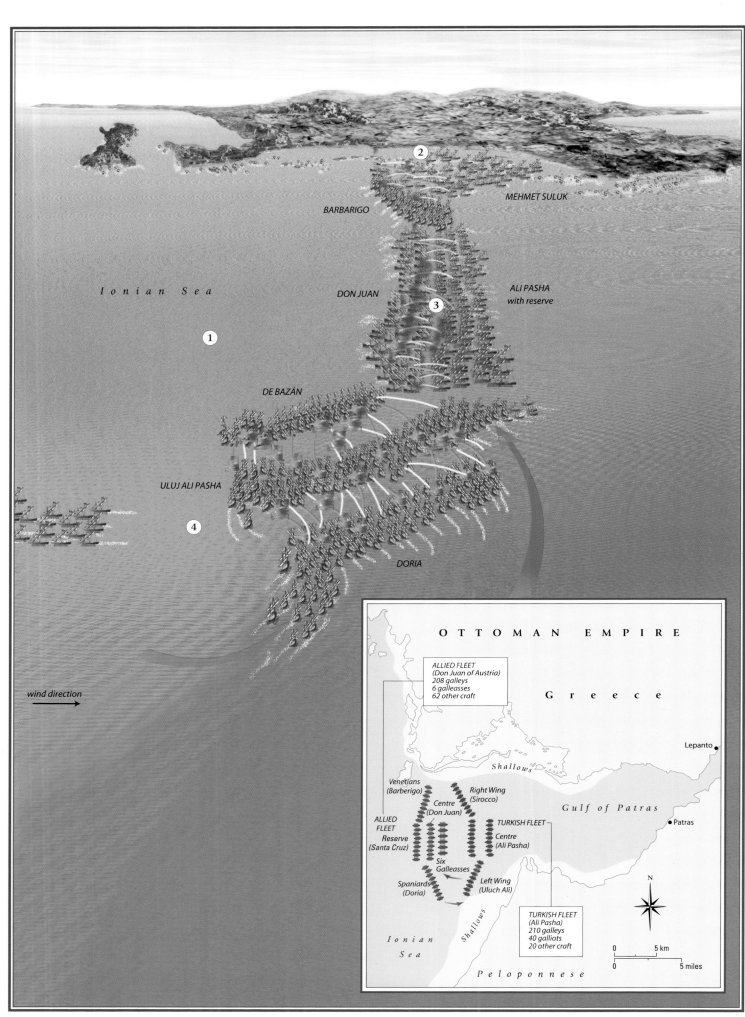

THE BATTLE OF
LEPANTO
7 OCTOBER 1571

1 The battle begins with the two sides
adopting a traditional Gallery formation,
with the Christian's left flank and the
Ottoman's right flank closest to the coast.
The wind direction is in favour of the
Christian fleet.

2 The Ottoman right tries to outflank the
Christian left by slipping around its
inshore flank, this is countered and driven
back by the Christians and the Ottoman
right flank is all but destroyed.

3 Both central sections engage, and despite
holding on for longer the Ottomans are
again overwhelmed by the superior
firepower of the Christians.

4 The Ottoman left flank holds the
Christians back, but on hearing of the
collapse of the rest of the force, soon beat
a retreat with the 47 remaining ships.

THE BATTLE OF
LEPANTO 1571

This battle is important because
it was the last major naval
battle in world history that took
place solely between rowing
vessels. The battle took place off
the western coast of Greece and
involved the galleys of the
Ottoman fleet and the galleys of
a Christian coalition known as
the Holy League. In a battle
lasting for five hours, the result
was a decisive victory for the
Holy League. Although the
Christians had 8,000 killed or
wounded and lost 12 galleys,
20,000 Ottomans were killed or
wounded and 137 of their ships
were captured, with 50 sunk.

THE SPANISH ARMADA

THE SPANISH
ARMADA MAY –
SEPTEMBER 1588

→ Route of the Armada

⇢ Individual or small
groups of ships
blown off course

✕ Site of battle

▢ Spanish Empire

▨ Provinces in revolt
against Spanish rule

1. 30 May: the Armada departs Lisbon numbering 128 ships and 29,453 men, heading north against adverse winds

2. 14 June: the Armada arrives off Cape Finisterre and waits for supplies to be sent out but nothing appears. Medina Sidonia decides to enter Corunna harbor with 40 ships, the rest to enter the next day. The waiting ships, however, are scattered by a violent storm, some even sailing as far as the Scilly Islands off the Cornish coast. They are found by a Spanish dispatch boat on 30 June and brought back to Corunna

3. 21 July: the Armada sails from Corunna now numbering, after recovering ships blown off course by the storm and receiving reinforcements, 131 ships and 24,607 men

4. 25 July: the Armada passes Ushant and makes a heading for England

5. 29 July: in the afternoon the Armada passes Lizard Point, Cornwall

6. 30 July: 54 ships of the English fleet sail out of Plymouth, managing during the night to take a position windward of the Spanish fleet. The Spanish are shocked to see eleven more English ships tacking into the wind at what seems incredible speed to join their fleet

7. 31 July: the English attack and inflict some damage on the Armada with no losses

8. 2–4 August: the English attack again and harry the Spanish

9. 6 August: the Spanish fleet anchors some 4 miles off Calais with the English fleet anchoring nearby. Later in the day English reinforcements arrive; the Spanish now face some 230 ships

10. 6 August: the intended link up with the Duke of Parma's forces in the Spanish Netherlands proves impossible. Parma has effectively deceived the Dutch as to his intentions. They are defending against an attack on Amsterdam. Parma will be ready to link up within 48 hours, but by then it will be too late

11. 7 August: fireships are sent against the anchored Spanish fleet around midnight on the 7th. The Spanish cut their anchor cables and set sail in disorder

12. 8 August: at dawn the Spanish fleet is scattered over some 12 miles of ocean. The English attack as the Spanish are reforming and the ensuing battle drags on all day with the English gaining the upper hand. Despite having better ammunition, the Spanish are suffering badly when a sudden squall blows, enabling them to draw away

13. The Spanish fleet, intending to refit at a Flemish port, is caught by unfavorable winds. Medina Sidonia decides to return to Spain by circling the British Isles. Regaining a close formation they head north, pursued by the English fleet

14. The English fleet, short of provisions, returns to its home ports

15. The Armada continues its long journey, battle-damaged and hit by storms, causing terrible hardships. Of the 131 ships that set out, 63 were lost in or as a result of battle or shipwrecked. Of the 34 others lost, their fate was unrecorded or unknown. The remaining 55 ships straggled into Spanish ports during September

THE SPANISH ARMADA 1588

The Armada was sent by King Philip II of Spain, who had been king consort of England until the death of his wife, Mary I of England, thirty years earlier. The purpose of the expedition was to escort the Duke of Parma's army from the Spanish Netherlands and land them in southeast England. It was hoped that this would put a stop to attacks against Spanish possessions in the New World and the Atlantic treasure fleets. It was also hoped that it would reverse the protestant revolution in England, and to this end the expedition was supported by Pope Sixtus V.

1683　　THE SIEGE OF VIENNA

THE SIEGE OF VIENNA 1683

The capture of Vienna had long been a strategic target of the Ottoman Empire and during two months in the late summer of 1683 a large Ottoman army laid siege to the city, cutting virtually every means of food supply, and mining the walls. The city was only saved after a relief army of some 70,000 men arrived to confront the Ottomans. At the resulting Battle of Kahlenberg the Ottomans were defeated and Vienna was saved from capture. The Ottomans carried on fighting for another 16 years, but this battle marked the end of Turkish expansion into southeastern Europe.

> THE SIEGE OF
> VIENNA, 1683

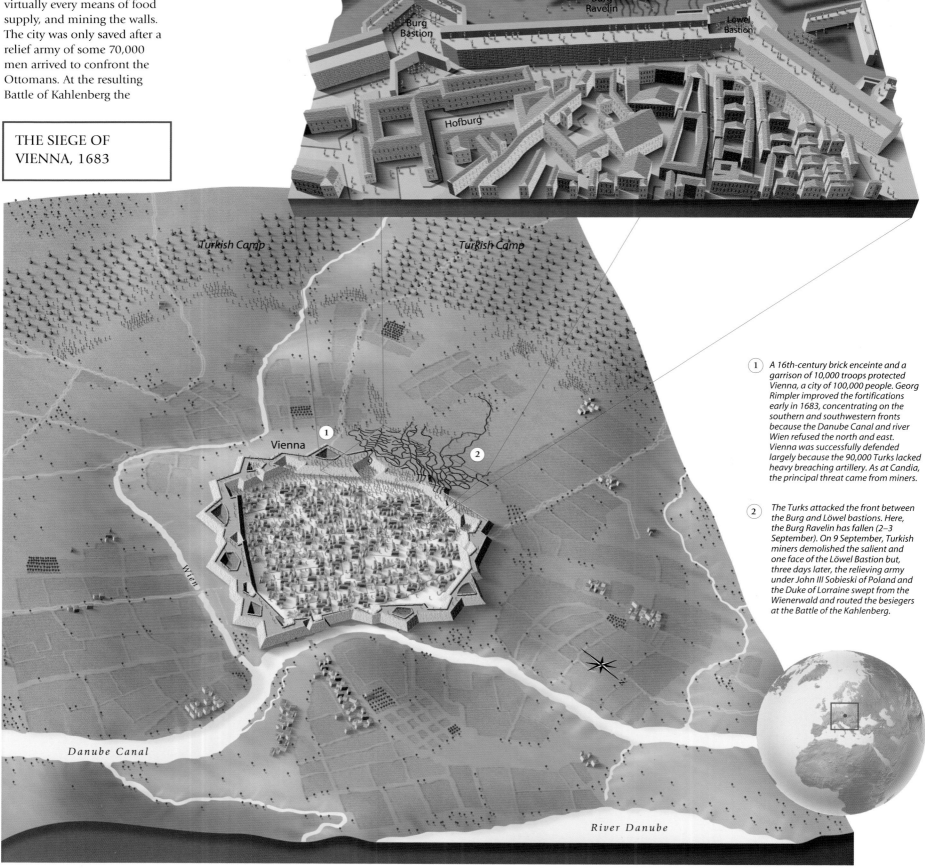

1　A 16th-century brick enceinte and a garrison of 10,000 troops protected Vienna, a city of 100,000 people. Georg Rimpler improved the fortifications early in 1683, concentrating on the southern and southwestern fronts because the Danube Canal and river Wien refused the north and east. Vienna was successfully defended largely because the 90,000 Turks lacked heavy breaching artillery. As at Candia, the principal threat came from miners.

2　The Turks attacked the front between the Burg and Löwel bastions. Here, the Burg Ravelin has fallen (2–3 September). On 9 September, Turkish miners demolished the salient and one face of the Löwel Bastion but, three days later, the relieving army under John III Sobieski of Poland and the Duke of Lorraine swept from the Wienerwald and routed the besiegers at the Battle of the Kahlenberg.

PART 4

KINGS AND REVOLUTIONS

THIS WAS A PERIOD WHERE well-established social traditions underwent considerable change. 1618 saw the start of the Thirty Years' War. This originally began as a civil war but it escalated into a pan-European conflict between the established Catholics and the emergent Protestants. Ferdinand II, King of Bohemia and Holy Roman Emperor was fiercely Catholic, but he was not able to stem a Bohemian Protestant revolt that rapidly spread throughout Europe, killing thousands of people and laying vast areas to waste.

In 1642, as the result of a build-up of tension between King Charles I and Parliament, a Civil War broke out in Britain. After a number of fierce and bloody battles, King Charles was eventually captured and in January 1649 was executed for high treason.

The monarchy was abolished and for the next ten years the country was ruled by Oliver Cromwell as Lord Protector. Cromwell is also remembered in Ireland for his brutal treatment of the population following signs of monarchist support.

In North America Britain had won the French colonies after the Seven Years' War, but then tried to offset some of the cost by taxing the thirteen British colonies. The colonies rebelled and gained their independence at the Treaty of Paris in 1783.

Elsewhere, the British were extending their territory in India, taking advantage of the weakened Maratha Confederacy, and a revolution in France and the subsequent rise of Napoleon together caused a massive social upheaval and ramifications that were felt throughout Europe.

1618 – 1639 THE THIRTY YEARS' WAR

THE THIRTY YEARS' WAR 1618–29

Imperial campaigns, with dates

→ Tilly

→ Wallenstein

→ Spínola

→ other Spanish armies

Protestant campaigns, with dates

→ Christian IV of Denmark

→ Mansfeld

→ Bethlen Gábor

✕ battle

▪ towns captured by Habsburgs, with dates

— border of Holy Roman Empire

  Spanish Habsburg territories

  Austrian Habsburg territories

THE THIRTY YEARS' WAR 1618–1629

This war began as a religious conflict between Protestants and Catholics. At that time Germany was a collection of states that ranged from the Austrian Habsburgs with eight million subjects, to tiny dukedoms that were little more than a single village. The fiercely Catholic Ferdinand II, Holy Roman Emperor and King of Bohemia, was not able to stem a Bohemian Protestant revolt that spread throughout Europe. The Lutheran Danes set out to help the Protestants, but were defeated and had to withdraw. The Treaty of Lübeck ensured that the Danes abandoned their support for the German Protestants.

THE THIRTY YEARS'
WAR 1630–39

Imperial campaigns

→ Gallas and Piccolomini
1636

Protestant campaigns

→ Gustav II Adolf

→ Banér 1637

✕ battle

— Border of Holy Roman
Empire

Spanish Habsburg
territories

Austrian Habsburg
territories

***THE THIRTY YEARS'
WAR 1630–1639***

In 1630 the Swedes appeared
on the scene. The Protestant
Swedes were anxious to
forestall any Catholic
aggression against their
homeland. They were also
motivated to help their fellow
Protestants and to obtain
economic influence in the
German states around the
Baltic Sea. For the next two
years Swedish King Gustavus
Adolphus waged an intensive
campaign, defeating the
Catholic League at the Battle
of Breitenfeld 1631, only to
be killed at the Battle of
Lützen in 1632. In 1634,
without Gustavus Adolphus's
leadership, the Protestant
forces were defeated at the
Battle of Nördlingen. The
following year Swedish
involvement in the war ended
with the Peace of Prague.

1631 – 1648   THE BATTLE OF BREITENFELD

THE BATTLE OF BREITENFELD 1631

This battle was fought near Leipzig in present-day Germany. On the Protestant side were the Swedes and the Saxons under the leadership of King Gustavus Adolphus of Sweden, while Counts Tilly and Pappenheim led the Catholic opposition. It was the first major Protestant victory of the Thirty Years' War and it confirmed the Swedish king as a great tactical leader. Many German states were encouraged to ally with Sweden against the Catholics as a result. In the battle Gustavus Adolphus inflicted more than 60 per cent casualties on his opponent and made up his own losses from captured mercenary soldiers who changed sides.

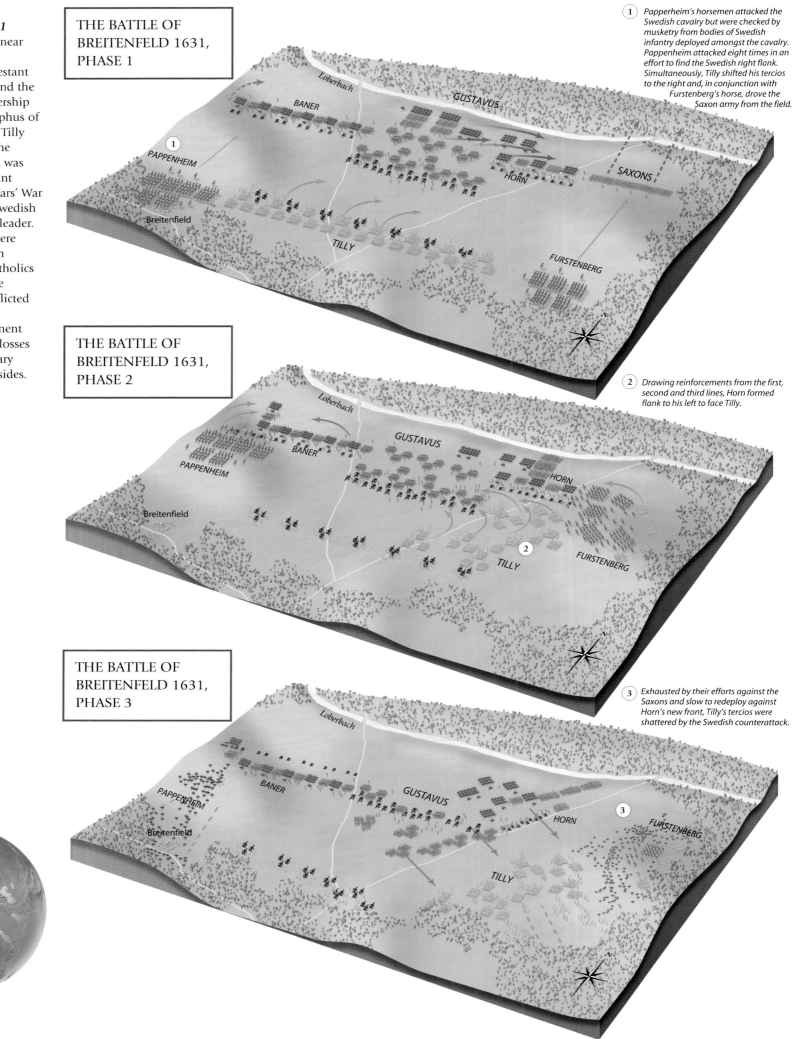

THE BATTLE OF BREITENFELD 1631, PHASE 1

THE BATTLE OF BREITENFELD 1631, PHASE 2

THE BATTLE OF BREITENFELD 1631, PHASE 3

1 Papperheim's horsemen attacked the Swedish cavalry but were checked by musketry from bodies of Swedish infantry deployed amongst the cavalry. Pappenheim attacked eight times in an effort to find the Swedish right flank. Simultaneously, Tilly shifted his tercios to the right and, in conjunction with Furstenberg's horse, drove the Saxon army from the field.

2 Drawing reinforcements from the first, second and third lines, Horn formed flank to his left to face Tilly.

3 Exhausted by their efforts against the Saxons and slow to redeploy against Horn's new front, Tilly's tercios were shattered by the Swedish counterattack.

THE THIRTY YEARS' WAR

THE THIRTY YEARS' WAR 1640–48

Swedish campaigns, with dates

→ Banér

→ Torstensson

→ Wrangel

→ other Swedish campaigns

other campaigns, with dates

→ Austrian

→ French

→ Dutch

→ George Rákóczy, Prince of Transylvania

✕ Swedish victory

✕ Swedish defeat

◼ towns captured by Swedes, with date

◼ towns captured by French, with date

◼ towns captured by Dutch, with date

✧ siege

— border of Holy Roman Empire

Spanish Habsburg territories

Austrian Habsburg territories

North Sea
Kristiansand
SWEDEN
Gothenburg
Arhus
Copenhagen • Malmö
Baltic Sea
DENMARK
Stralsund
1644
Wismar
POMERANIA
Stettin
Emden
Bremen
Hamburg 1643
Elbe
Verden 1643
Hanover
BRANDENBURG
Berlin
1648
Jüterbok Nov. 1644
NETHERLANDS
Amsterdam
Rotterdam
Venlo 1646
Ghent 1644
Hulst 1645 1644–5
Breda 1637
Dunkirk 1646
1646
1644
1647
1644
Düsseldorf
Magdeburg
Wolfenbüttel 29 June 1641
Breitenfeld 2 Nov. 1642
Leipzig
Antwerp
Cologne
Brussels
1645
SPANISH NETHERLANDS
Arras 1640
Rhine
1646
Giessen 1646
Erfurt 1640
SAXONY
1642
Breslau
POLAND
Rocroi 19 May 1643
Luxembourg
1646
Frankfurt
1640
1640
1646
1642
1642
Triebel 25 Aug. 1647
Prague
1645
Schweidnitz 9 June 1642
Cracow
Herbshausen 4 May 1645
1645
Nuremberg
1643
Pilsen
BOHEMIA
Olmütz 1642
Heidelberg
Allerheim 3 Aug. 1645
1641
Jankov 6 March 1645
Brno 1645
1642
Mannheim
Strasbourg
Stuttgart
1647
Danube
MORAVIA
1645
Banska Bystrica
Freiburg 3–4 Aug. 1644
Zusmarshausen 17 May 1648
1645
AUSTRIA
1645
1644
Kosice
FRANCE
Freiburg-im-Breisgau
Tuttlingen 24–5 Nov. 1643
BAVARIA
Munich
Krems 1645
Vienna
Levice
Szerencs
Dijon
FRANCHE-COMTÉ
Bregenz 1647
Salzburg
Linz 1648
Bratislava
1644
Basel
Zürich
SWISS CONFEDERATION
Berne
STYRIA
Kösseg
Pest
IMPERIAL HUNGARY
Papa
Geneva
CARINTHIA
Lyon
SAVOY
CARNIOLA
Ljubljana
Zagreb
OTTOMAN EMPIRE
Milan
REPUBLIC OF VENICE
Venice
Casale
Mantua
Pinerolo
Modena
Genoa
Bologna
Adriatic Sea
1646
Finale
Belgrade
Rhône

THE THIRTY YEARS' WAR 1640–1648

France was unhappy about the renewed strength that had been given to the Habsburgs by the Treaty of Prague and now entered the War. Although largely a Catholic country, France came in on the side of the Protestants because Cardinal Richelieu, the chief minister of King Louis XIII of France, felt that the Habsburgs were too powerful and posed a threat in the region. In retaliation Spain, a Habsburg ally, attacked French territory and even threatened Paris, before being repulsed. Richelieu died in 1642 and his successor began to work for peace. The Thirty Years' War ended with the Peace of Westphalia in 1648.

1642 – 1651   ENGLISH CIVIL WAR

ENGLISH CIVIL WAR 1642–3

→ March of Charles I in 1642

→ Royalist campaigns in 1643

✕ Royalist victories

✕ Parliamentary victories

✕ Inconclusive battles

▮ Royalist areas by the end of 1642

▯ Parliamentary areas by the end of 1642

◣ Royalist gains in 1643

▨ Royalist losses in 1643

ENGLISH CIVIL WAR 1642–1646

The English Civil War resulted from a build-up of tension between King Charles I and the English Parliament. It consisted of a series of armed conflicts and political machinations that took place between Parliamentarians, who were known as Roundheads, and Royalists, who were known as Cavaliers. The maps on these pages deal with what became known as the "First War." Charles officially began the war by raising his standard at Nottingham in August 1642. The first battle was at Edgehill in October. Although the battle was inconclusive another at Turnham Green the following month prevented Charles from reaching London and he withdrew to Oxford, which became his base. 1643 saw many battles all over the country, with early victories for the Royalists. The turning point came in the late summer and early autumn of that year, when the Earl of Essex's army inflicted a heavy defeat on the Royalist army at the First Battle of Newbury. In 1644 actions were fairly evenly balanced, with Parliament gaining large areas of the north while losing large areas of the west. However, in 1645, after the restructuring of Parliamentary forces into the New Model Army, Charles's armies were effectively destroyed at the battles of Naseby and

Langport and Charles was forced to leave Oxford and flee north. Royalist uprisings, largely in the north of England and Scotland, took place in the summer or 1648, but these were quickly put down by Parliament; this came to be known as the "Second War."

ENGLISH CIVIL WAR 1644

→ Campaigns of Montrose

→ Other Royalist campaigns

→ Campaigns of Scottish Covenanters

→ Other Parliamentary campaigns

✕ Royalist victories

✕ Parliamentary victories

✕ Inconclusive battles

▪ Town captured, with date

▮ Royalist areas by the end of 1643

▯ Parliamentary areas by the end of 1643

◣ Royalist gains in 1644

▨ Royalist losses in 1644

CROMWELL IN IRELAND

ENGLISH CIVIL WAR 1645–6

→ Campaigns of Montrose

→ Other Royalist campaigns

→ Scottish army

→ Other Parliamentary campaigns

✕ Royalist victories

✕ Parliamentary victories

▨ Royalist areas by the end of 1645

▨ Parliamentary areas by the end of 1644

▨ Royalist losses in 1645

CROMWELL IN IRELAND
In 1649 the Irish Confederate Catholics signed an alliance with the English Royalists, releasing an additional 18,000 troops to fight for the king. As a result, the English House of Commons sent an army to Ireland, under the command of Oliver Cromwell, one of the key leaders of the Roundheads during the Civil War. One of Cromwell's first acts was to storm the town of Drogheda, brutally killing around 3500 of the population. He then moved his army south and stormed and sacked Wexford, again with great brutality. This set the pattern for the rest of a bloody campaign, which has made Cromwell's name one of the most hated in Irish history.

CROMWELL IN IRELAND

✕ Battles with dates

→ Main route of Cromwell's campaign, August 1649–May 1650

→ Ireton, 1649–51

Westward limits of territory held by Cromwell's forces

▨ December 1649

▨ May 1650

▨ End 1650

BATTLE OF NASEBY

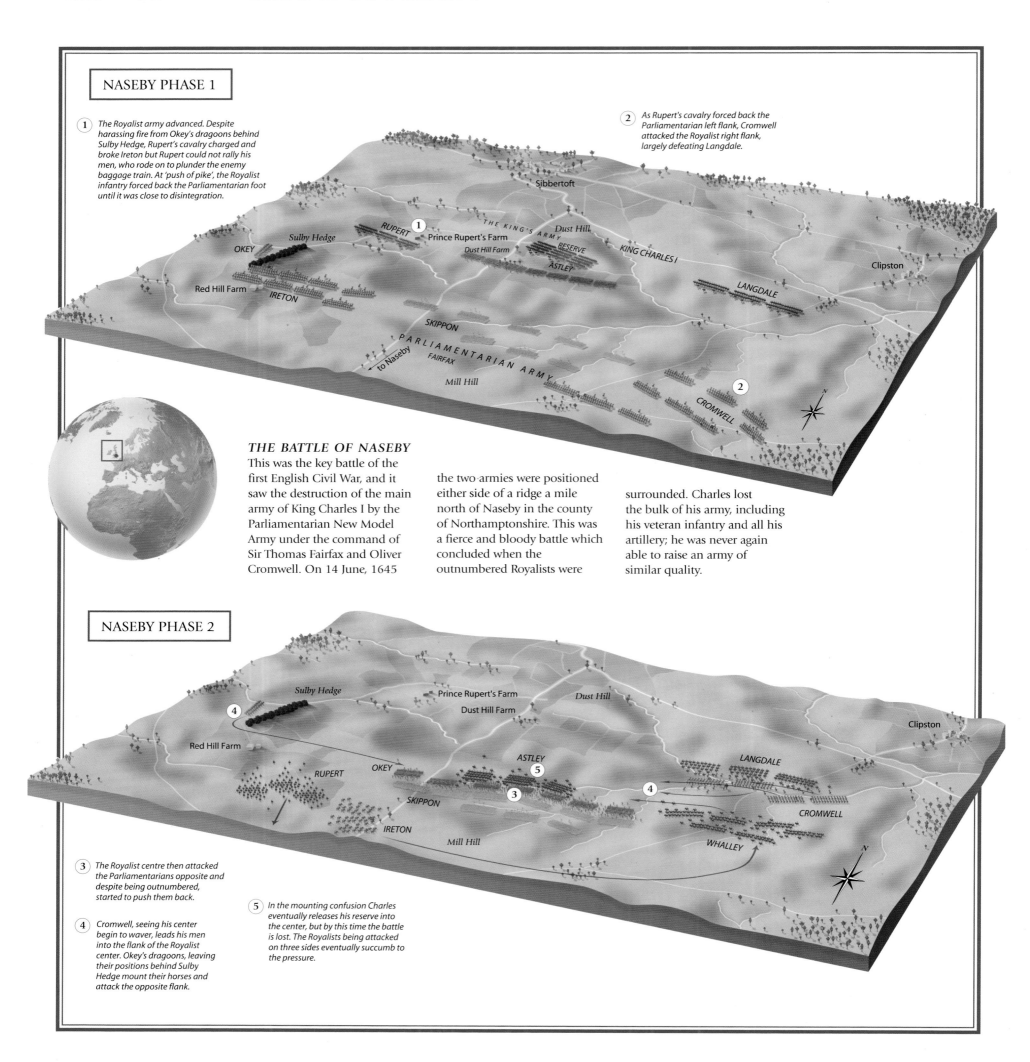

NASEBY PHASE 1

1 *The Royalist army advanced. Despite harassing fire from Okey's dragoons behind Sulby Hedge, Rupert's cavalry charged and broke Ireton but Rupert could not rally his men, who rode on to plunder the enemy baggage train. At 'push of pike', the Royalist infantry forced back the Parliamentarian foot until it was close to disintegration.*

2 *As Rupert's cavalry forced back the Parliamentarian left flank, Cromwell attacked the Royalist right flank, largely defeating Langdale.*

Sibbertoft

RUPERT

OKEY

Sulby Hedge

Prince Rupert's Farm

THE KING'S ARMY

Dust Hill

Dust Hill Farm

RESERVE

KING CHARLES I

Clipston

Red Hill Farm

IRETON

ASTLEY

LANGDALE

SKIPPON

PARLIAMENTARIAN ARMY

to Naseby

FAIRFAX

Mill Hill

CROMWELL

2

N

THE BATTLE OF NASEBY
This was the key battle of the first English Civil War, and it saw the destruction of the main army of King Charles I by the Parliamentarian New Model Army under the command of Sir Thomas Fairfax and Oliver Cromwell. On 14 June, 1645 the two armies were positioned either side of a ridge a mile north of Naseby in the county of Northamptonshire. This was a fierce and bloody battle which concluded when the outnumbered Royalists were surrounded. Charles lost the bulk of his army, including his veteran infantry and all his artillery; he was never again able to raise an army of similar quality.

NASEBY PHASE 2

Sulby Hedge

4

Prince Rupert's Farm

Dust Hill Farm

Dust Hill

Clipston

Red Hill Farm

RUPERT

OKEY

ASTLEY

5

LANGDALE

3

4

SKIPPON

IRETON

Mill Hill

CROMWELL

WHALLEY

N

3 *The Royalist centre then attacked the Parliamentarians opposite and despite being outnumbered, started to push them back.*

4 *Cromwell, seeing his center begin to waver, leads his men into the flank of the Royalist center. Okey's dragoons, leaving their positions behind Sulby Hedge mount their horses and attack the opposite flank.*

5 *In the mounting confusion Charles eventually releases his reserve into the center, but by this time the battle is lost. The Royalists being attacked on three sides eventually succumb to the pressure.*

DAHLBERG'S FORTIFICATIONS AT GOTHENBURG; VAUBAN'S TRENCH ATTACK WITH FIELDS OF FIRE

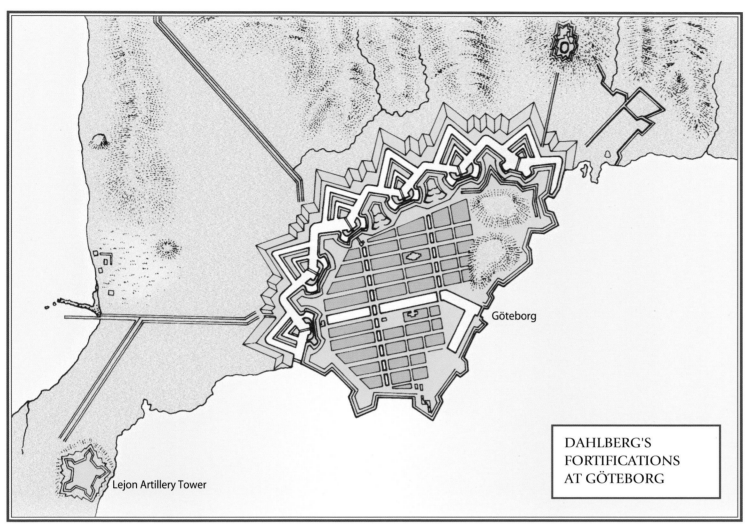

DAHLBERG'S FORTIFICATIONS AT GÖTEBORG

Göteborg

Lejon Artillery Tower

DAHLBERG'S FORTIFICATIONS AT GOTHENBURG

In 1621 the Swedish king Gustavus Adolphus II decided on the location of present-day Gothenburg. It was a very marshy area and, because of their experience in building on such terrain, Dutch planners were contracted to build the city. As a result, a town was planned with canals like Amsterdam. The city was also heavily fortified by Erik Dahlberg, Sweden's foremost military engineer. The defenses were planned using the star principle and, as a consequence, Gothenburg became one of the best-defended cities in Europe.

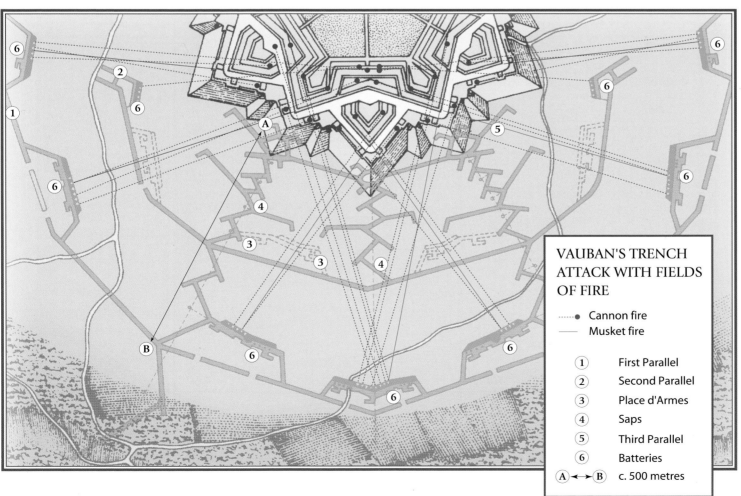

VAUBAN'S TRENCH ATTACK WITH FIELDS OF FIRE

- - - • Cannon fire
——— Musket fire

①	First Parallel
②	Second Parallel
③	Place d'Armes
④	Saps
⑤	Third Parallel
⑥	Batteries
Ⓐ ←→ Ⓑ	c. 500 metres

VAUBAN'S TRENCH ATTACK WITH FIELDS OF FIRE

Sebastien de Vauban spent more than half a century on active service in the campaigns of Louis XIV of France during the 17th century. He was an expert in siege warfare and developed a particular technique for attacking fortresses. He would arrange his artillery about 1500 feet from the fortress and dig a parallel trench behind them. Musketeers would be positioned in the trench to protect the artillery from attack. Sappers would dig zigzag trenches toward the fort for about 500 feet, then another parallel trench would be dug and everything moved forward. This would be repeated until the walls were close enough to be smashed by the artillery.

COLONIAL FRONTIERS

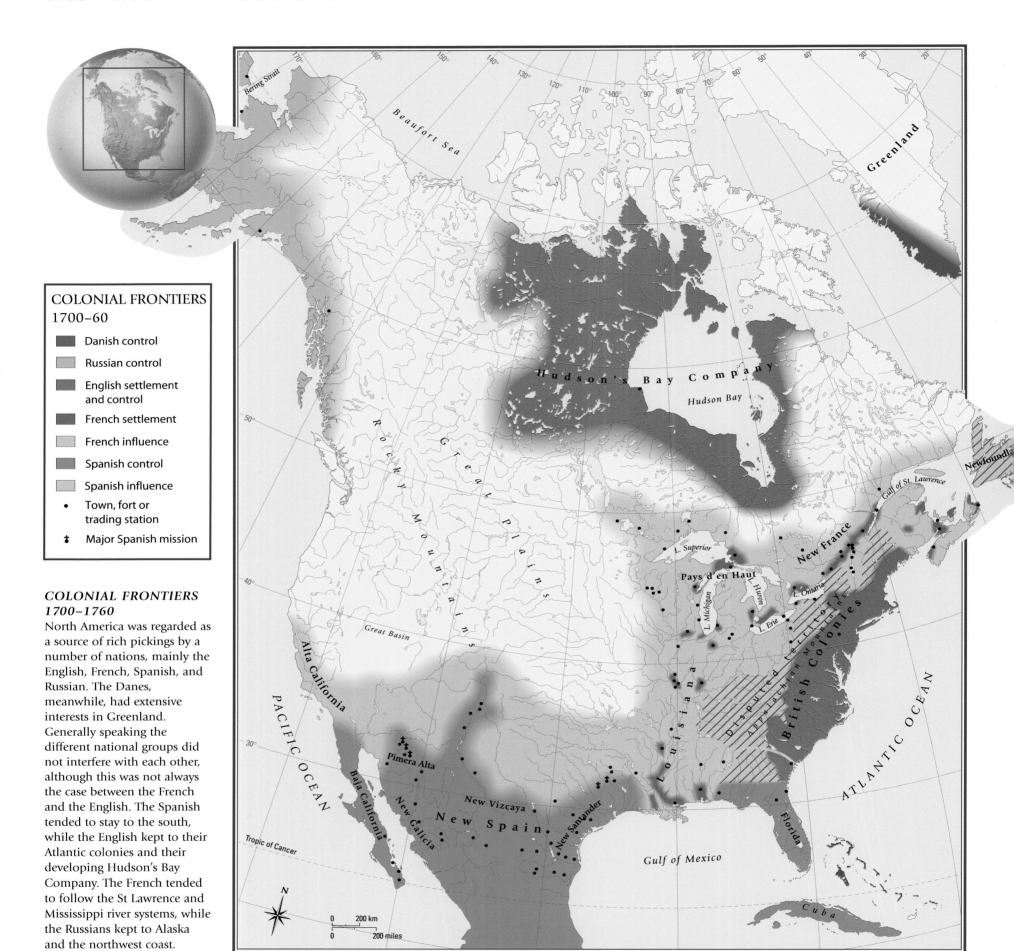

COLONIAL FRONTIERS
1700–60

- ■ Danish control
- ■ Russian control
- ■ English settlement and control
- ■ French settlement
- ■ French influence
- ■ Spanish control
- ■ Spanish influence
- • Town, fort or trading station
- ⚓ Major Spanish mission

COLONIAL FRONTIERS
1700–1760

North America was regarded as a source of rich pickings by a number of nations, mainly the English, French, Spanish, and Russian. The Danes, meanwhile, had extensive interests in Greenland. Generally speaking the different national groups did not interfere with each other, although this was not always the case between the French and the English. The Spanish tended to stay to the south, while the English kept to their Atlantic colonies and their developing Hudson's Bay Company. The French tended to follow the St Lawrence and Mississippi river systems, while the Russians kept to Alaska and the northwest coast.

DISCONTENT IN THE COLONIES ON THE EVE OF WAR

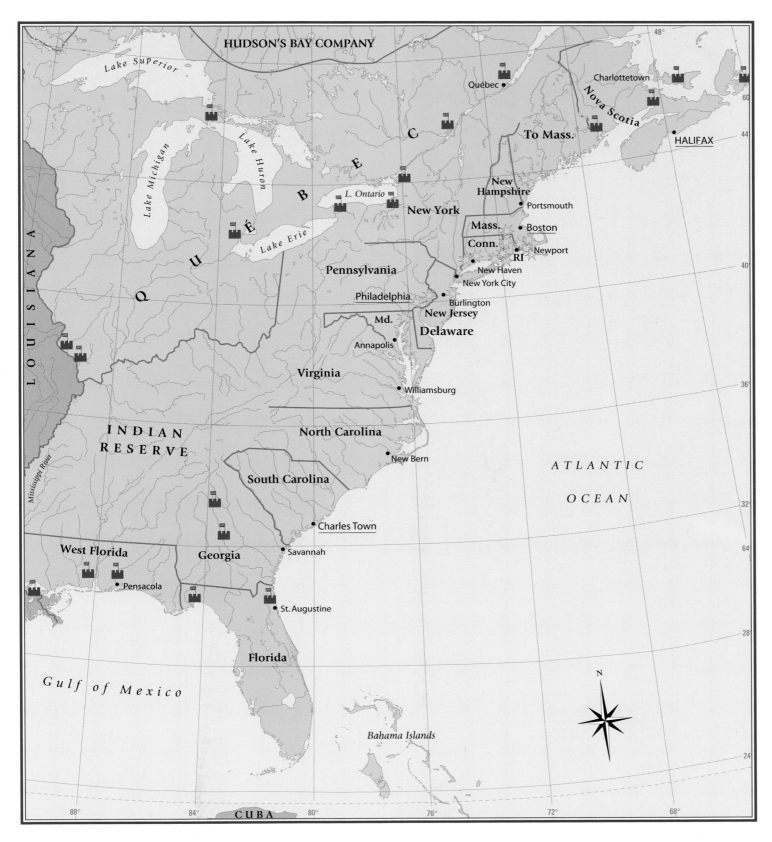

DISCONTENT IN THE COLONIES ON THE EVE OF WAR 1764–76

	British territory
	Army garrison, 1766
HALIFAX	Vice-Admiralty Court, 1764–68
Boston	Additional Vice-Admiralty Court, 1768
New Bern	Colonial capital
✳	Anticustoms riot, 1764–74
	Spanish territory

DISCONTENT IN THE COLONIES ON THE EVE OF WAR 1764–1776

In the mid-1700s Britain and France were at war, and this conflict spilled over to North America. At its conclusion in 1763, Britain had won control of Canada and kept the Thirteen Colonies. The following year the Colonists were angered when Britain introduced new taxes and restrictions. Although some of these were repealed, further taxes and restrictions were progressively added, leading to increased Colonial anger. British troops were mobilized and in 1774 the Colonists formed special groups of militia known as Minute Men. In 1775 George Washington was appointed commander-in-chief of the new army and in 1776 the Colonies declared their independence from British rule.

1776 – 1781 THE BATTLE OF TRENTON

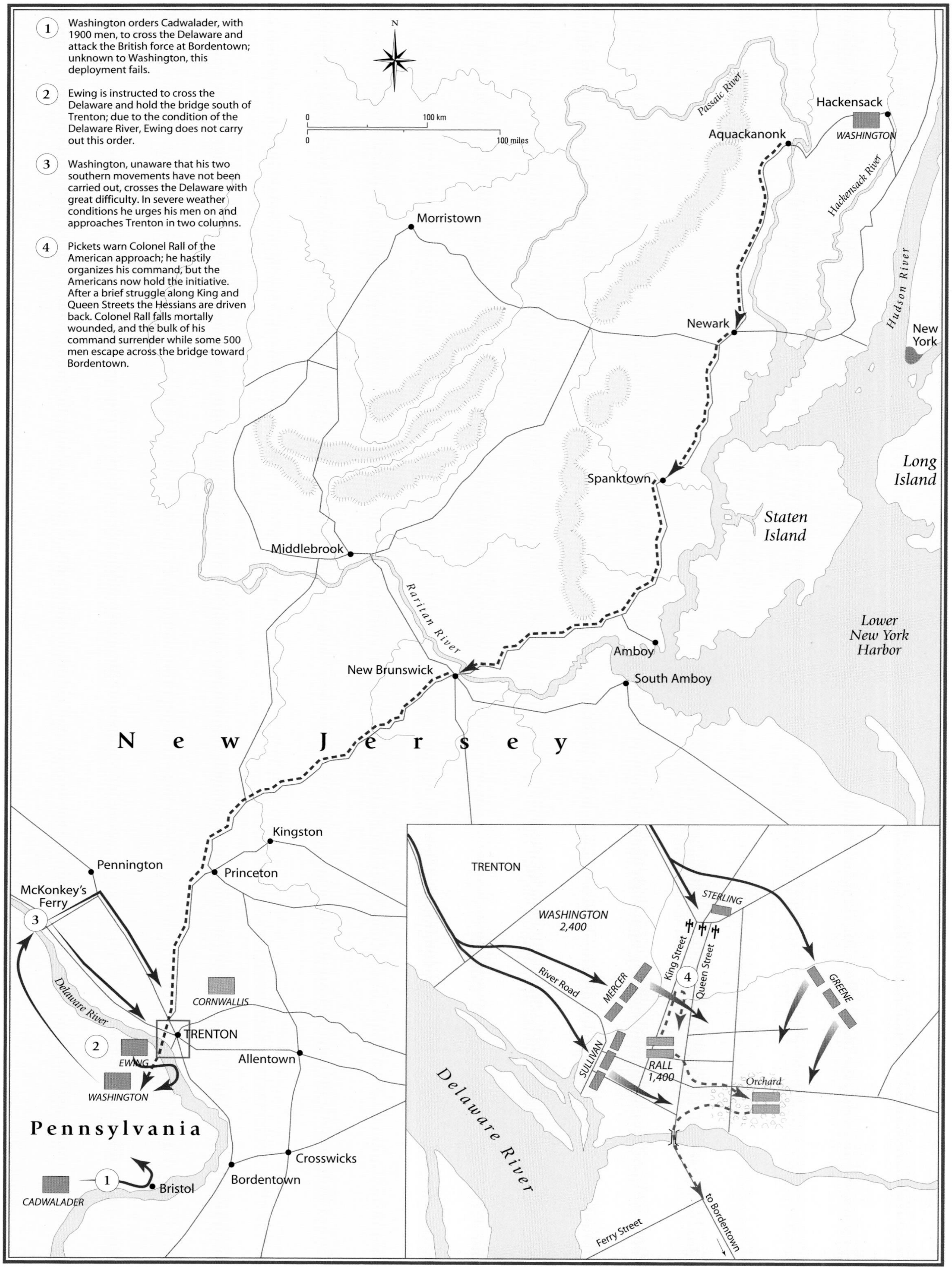
1 Washington orders Cadwalader, with 1900 men, to cross the Delaware and attack the British force at Bordentown; unknown to Washington, this deployment fails.
2 Ewing is instructed to cross the Delaware and hold the bridge south of Trenton; due to the condition of the Delaware River, Ewing does not carry out this order.
3 Washington, unaware that his two southern movements have not been carried out, crosses the Delaware with great difficulty. In severe weather conditions he urges his men on and approaches Trenton in two columns.
4 Pickets warn Colonel Rall of the American approach; he hastily organizes his command, but the Americans now hold the initiative. After a brief struggle along King and Queen Streets the Hessians are driven back. Colonel Rall falls mortally wounded, and the bulk of his command surrender while some 500 men escape across the bridge toward Bordentown.
N
0 100 km
0 100 miles
Passaic River
Hackensack
WASHINGTON
Aquackanonk
Hackensack River
Hudson River
New York
Morristown
Newark
Long Island
Spanktown
Staten Island
Middlebrook
Raritan River
Lower New York Harbor
Amboy
New Brunswick
South Amboy
New Jersey
Kingston
Pennington
Princeton
McKonkey's Ferry
Delaware River
CORNWALLIS
TRENTON
EWING
Allentown
WASHINGTON
Pennsylvania
Crosswicks
CADWALADER
Bristol
Bordentown
TRENTON
STERLING
WASHINGTON 2,400
King Street
Queen Street
River Road
MERCER
GREENE
SULLIVAN
RALL 1,400
Orchard
Delaware River
Ferry Street
to Bordentown

THE BATTLE OF TRENTON
26 DECEMBER 1776

- British advance
- American retreat
- British unit
- American unit
- Road
- Higher ground

THE BATTLE OF TRENTON DECEMBER 26 , 1776

This battle, which was part of the American War of Independence, took place in a fierce snowstorm on Boxing Day. Three regiments of about 1400 Hessian soldiers (German troops who were in service to the British Empire) occupied Trenton, New Jersey. The British forces felt fairly secure because they had been told that the Americans were in a state of confusion and in no condition to attack. In addition, because of the violent storm, it was felt that it would be impossible for Washington's forces to cross the Delaware River. However, Washington crossed during the night and fighting began at around 8.00 am and was over by 9.00 am. The Hessian army was virtually eliminated and Washington's victory helped to set the stage for the Battle of Princeton the following week, which effectively ended the British presence in New Jersey.

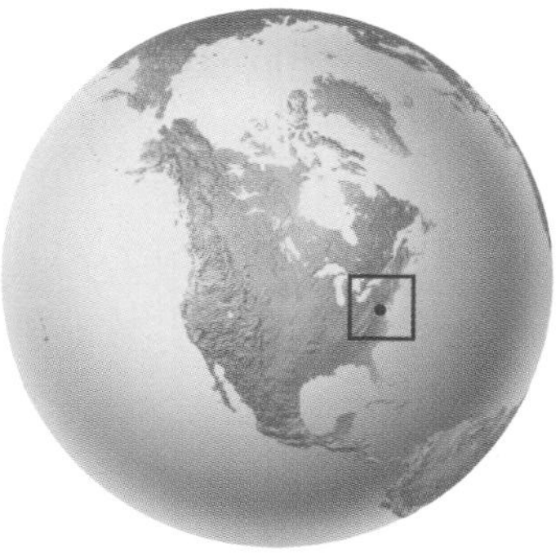

THE SIEGE OF YORKTOWN

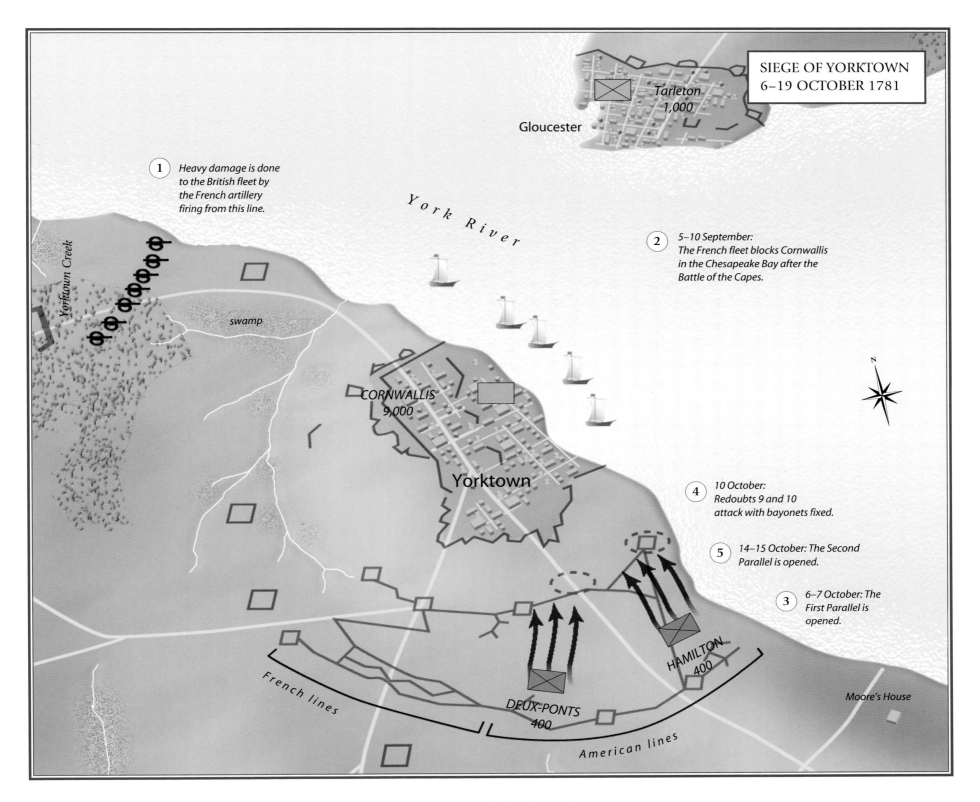

SIEGE OF YORKTOWN
6–19 OCTOBER 1781

Tarleton
1,000

Gloucester

1 Heavy damage is done
to the British fleet by
the French artillery
firing from this line.

York River

2 5–10 September:
The French fleet blocks Cornwallis
in the Chesapeake Bay after the
Battle of the Capes.

Yorktown Creek

swamp

CORNWALLIS
9,000

Yorktown

4 10 October:
Redoubts 9 and 10
attack with bayonets fixed.

5 14–15 October: The Second
Parallel is opened.

3 6–7 October: The
First Parallel is
opened.

French lines

HAMILTON
400

Moore's House

DEUX-PONTS
400

American lines

THE SIEGE OF YORKTOWN

This was a decisive victory by a joint French and American army over a British army commanded by General Lord Cornwallis. Cornwallis had been campaigning in the southern states and had taken up a defensive position in Yorktown hoping to be evacuated by the Royal Navy. After being completely surrounded, with little hope of relief and with food and ammunition running low, Cornwallis surrendered on 19th October. 7000 British troops became prisoners, about a quarter of all the British soldiers in America. As a result the British government decided to end the war and the Treaty of Paris was signed in September 1783.

THE TREATY OF PARIS

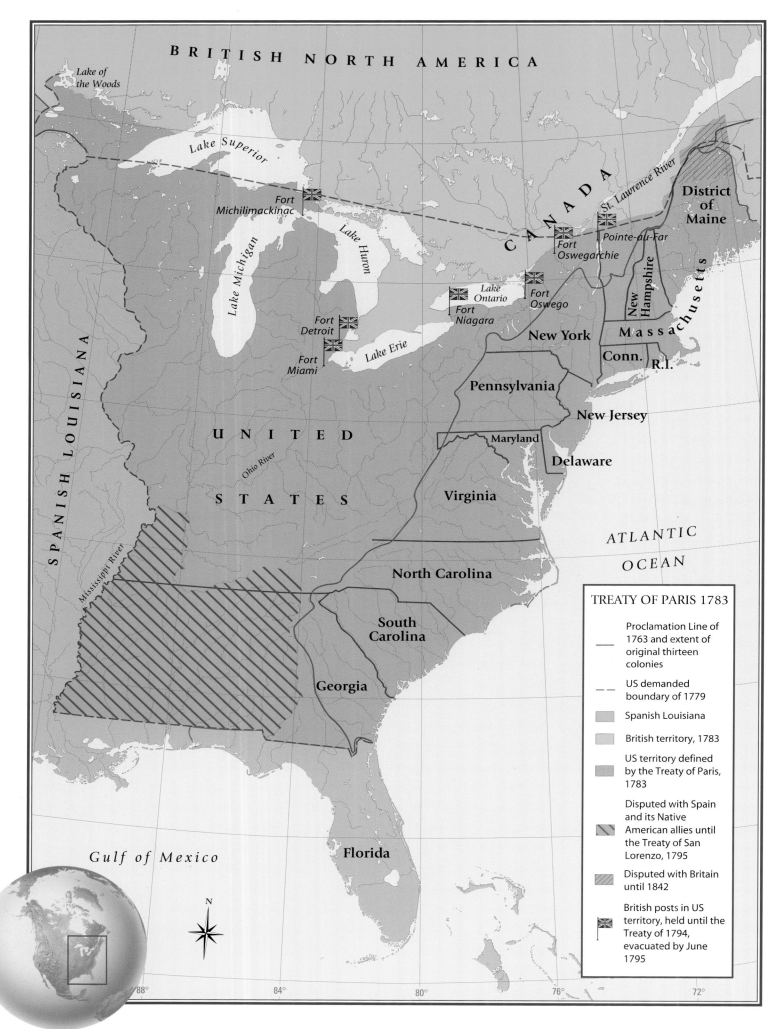

TREATY OF PARIS 1783
Although the British
Parliament decided in April
1783 that the American
Revolutionary War was a war
that was no longer worth
fighting, it still did not
recognize American
independence. However, in
September 1783, a treaty was
signed in Paris that formally
ended the war. The 13
colonies were now officially
recognized as free and
sovereign states and
boundaries were established
between the United States,
British North America and
Spanish Louisiana. US
fishermen were also granted
fishing rights off
Newfoundland and in the
Gulf of St Lawrence. The
United States and Britain
both formally recognized
the Treaty early in 1784.

**INDIA, INVASIONS, AND
REGIONAL POWERS
1739–1760; THE BATTLE
OF PLASSEY (RIGHT)**
In the mid-1700s the Maratha
Empire dominated India. It was
a Hindu state and at its height
it ruled over 600,000 square
miles, or one third of South
Asia. It was strong enough to
resist the Mughal invasions
from the north and to keep the
British East India Company at
bay. The Battle of Plassey was
pitched between the British East
India Company and the French
East India Company, who had
sided with the Nawab of
Bengal. The result was a victory
for the British that gave them
control of Bengal and paved the
way for the complete British
conquest of India.

Map Legend

TREATY OF PARIS 1783

— Proclamation Line of
1763 and extent of
original thirteen
colonies

– – US demanded
boundary of 1779

Spanish Louisiana

British territory, 1783

US territory defined
by the Treaty of Paris,
1783

Disputed with Spain
and its Native
American allies until
the Treaty of San
Lorenzo, 1795

Disputed with Britain
until 1842

British posts in US
territory, held until the
Treaty of 1794,
evacuated by June
1795

INDIA INVASIONS; THE BATTLE OF PLASSEY

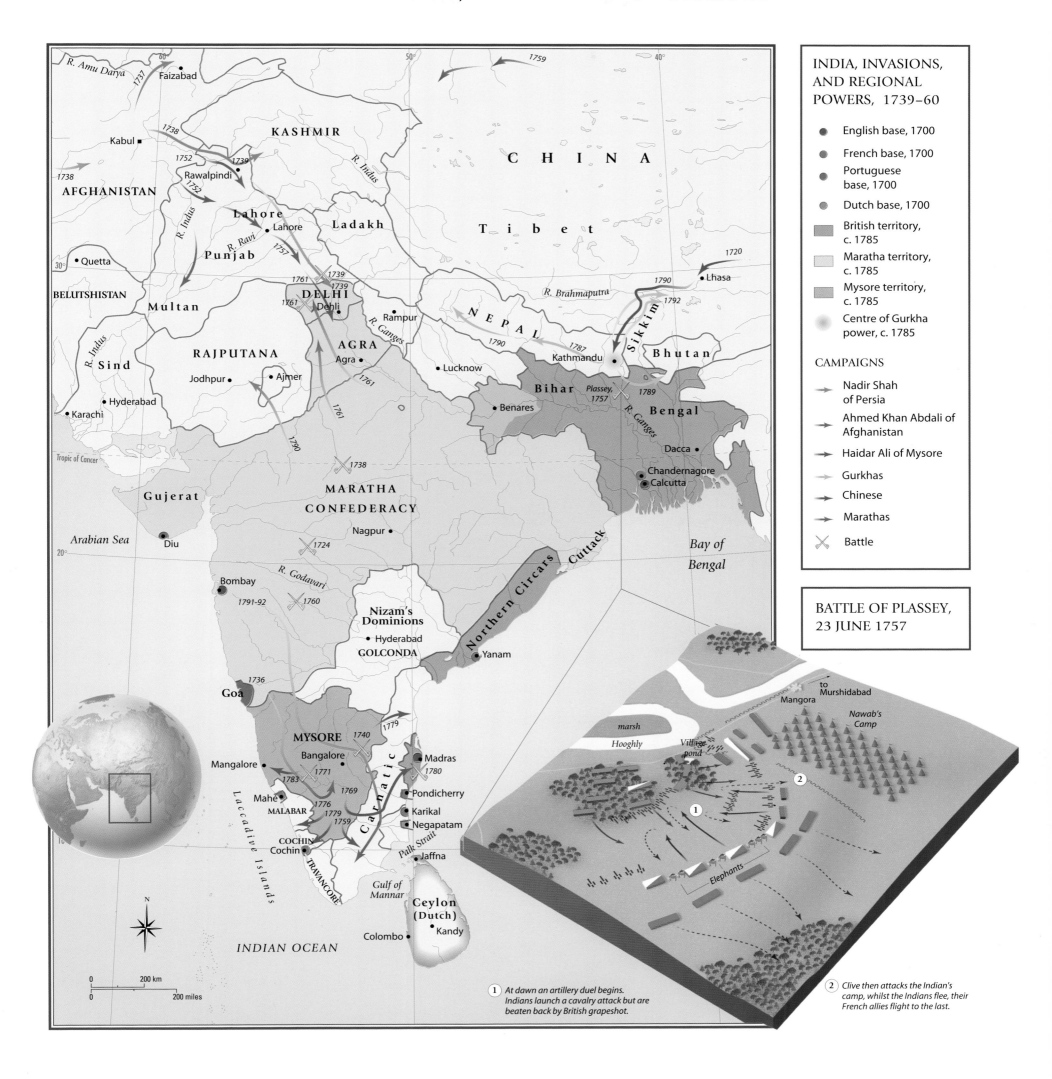

INDIA, INVASIONS, AND REGIONAL POWERS, 1739–60

- English base, 1700
- French base, 1700
- Portuguese base, 1700
- Dutch base, 1700
- British territory, c. 1785
- Maratha territory, c. 1785
- Mysore territory, c. 1785
- Centre of Gurkha power, c. 1785

CAMPAIGNS

- Nadir Shah of Persia
- Ahmed Khan Abdali of Afghanistan
- Haidar Ali of Mysore
- Gurkhas
- Chinese
- Marathas
- Battle

BATTLE OF PLASSEY, 23 JUNE 1757

1. At dawn an artillery duel begins. Indians launch a cavalry attack but are beaten back by British grapeshot.

2. Clive then attacks the Indian's camp, whilst the Indians flee, their French allies flight to the last.

1789 – 1795

FRENCH REVOLUTION 1789 – 1795

FRENCH REVOLUTION 1789–1795

The French Revolution was a period of political and social upheaval in the history of France and of Europe as a whole. During this time the French governmental structure, which had previously been an absolute monarchy with feudal privileges for the aristocracy and the Catholic clergy, underwent a radical change. These changes were accompanied by violent turmoil, executions, and repression during the Reign of Terror. There was also warfare, and eventually every major European power was caught up in this. These wars involved enormous numbers of soldiers, mainly due to the application of modern mass conscription.

EUROPE IN 1789
(FACING PAGE)

In 1789 Europe was made up of a range of large and small countries. Spain, France, and Great Britain were similar to how they are today, but others were quite different. The eastern Mediterranean was dominated by the Ottoman Empire, the vast area of Russia stretched away to the east, while much of central Europe was a mish-mash of small states, some little larger than villages. These regularly changed hands as a result of marriage alliance or conquest; for instance, large parts of the Netherlands belonged to the Austrian Habsburg Empire. The Habsburgs had built a huge empire that covered most of south-central and eastern Europe.

FRENCH REVOLUTION
1789–1795

→ Advance of French revolutionary armies

→ Attacks by Allied armies

✕ French victory

✕ Allied victory

--- Naval blockade

● Major town where council was replaced by revolutionary committee

● Major town where council shared power with revolutionary committee

▦ France in 1789

▦ Annexed by France in 1792–93

▦ Annexed by France in 1795

▨ Center of counterrevolution

EUROPE 1789

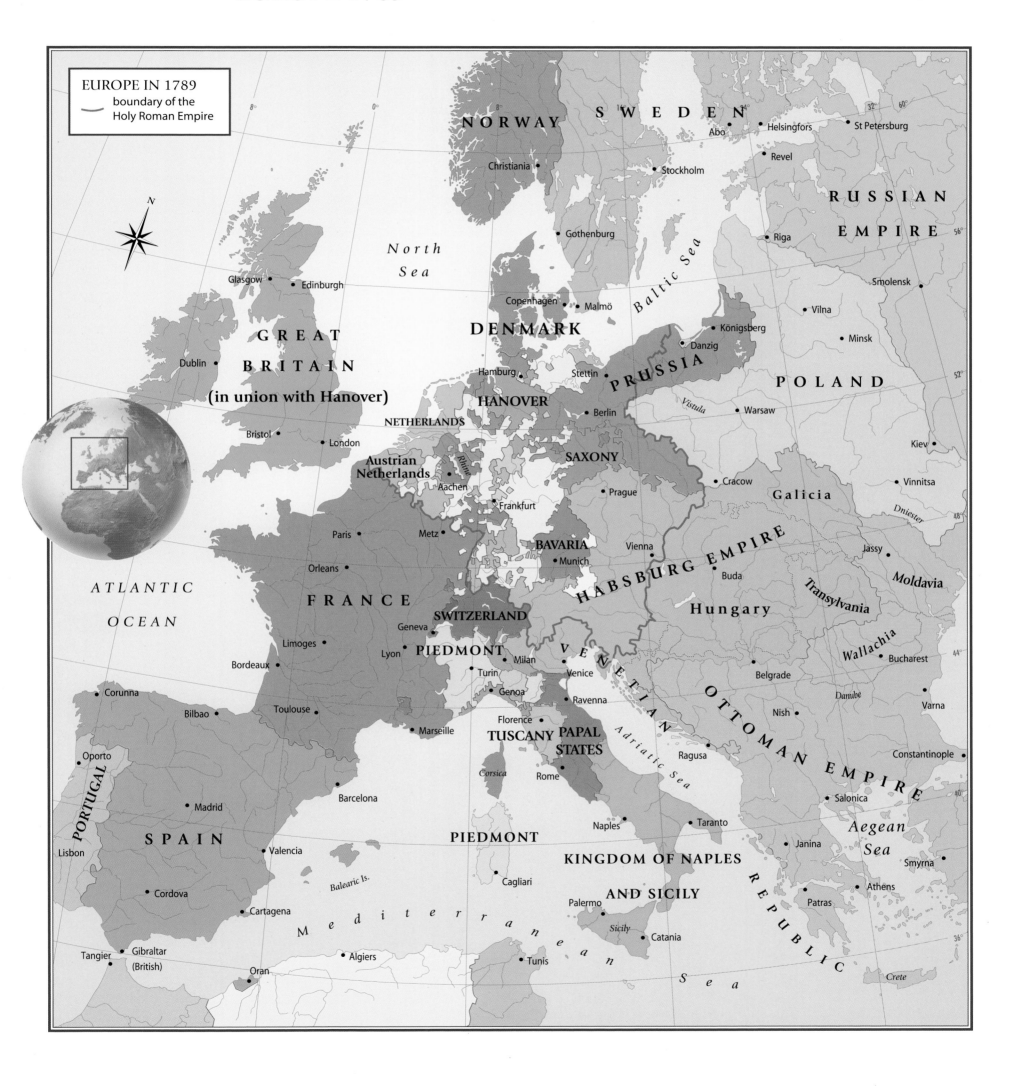

EUROPE IN 1789
— boundary of the
Holy Roman Empire

NORWAY

SWEDEN

RUSSIAN

EMPIRE

Christiania

Åbo

Helsingfors

St Petersburg

Stockholm

Revel

*North
Sea*

Glasgow

Edinburgh

Gothenburg

Riga

Smolensk

Baltic Sea

Copenhagen

Malmö

Vilna

Minsk

DENMARK

Königsberg

Dublin

GREAT

BRITAIN

Danzig

Hamburg

Stettin

PRUSSIA

POLAND

Bristol

London

HANOVER

Berlin

Warsaw

(in union with Hanover)

NETHERLANDS

Kiev

Austrian
Netherlands

SAXONY

Aachen

Rhine

Prague

Cracow

Vinnitsa

Frankfurt

Galicia

Dniester

Paris

Metz

Vienna

HABSBURG EMPIRE

Jassy

Orleans

BAVARIA

Munich

Buda

Moldavia

ATLANTIC

FRANCE

SWITZERLAND

Hungary

Transylvania

OCEAN

Geneva

Limoges

Lyon

PIEDMONT

Milan

VENETIAN

Wallachia

Bucharest

Bordeaux

Turin

Venice

Belgrade

Danube

Varna

Toulouse

Genoa

Ravenna

Nish

Corunna

Marseille

TUSCANY

Florence

PAPAL
STATES

*Adriatic
Sea*

Ragusa

OTTOMAN EMPIRE

Constantinople

Bilbao

Corsica

Rome

PORTUGAL

Oporto

Madrid

Barcelona

PIEDMONT

Naples

Taranto

Salonica

*Aegean
Sea*

Janina

Smyrna

Lisbon

SPAIN

Valencia

KINGDOM OF NAPLES

Cagliari

AND SICILY

Palermo

Cordova

Balearic Is.

Catania

Sicily

REPUBLIC

Patras

Athens

Cartagena

Mediterranean

Tangier

Gibraltar
(British)

Oran

Algiers

Tunis

Sea

Crete

1800 THE BATTLE OF MARENGO

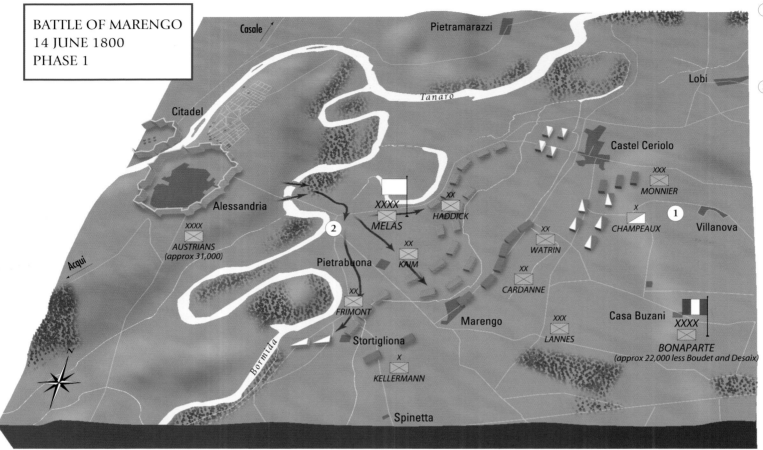

BATTLE OF MARENGO
14 JUNE 1800
PHASE 1

① In the belief that the Austrians intend to escape, Bonaparte detaches three divisions, including two under Desaix, to block their movement. On the night of 13th–14th June, the French camp around Marengo but take no precautions against Austrian attack.

② Melas, who had retained a small bridgehead across the Bormida, attacks around 8 a.m. but with only two bridges, the attack is slow to develop. Still, by 10 a.m. the advanced French formations have been pushed back and the Austrians have formed a strong fighting line supported by superior artillery. Shortly thereafter Bonaparte recognizes his danger and calls for his detached divisions to return. Fighting a stubborn defensive action, the French continue to retire east.

THE BATTLE OF MARENGO JUNE 14, 1800

This battle took place near the city of Alessandria in Piedmont, Italy between the armies of Austria and France. Napoleon thought that the Austrians were intending to escape so he sent three divisions of his army to stop them. In actual fact the Austrians attacked, taking the French by surprise. Things began to look very bad for Napoleon, but fortunately for him he was able to recall his three divisions. The French counterattacked, executed an artillery bombardment and mounted a cavalry charge, leaving the Austrians completely defeated, with 9500 of their troops killed, wounded, or captured. The Austrians were forced out of most of Italy.

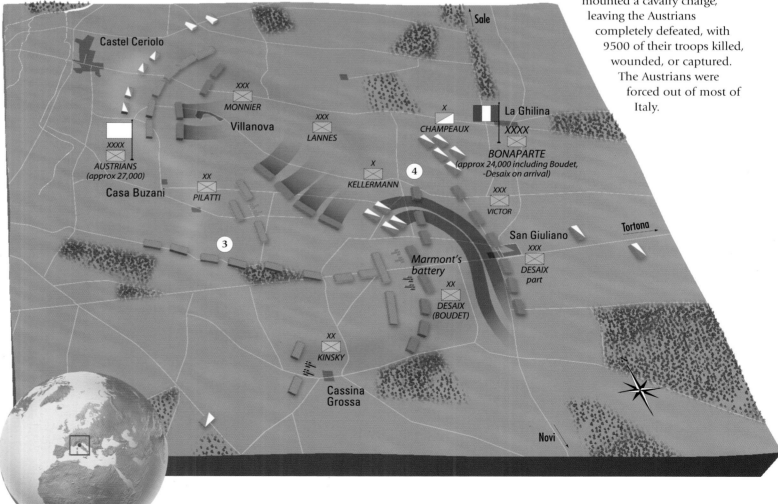

BATTLE OF MARENGO
14 JUNE 1800
PHASE 2

③ Afternoon: the Austrians believing themselves victorious, form march formation and proceed eastward. Melas retires, handing command to Zach, thus delaying the advance until 4 p.m. Bonaparte throws in reserves and tries to stem Austrian advance around San Giuliano but his troops are exhausted.

④ Desaix had already heard the sound of the guns and returned on his own initiative, arriving in the mid-afternoon. Marmont now forms remaining 18 cannon into a battery to blast closest Austrian column. Desaix counterattacks at the head of Boudet's division but is mortally wounded. General Kellermann exploits temporary Austrian disarray and charges with 400 troopers. The Austrian center crumbles and their army is pushed back into the bridgehead by 9 p.m., suffering heavy losses.

PART 5

WARS OF THE
INDUSTRIAL AGE

BY THE END OF THE EIGHTEENTH century the Industrial Revolution was in full swing and this was being reflected in battles and warfare. Mass-produced weapons had transformed the battlefield and human-powered weapons had been completely replaced by firearms. Progressive improvements had made these weapons lighter, safer and more accurate. Heavy guns on the battlefield had become capable of massive destruction.

The turn of the 18th–19th centuries was the age of Napoleon. His innovative battle techniques ensured a series of victories that by 1810 had given him effective control of much of Europe. He was finally defeated at the Battle of Waterloo in 1815.

The American Civil War that took place some 45 years later was a true war of the industrial age. Both sides had factories that mass-produced weapons in vast numbers. A problem was that technology had advanced so quickly that battlefield techniques had not kept pace. Generals were still trying to fight using outdated strategies and the result was that many of the Civil War battles ended in complete carnage. The Battle of Gettysburg, for instance, resulted in around 51,000 casualties, and at the Battle of Antietam 23,000 soldiers were killed in a single day. In all there were 970,000 casualties in the Civil War, or 3 per cent of the American population. 620,000 of these were fatalities and around two-thirds of this number were the result of disease. The American Civil War accounted for more casualties than all other US wars combined.

1810 – 1815 FRENCH EMPIRE

FRENCH EMPIRE 1810
The French Empire began after Napoleon Bonaparte became Emperor in 1804 and it lasted until his abdication in 1814. His defeats of the Prussian armies at Austerlitz in 1806 and the Russians at Friedland in 1807 were two of his early victories. He then turned his attention to the Iberian Peninsula. The Peninsula War, which began in 1808, was particularly vicious and was to drag on for six years, severely weakening the Empire and eventually contributing to Napoleon's downfall, but in 1810 France was the major force in Europe, with enormous areas of the continent being ruled by Napoleon or members of his family.

FRENCH EMPIRE 1810

- Under direct rule by Napoleon
- Under rule by members of Napoleon's family
- Dependent state
- → Napoleon's European campaigns

THE BATTLE OF WATERLOO

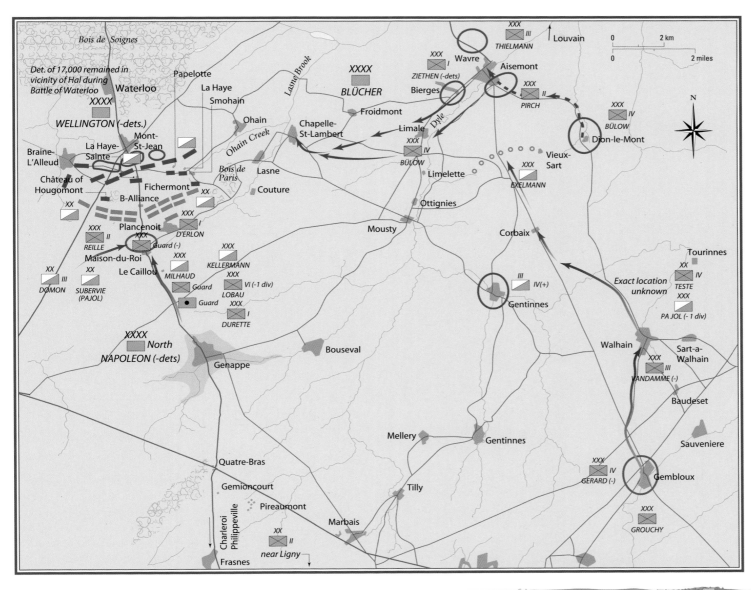

BATTLE OF WATERLOO
10:00 HRS, 18 JUNE
1815

→ French advance
→ Allied advance
⇢ Allied retreat
◯ French concentration
◯ Allied concentration

***THE BATTLE OF
WATERLOO JUNE 18, 1815***
This was Napoleon Bonaparte's
last battle. It also marked the
end of the period known as
the "Hundred Days", which
started in March 1815 when he
returned to France from his
exile in Elba. Many countries
that had previously resisted his
rule began to assemble armies
to oppose him. His principal
opponents were the British,
commanded by the Duke of
Wellington, and the Prussians,
commanded by Gebhard
Leberecht von Blücher. The
battle lasted all day and was
very closely fought with heavy
losses on both sides, but
eventually the French were
defeated by the combined
British and Prussian forces.

BATTLE OF WATERLOO
13:30 HRS, 18 JUNE
1815

① Shortly after 3:30p.m. on the 18 June, his
attack on La Haye Sante repulsed, Ney
ordered General Milhaud's Cuirassiers to
attack. Milhaud in turn asked for support
from the Imperial Guard's Light Cavalry
and some 4,000 French troopers were
advancing in an unsupported attack
against the Allied line. At first Napoleon
was angry about Ney's move, but then
reinforced with Kellermann's cuirassiers
and the heavy cavalry of the Guard. Most
of Napoleon's Cavalry was committed to
unsupported charges that achieved little
but suffered heavy losses against firm
infantry squares. Around 4p.m. Ney
launches a series of cavalry charges on
the allied center.

② The British infantry formed squares
with artillery between and after
facing cavalry charges for more than
an hour eventually drove them off.

③ Ney attacks and captures the
farm of La Haye Sainte.

④ Napoleon orders units of the Guard
eastward to face the Prussians
ignoring Neys call for
reinforcement at La Haye Sainte.

⑤ Ziethen's Prussian Corps arrive
just in time to reinforce the
allied position.

⑥ Napoleon, now reassured that
his right was safe, ordered his
remaining Guards units to
attack the allied center,
they were driven off with
heavy losses.

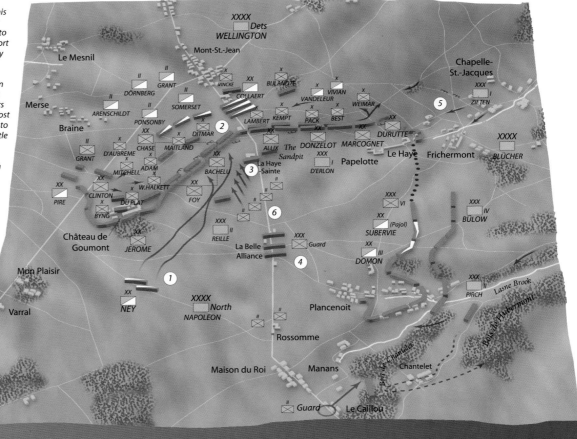

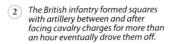

THE CAMPAIGNS OF THE AMERICAN CIVIL WAR

1861 – 1863

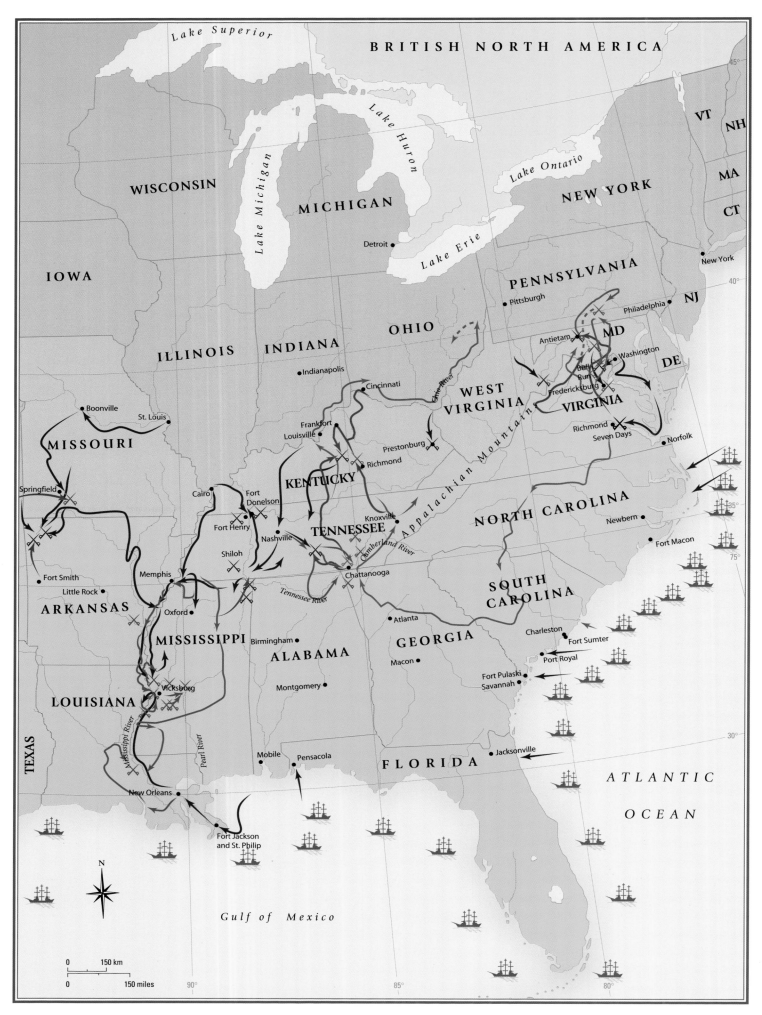

THE CAMPAIGNS OF 1861–1863

	Union blockade
	Union state
	Slave state staying loyal to the Union
	Confederate state

CAMPAIGNS 1861–62

→	Union offensive
→	Confederate offensive
✕	Union victory
✕	Confederate victory

CAMPAIGNS 1863

→	Union offensive
→	Confederate offensive
✕	Union victory
✕	Confederate victory
✕	Inconclusive outcome

THE CAMPAIGNS OF 1861–1863

During the first year of the American Civil War, as both sides raised huge armies, the Union assumed control of the border states and established a naval blockade. The major battles began the following year in 1862. These were large and bloody and resulted in massive casualties, due largely to the incompatibility between new weapons and old battlefield techniques. In December 1862 more than 12,000 Union soldiers were killed or wounded at the Battle of Fredericksburg, but the bloodiest battle was at Gettysburg in the following July with some 51,000 casualties on both sides. This battle is credited with turning the war in the Union's favor.

THE BATTLE OF ANTIETAM

ANTIETAM
SEPTEMBER 17 , 1862

This was the first major Civil War engagement on Northern soil and the bloodiest single-day battle in American history. 23,000 soldiers were killed, and the huge loss of life shocked both sides. The battle lasted late into the evening, and the following day, after an exchange of wounded, General Lee of the Confederacy withdrew his army across the Potomac and returned to Virginia. The battle sealed the fate of the Confederacy, halting Lee's bold invasion of the North and his efforts to force Abraham Lincoln to sue for peace. It also provided Lincoln with the victory he needed to announce the abolition of slavery in the South.

1 After hours of delay, Major General Ambrose Burnside finally launched elements of his Ninth Corps in an assault that captured the bridge that has since borne his name.

2 Brigadier General Rodman's division of the Ninth Corps crossed Antietam Creek via Snavely's Ford and provided cover for the rest of the corps as it crossed the bridge and deployed on the west side of the creek.

3 Burnside's Ninth Corps mounted an assault toward Sharpsburg, driving the Confederate defenders to the outskirts of the town.

4 Ambrose Powell Hill's Confederate division arrived after a day-long forced march from Harpers Ferry, just in time to flank and drive back Burnside's attackers.

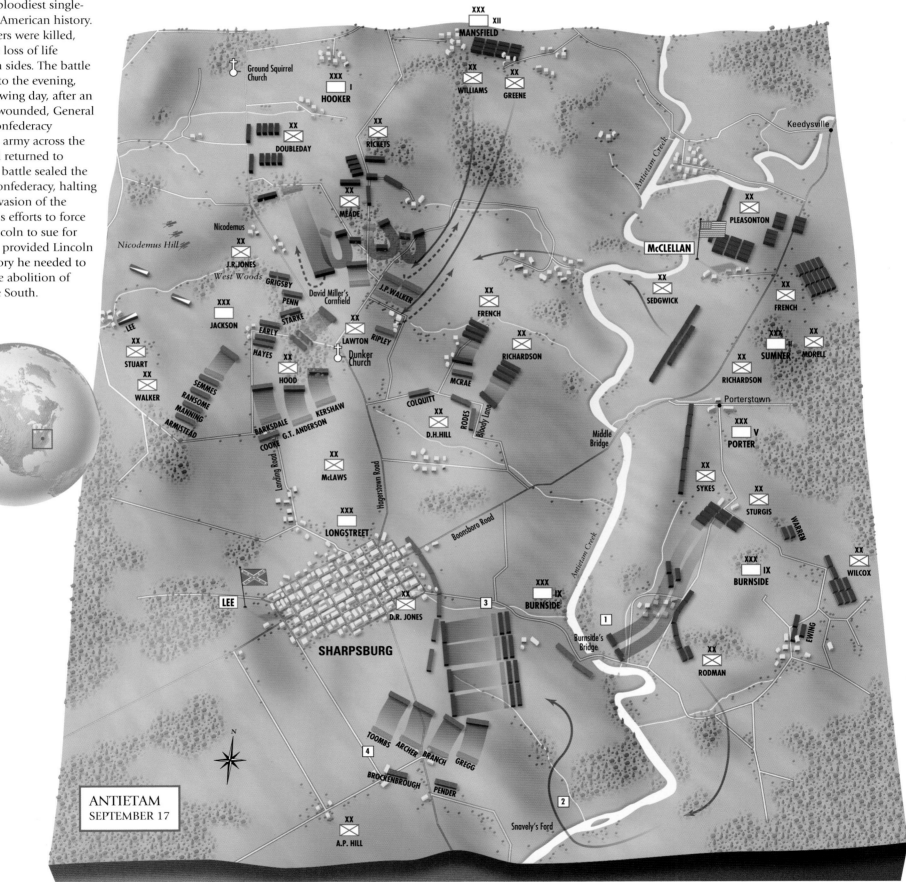

ANTIETAM
SEPTEMBER 17

1863 BATTLE OF GETTYSBURG

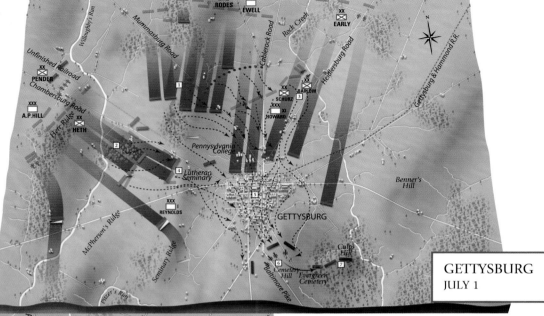

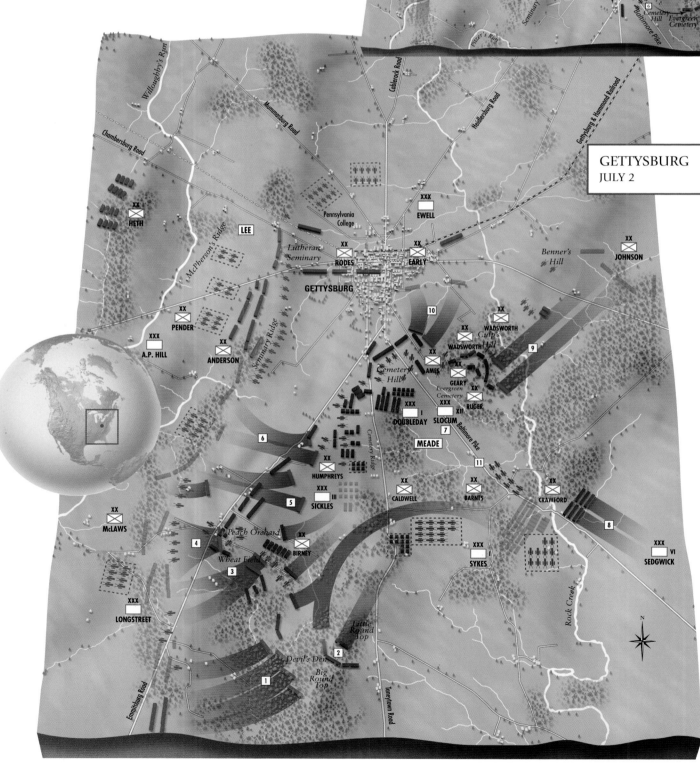

1. July 1, 1:00 p.m.: Having rallied from its earlier repulse, Rodes's division renewed its attack and this time succeeded in driving in the right flank of the First Corps.

2. Heth's division also renewed its assault on McPherson's Ridge and finally succeeded in driving back the First Corps after ferocious fighting in which some regiments suffered 80 percent casualties.

3. Early's division attacked almost simultaneously from the north and northeast, crumbling the line of Eleventh Corps north of Gettysburg.

4. Elements of the First Corps made a stand on Seminary Ridge and inflicted ruinous casualties on two brigades of Major General William Dorsey Pender's division before being driven back toward the town.

5. About 4:00 p.m.: The fugitives of the First and Eleventh Corps streamed through Gettysburg in retreat. Some were captured by pursuing Confederates.

6. About 6:00 p.m.: Major General Oliver O. Howard and newly arrived Major General Winfield S. Hancock rallied the First and Eleventh Corps on Cemetery Hill, where Howard had posted a reserve brigade.

7. Hancock dispatched elements of the First Corps to hold vital Culp's Hill nearby.

GETTYSBURG
JULY 1

GETTYSBURG
JULY 2

1. July 2, 4:00 p.m.: Major General John B. Hood's division led off Longstreet's attack, crushing the poorly deployed troops of Major General Daniel E. Sickles's Third Corps on the extreme Union left.

2. 5:00 p.m.: Colonel Strong Vincent's brigade of the Fifth Corps arrived just in time to hold Little Round Top.

3. Brigadier General George T. Anderson's brigade of Hood's division waged a long and intense struggle for the Wheat Field, which changed hands four times before nightfall.

4. Major General Lafayette McLaws's division joined the assault and drove Union troops out of the Peach Orchard.

5. Brigadier General William Barksdale's brigade of McLaws's division broke through the Union line and penetrated deeply before being stopped by Union reinforcements.

6. Major General Richard H. Anderson's division joined the attack and penetrated almost all the way to Cemetery Ridge before being stopped by a Union counterattack.

7. Meade ordered Major General Henry W. Slocum to take the entire Twenty-first Corps off of Culp's Hill and march to the support of the Union left. Slocum protested, and Meade allowed him to leave a single brigade.

8. Major General John Sedgwick's Sixth Corps arrived after a forced march, provided Meade with much needed reserves.

9. Confederate troops of Major General Edward Johnson's division attacked and took some of the abandoned Twelfth Corps positions on Culp's Hill but were prevented from taking the summit by the well-entrenched brigade of Brigadier General George S. Greene.

10. In the gathering darkness, Early's division assaulted Cemetery Hill and got among some of the cannons there before Union infantry drove them back.

11. Major General Geary's division of the Twelfth went astray, marching down the Baltimore Pike for some distance before turning and marching back. None of the Twelfth Corps units became engaged on the left and all returned late in the night to find their former positions held by Johnson's Confederates.

BATTLE OF GETTYSBURG

BATTLE OF GETTYSBURG – DAY 3

In spite of fierce fighting and significant losses on both sides, there was no decisive result on the first two days of the Battle. On Day 3 fighting began at 4.30 am on Culps Hill, which the Unionist managed to hold. Cavalry battles raged to the east and the south and just after 1.00 pm a Confederate artillery barrage of 164 guns began to bombard the Union lines. This was followed by an infantry assault of 12,500 Confederates against the Unionists on Cemetery Ridge. The Confederates suffered massive losses and General Lee was forced to lead the remnants of his defeated army back to Virgina.

1. July 3, 4:30 a.m.: The Twefth Corps's artillery opened a barrage in preparation for an attack to retake the positions Johnson's Confederates had seized the night before in the corps's absence.

2. 4:45 a.m.: As Twelfth Corps infantry prepared to advance, Johnson's Confederates pre-empted them with an attack of their own. The Union troops went over to the defensive and beat off repeated Confederate attacks until at 10:00 a.m. Johnson gave up the attempt to take the rest of Culp's Hill.

3. 1:07 p.m.: Confederate artillery opened a massed barrage on Union lines with one hundred and sixty-four guns.

4. 2:30 p.m.: Pickett's and Pettigrews's divisions, along with two brigades of Major General Isaac Trimble's advance toward the Union center, all under the command of Longstreet.

5. 3:00 p.m.: The Eighth Ohio Regiment attacked the left flank of the advancing Confederate line.

6. 3:15 p.m.: Brigadier General George Stannard's Vermont brigade attacked to the right flank of Pickett's division.

7. 3:15 p.m.: The Confederate attackers reached Union lines and a few of them briefly got in amongst a battery of guns before being driven back with heavy losses.

8. 5:30 p.m.: Brigadier General Judson Kilpatrick, without orders from Meade, launched an ill-conceived cavalry attack on the extreme right flank of the confederate line, which accomplished nothing beyond getting some of his men shot.

GETTYSBURG
JULY 3

THE OCCUPIED SOUTH

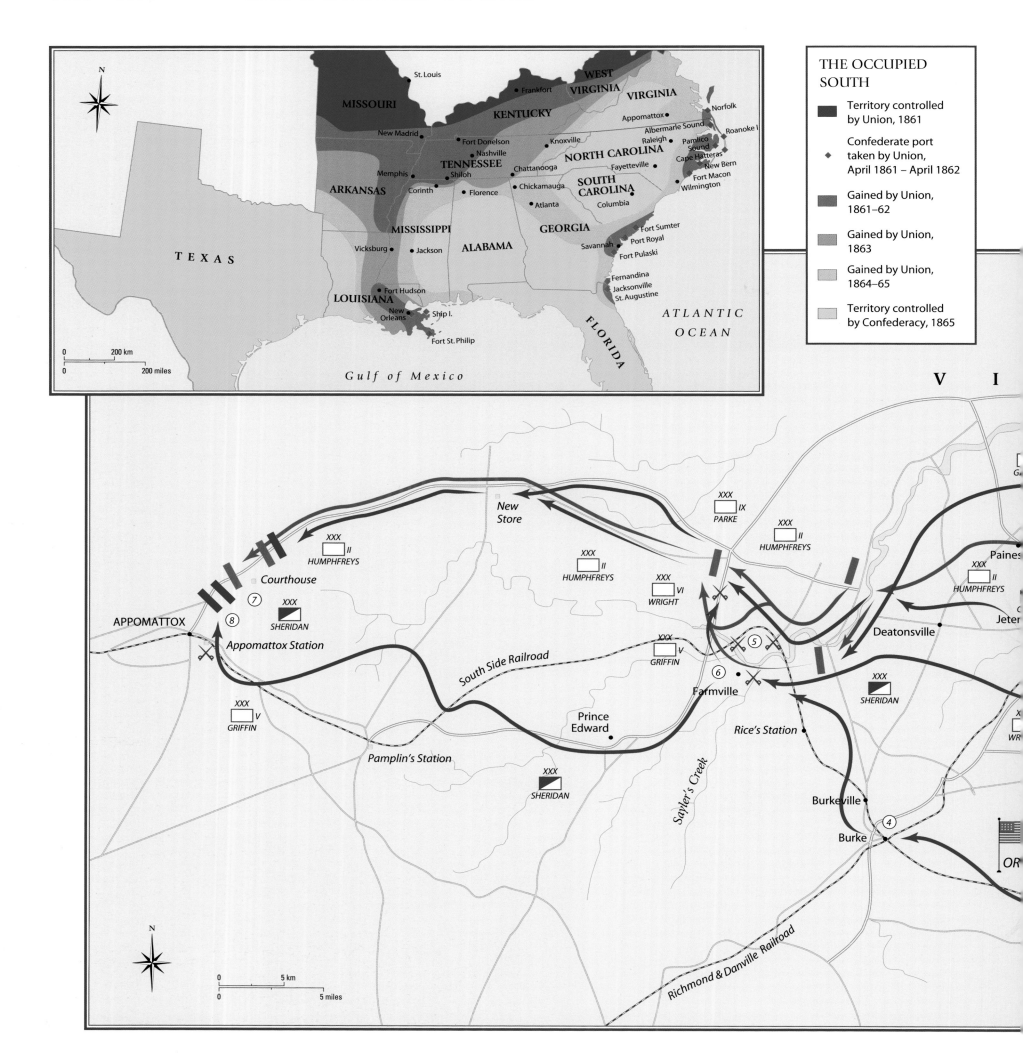

THE OCCUPIED SOUTH

- Territory controlled by Union, 1861
- ♦ Confederate port taken by Union, April 1861 – April 1862
- Gained by Union, 1861–62
- Gained by Union, 1863
- Gained by Union, 1864–65
- Territory controlled by Confederacy, 1865

St. Louis
Frankfort
WEST VIRGINIA
MISSOURI
KENTUCKY
VIRGINIA
Norfolk
Appomattox
New Madrid
Albermarle Sound
Roanoke I.
Fort Donelson
Knoxville
Raleigh
Pamlico Sound
Nashville
NORTH CAROLINA
TENNESSEE
Chattanooga
Fayetteville
New Bern
Memphis
Shiloh
Fort Macon
ARKANSAS
Corinth
Chickamauga
Florence
SOUTH CAROLINA
Wilmington
Atlanta
Columbia

MISSISSIPPI
ALABAMA
GEORGIA
Fort Sumter
Vicksburg
Jackson
Savannah
Port Royal
Fort Pulaski

TEXAS

LOUISIANA
Fort Hudson
Fernandina
Jacksonville
St. Augustine
New Orleans
Ship I.
FLORIDA
ATLANTIC OCEAN
Fort St. Philip

Gulf of Mexico

0   200 km
0   200 miles

V   I

New Store

XXX IX PARKE
XXX II HUMPHFREYS
XXX II HUMPHFREYS
XXX II HUMPHFREYS
XXX VI WRIGHT

Courthouse

⑦
⑧ XXX SHERIDAN

APPOMATTOX
Appomattox Station

XXX V GRIFFIN

Paines
XXX II HUMPHFREYS
Jeter
Deatonsville

⑤
⑥
XXX V GRIFFIN
Farmville
XXX SHERIDAN

South Side Railroad

XXX V GRIFFIN

Prince Edward

Pamplin's Station

Rice's Station

Sayler's Creek

XXX SHERIDAN

Burkeville

Burke ④

OR

Richmond & Danville Railroad

0   5 km
0   5 miles

THE BATTLE OF APPOMATTOX

BATTLE OF APPOMATTOX APRIL 3–9, 1865
This was the final engagement of Confederate General Robert E. Lee before he surrendered to Union Lt. General Ulysses S. Grant. Lee's army was in retreat and badly needed supplies. The Unionists destroyed the supply trains and offered Lee terms of surrender, which Lee initially refused. Fighting continued, but the situation was hopeless and Lee was eventually forced to accept Grant's terms. The surrender took place at Appomattox; the terms were very generous and there was great chivalry shown by the Unionists toward the defeated Confederates. For the rest of his life Lee would never tolerate a bad word about Grant.

APPOMATTOX
APRIL 3–9, 1865

① April 3: Confederate forces moved west on various routes, fleeing Richmond and Petersburg.

② April 4–5: Lee's army concentrated around Amelia Court House, pausing to gather much-needed supplies.

③ April 5: The Army of the Potomac reached Jetersville, cutting off Lee's avenue of flight to the south.

④ April 5: Ord's Army of the James reached Burke.

⑤ April 6: At Sayler's Creek Union troops caught and cut off part of Lee's rear guard, taking 6000 prisoners.

⑥ April 7: The Confederate rear guard succeeded in beating off a Union attack and crossing the Appomattox River.

⑦ April 8: Lee's army reached Appomattox Court House.

⑧ April 9: Lee surrendered to Grant.

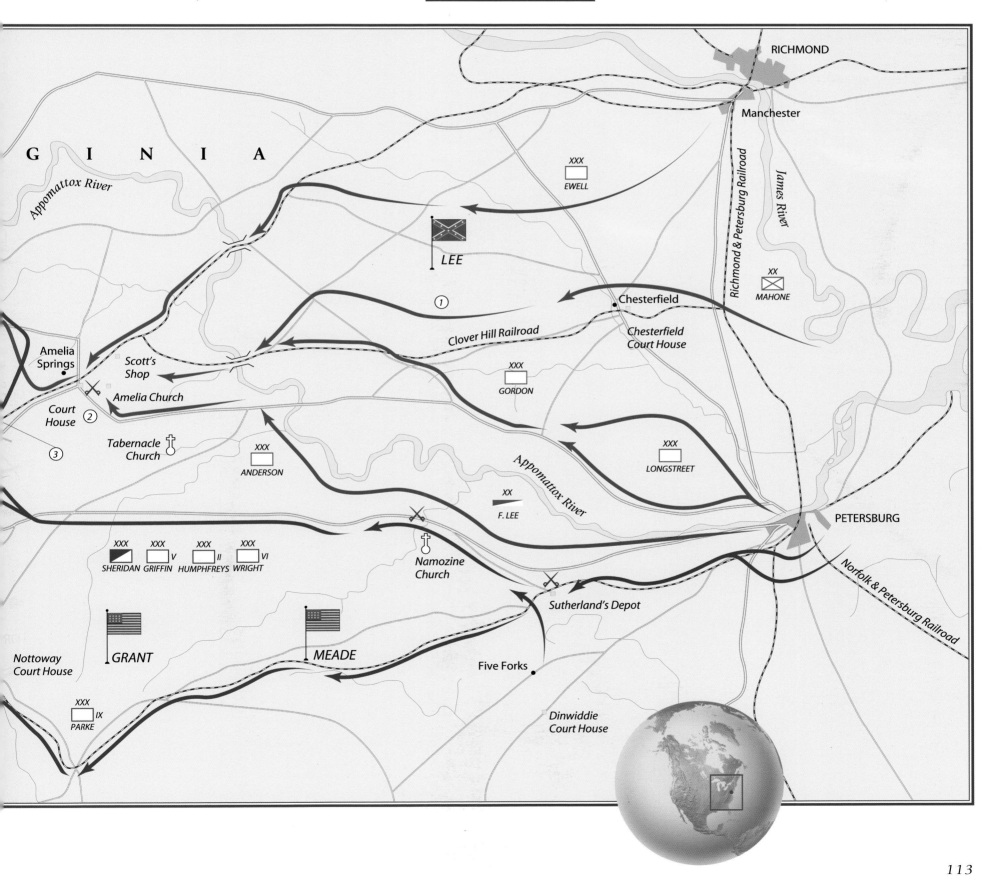

THE FRANCO-PRUSSIAN WAR; THE BATTLE OF SEDAN

THE FRANCO-PRUSSIAN WAR 1870–1871

The Franco-Prussian War marked the culmination of tension between the two powers following Prussia's rise to dominance in Germany. The French felt that they had been insulted by the Prussian king regarding the nomination of a Prussian Prince for the vacant Spanish throne. The alleged insult was contained in a document that came to be known as the "Ems Dispatch," which purported to be an account between King Wilhelm I of Prussia and the French Ambassador. However, the account had actually been edited by Bismarck, Minister-President of Prussia, to insult the French and to force them to declare war on Prussia—the tactic worked. The German armies rapidly mobilized, and by a combination of good leadership, swift rail transport, and innovative Krupp artillery, within a short time they controlled large areas of eastern France. Napoleon III and his entire army were captured at the Battle of Sedan and the Third Republic was proclaimed. A peace treaty was signed in May 1871.

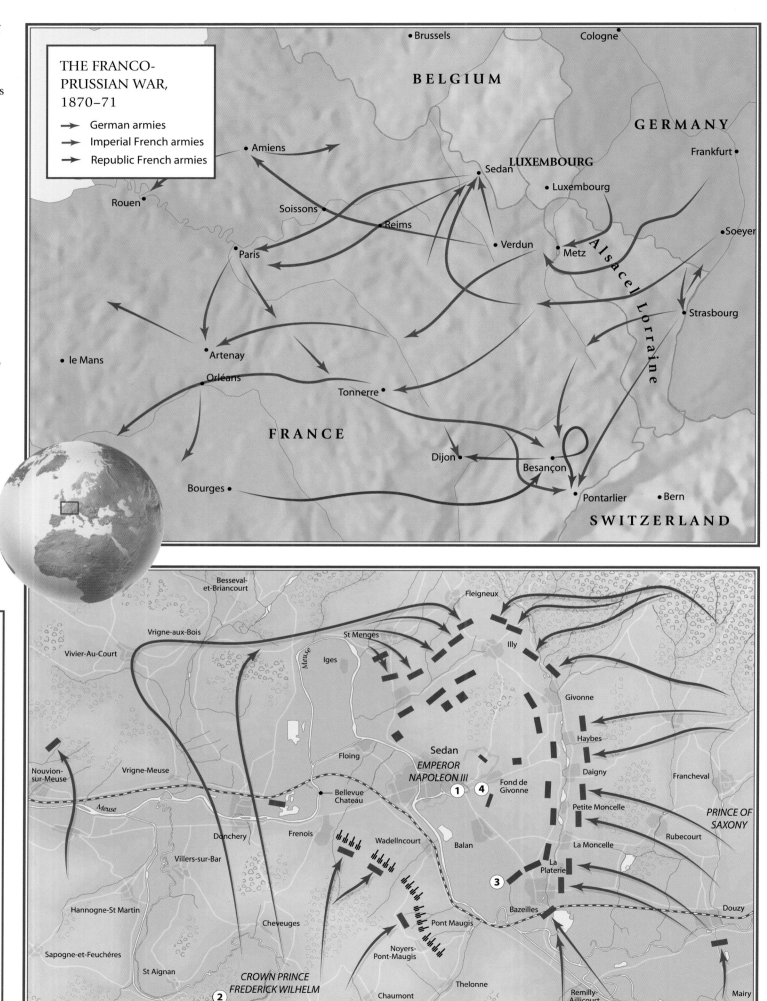

SEDAN, 1870

■ Prussian army
■ French army
→ Prussian movements
→ French movements
⊨ Artillery

Key phases

① 29 August: Prussian maneuvers force French commanded by MacMahon to fall back toward the borders fortress of Sedan.

② 1 September: Prussian forces under the command of Moltke surround the French army and begin an artillery bombardment of the town.

③ Afternoon: the French forces attempt a breakout. After a violent fight they are forced back into Sedan, losing some 17,000 casualties and 20,000 prisoners.

④ 2 September: Napoleon decides to surrender. The surviving 83,000 French troops march out into captivity.

RUSSO-JAPANESE WAR

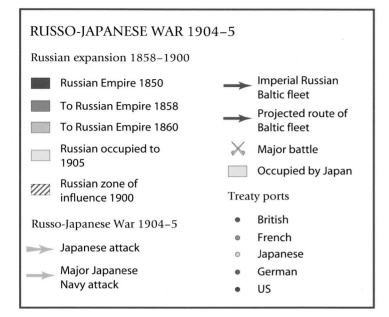

RUSSO-JAPANESE WAR 1904–5

Russian expansion 1858–1900

- ■ Russian Empire 1850
- ■ To Russian Empire 1858
- ■ To Russian Empire 1860
- □ Russian occupied to 1905
- ▨ Russian zone of influence 1900

Russo-Japanese War 1904–5

- → Japanese attack
- → Major Japanese Navy attack

- → Imperial Russian Baltic fleet
- → Projected route of Baltic fleet
- ✕ Major battle
- □ Occupied by Japan

Treaty ports
- ● British
- ● French
- ○ Japanese
- ● German
- ● US

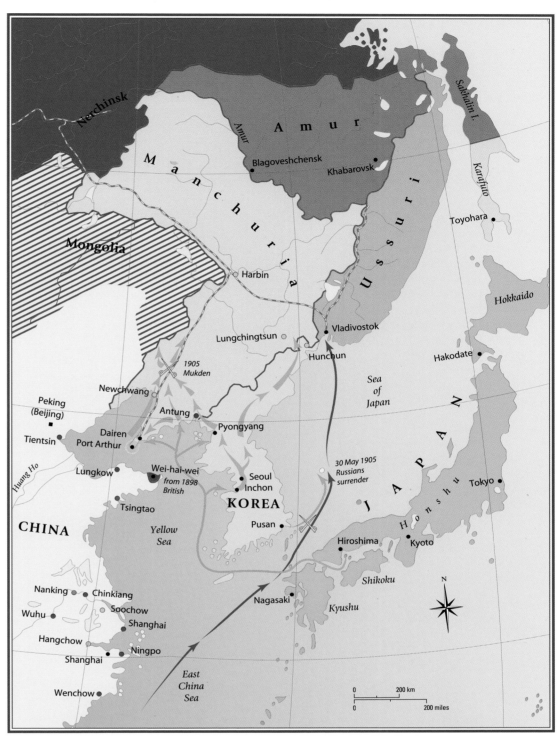

RUSSO-JAPANESE WAR 1904–1905

This war began in February 1904 and lasted until September 1905. Although the war was declared by Japan, it grew out of the rival imperialist ambitions of both countries. The Russians had always wanted a warm-water port, not only for their navy, but to develop maritime trade. The recently-established port of Vladivostok was the only Russian port that was reasonably operational during the winter, but Port Arthur on the southern tip of Manchuria could be operational all year. The Japanese victory was a humiliating defeat for Russia and contributed to the dissatisfaction that was brewing among the Russian population.

THE BATTLE OF SEDAN 1870 (LEFT)

Napoleon III was personally leading an army to relieve Metz, which had been besieged by the Prussians. They were intercepted and after a hard-fought battle at Beaumont the French withdrew toward Sedan, where they were encircled by the Prussian army.

On 1st September, after fierce Prussian artillery bombardment, the French unsuccessfully tried to break out. The attempt was called off after 17,000 of the French were killed or wounded and 21,000 were taken prisoner. On 2nd September, realizing the hopelessness of his situation, Napoleon decided to surrender and was taken prisoner together with the remaining 83,000 men of his army.

1913 – 1914   EUROPE 1914

EUROPE IN 1914

In 1914 Central Europe was dominated by the vast German and Austro-Hungarian Empires. Germany was a relatively young power, having only been united after a series of wars in 1871. Germany's Chancellor, Bismarck, always maintained that in any dispute among the five Great Powers, Germany must be in a majority of three. When Kaiser Wilhelm II came to power he retired Bismarck and upset the balance of power by refusing to renew Germany's alliance with Russia. Germany soon found itself in a minority of two, with its only ally being the weakest of the Great Powers, Austria-Hungary.

THE SCHLIEFFEN PLAN

THE SCHLIEFFEN PLAN
When Wilhelm II became Kaiser in 1888 he upset the European balance of power by cooling his alliance with Russia. With this move, it was now clear that in any future war Germany would find itself fighting on two fronts. As early as 1905 a plan had been devised by Alfred von Schlieffen, Chief of the

Imperial German General Staff, to win a quick war in the West, before sending a major force to conquer Russia. The plan scheduled 39 days for the conquest of Paris and for France to be defeated in six weeks. Ninety-one percent of German troops would be sent to France and the remaining 9 percent to Russia. It was felt that it would take at least six

weeks for the Russian army to mobilize, by which time the troops in France could be transferred east. There was a complete disregard for the neutrality of Belgium and Luxembourg and, in the event, it was the violation of Belgium's neutrality that brought Britain into the war. The plan failed for a number of reasons, including: Belgian

resistance being tougher than expected; Britain unexpectedly entering the war; delays caused by Belgian resistance that enabled the French to be ready for the Germans when they arrived; and the Russians mobilizing their forces quicker than had been anticipated.

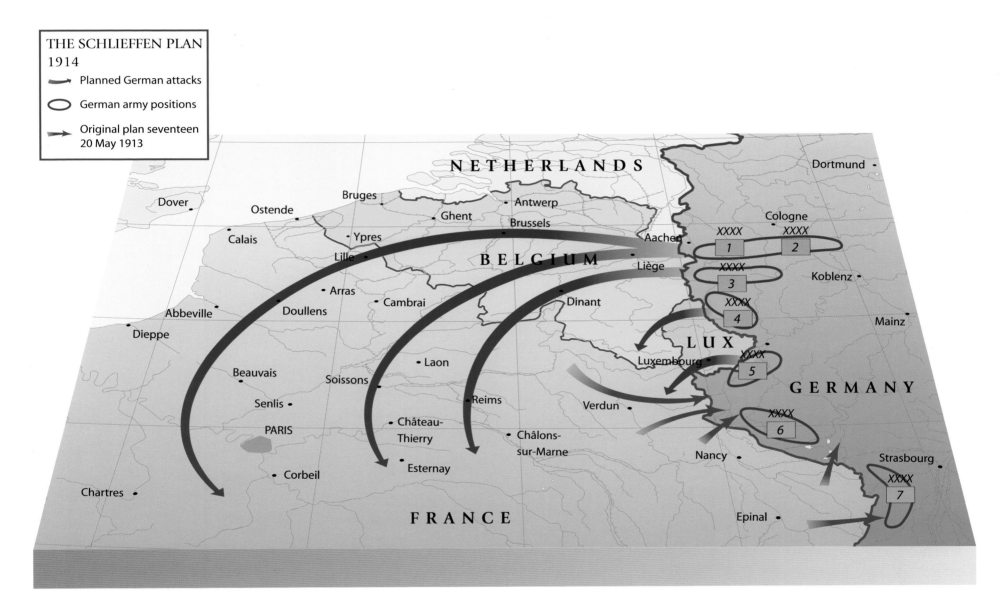

THE SCHLIEFFEN PLAN
1914

→ Planned German attacks

◯ German army positions

→ Original plan seventeen
20 May 1913

1914

THE EASTERN FRONT

***THE EASTERN FRONT
1914***

German planning had
anticipated that it would take
six weeks for the Russian army
to mobilize. In the event the
Russian advance on East
Prussia began in little over a
week, causing a German retreat
by mid-August. One of the
features of the Eastern Front
was that it was very long, so
aggressors and defenders had
to be spread much more
thinly than in the West. The
terrain was such that it was
very difficult to "dig in." The
result was that, once broken,
it was much more difficult to
rush in reinforcements, which
meant that the front was
continually moving.

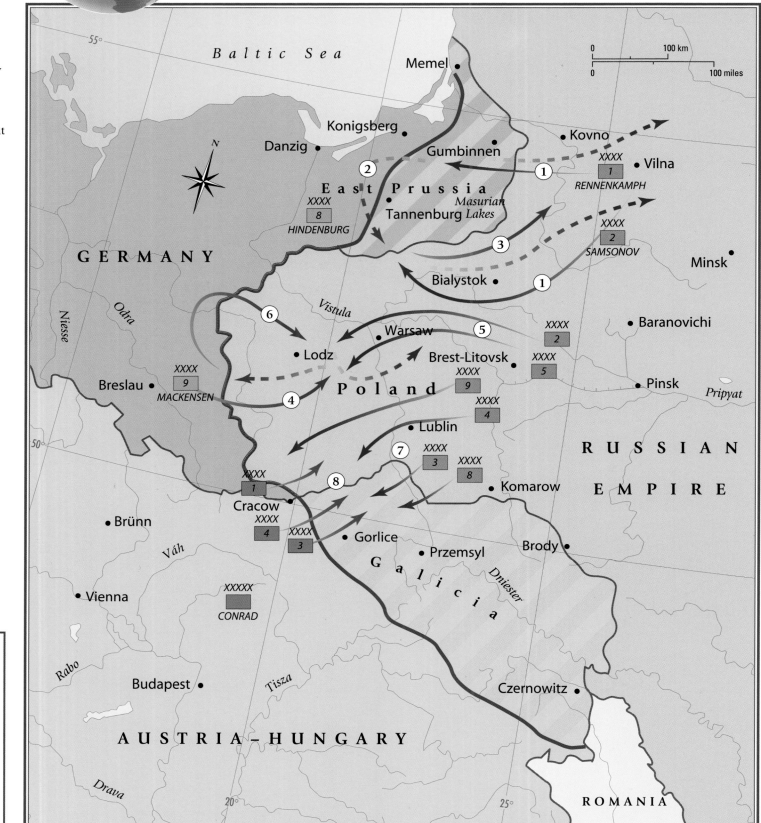

THE EASTERN FRONT
1914

→ Russian advance

⇢ Russian retreat

→ German advance

⇢ German retreat

→ Austro-Hungarian
advance

▬ Furthest Russian
advance

BATTLE OF THE MARNE

BATTLE OF THE MARNE SEPTEMBER 5–10, 1914
The German Schlieffen Plan depended on a quick victory on the Western Front. By the end of August 1914 the Allies were being driven back toward Paris. As the Germans approached Paris they began to swerve to the southeast, exposing their right flank. The Allies took advantage of this and a battle began along the Marne River. Fierce fighting lasted for several days before the Germans retreated about 40 miles and dug in, preparing trenches that were to last for several years. Over 2,000,000 men fought in the battle, of whom more than 500,000 were killed or wounded. The Schlieffen Plan was in ruins.

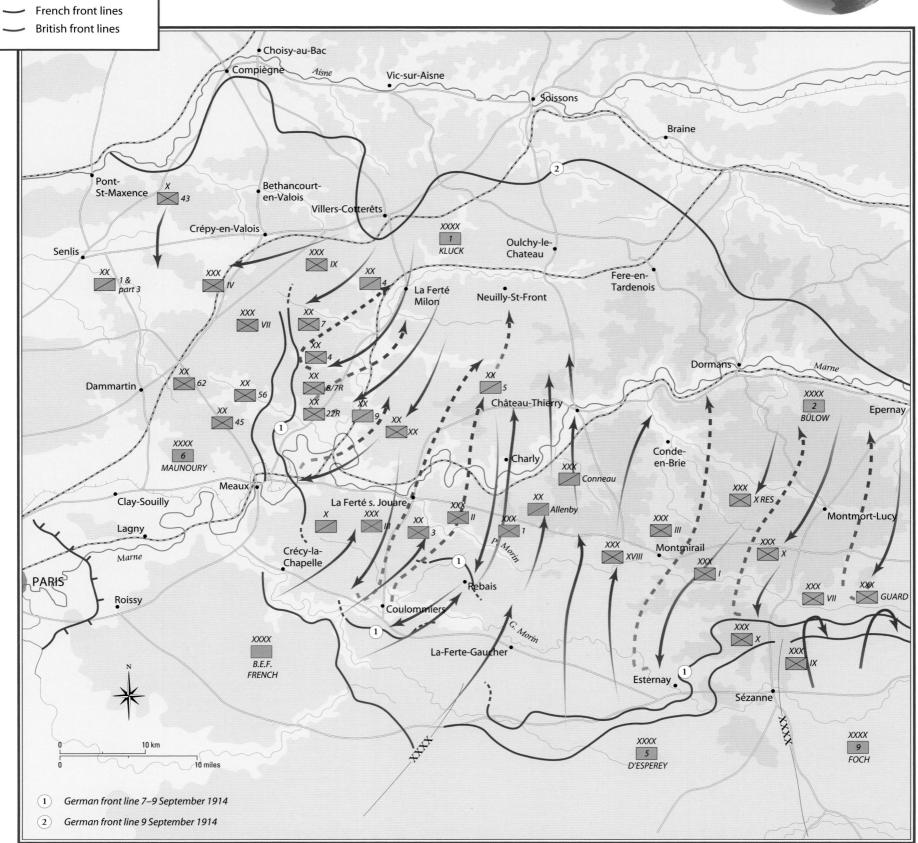

BATTLE OF THE MARNE
5–10 SEPTEMBER 1914

→ German advance
⇢ German retreat
→ French advance
→ British advance
⌐ German front lines
⌐ French front lines
⌐ British front lines

① German front line 7–9 September 1914
② German front line 9 September 1914

1916 THE BATTLE OF VERDUN

THE BATTLE OF VERDUN FEBRUARY–JUNE, 1916
This was one of the most important battles of World War I and was fought between the German and French armies. It was one of the longest battles in history, lasting for ten months. The Germans believed that victory was still possible if there were enough French casualties. The battle began with a nine-hour bombardment in which over a million shells were fired. The Germans

advanced three miles. Assault followed assault, and it was not until December that a last offensive by the French drove the Germans back to their original starting position. By then French casualties numbered 378,000, including 120,000 dead, while German losses stood at 337,000, including 100,000 dead.

① 21 February: position of German and French lines. Operation "Gericht" begins with the bombardment of the French positions by 1200 German guns

② German gains by 23 February

③ German gains by 25 February

④ 6–16 March: French hold off German attempts to seize "le Mort Homme" for two weeks

⑤ 3 May: German attacks eventually secure Cote 304

⑥ Lines held by Germans March–June

BATTLE OF VERDUN FEBRUARY–JUNE 1916

- German/French lines 21 February
- German lines 23 February
- German lines 25 February
- German lines 8 March
- field works
- major fort
- major engagements
- French counter-attacks 22–23 May

THE BATTLE OF THE SOMME

THE BATTLE OF THE SOMME JULY–NOVEMBER 1916

The Battle of the Somme was intended to secure a decisive Allied victory, but with over a million casualties it was also one of the bloodiest in human history. On its first day alone, 1st July, there were 57,470 British casualties, including 19,240 dead. Throughout the summer, casualties continued to mount on both sides. Aside from being one of the the most brutal battles ever fought, the Somme is also notable for being the first battle in which tanks were used, making their debut in September. By November winter had set in and the last action took place in the Ancre sector. The British gained approximately 2 miles, but lost about 420,000 soldiers in the process.

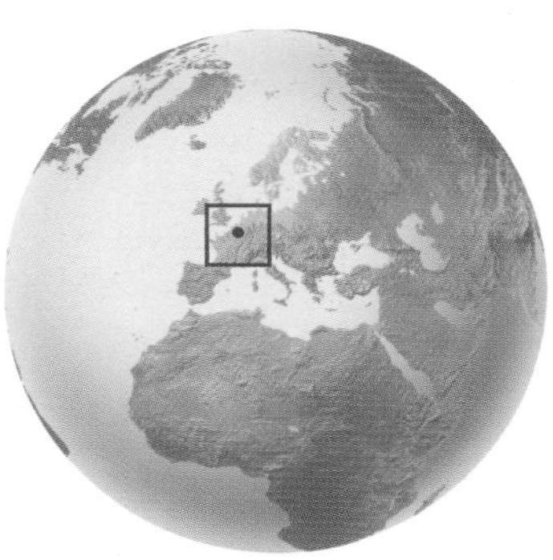

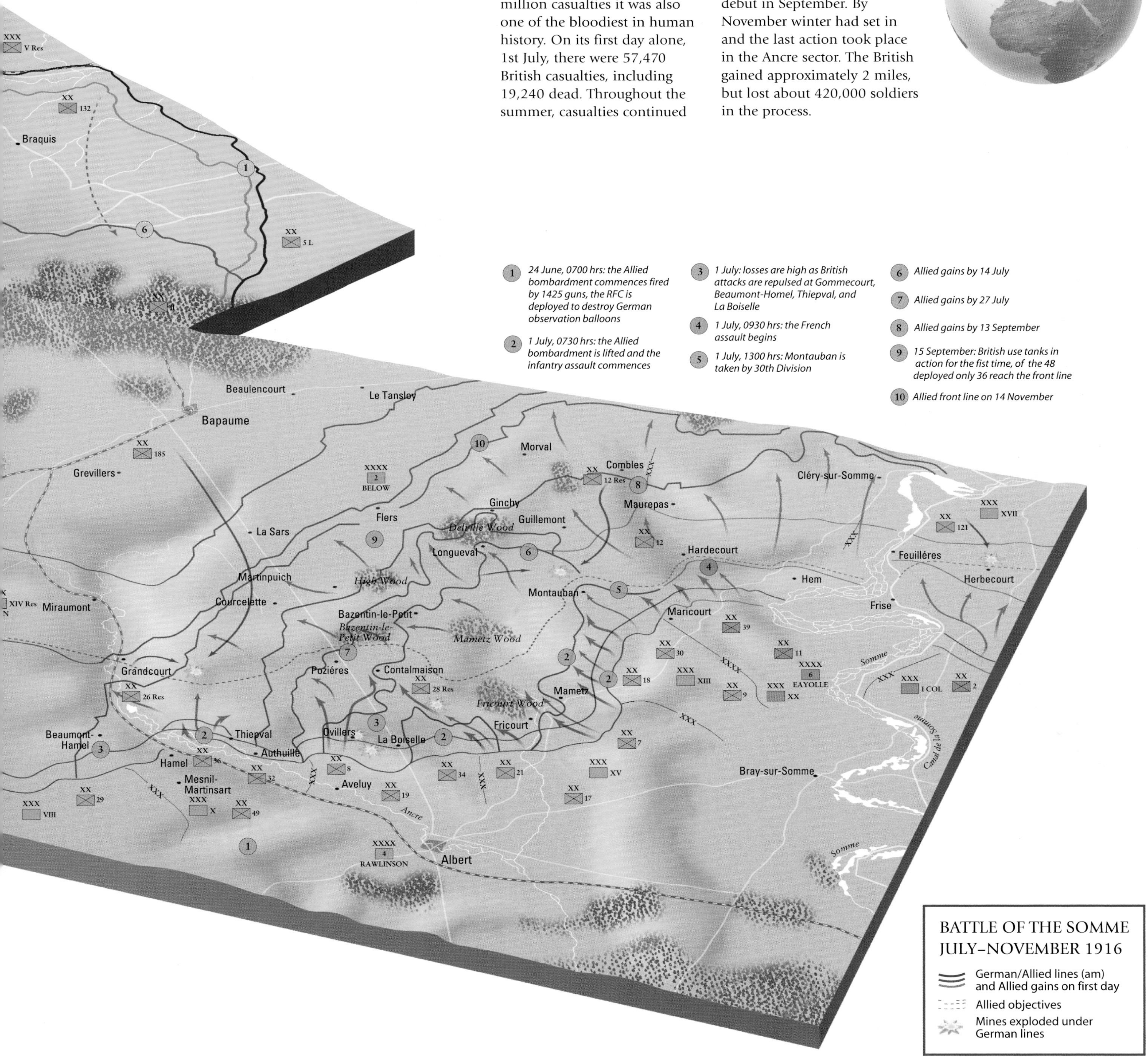

1. 24 June, 0700 hrs: the Allied bombardment commences fired by 1425 guns, the RFC is deployed to destroy German observation balloons

2. 1 July, 0730 hrs: the Allied bombardment is lifted and the infantry assault commences

3. 1 July: losses are high as British attacks are repulsed at Gommecourt, Beaumont-Homel, Thiepval, and La Boiselle

4. 1 July, 0930 hrs: the French assault begins

5. 1 July, 1300 hrs: Montauban is taken by 30th Division

6. Allied gains by 14 July

7. Allied gains by 27 July

8. Allied gains by 13 September

9. 15 September: British use tanks in action for the fist time, of the 48 deployed only 36 reach the front line

10. Allied front line on 14 November

BATTLE OF THE SOMME
JULY–NOVEMBER 1916

German/Allied lines (am) and Allied gains on first day

Allied objectives

Mines exploded under German lines

(Map labels: Braquis, Beaulencourt, Le Tansley, Bapaume, Grevillers, La Sars, Martinpuich, Courcelette, Miraumont, Grandcourt, Beaumont-Hamel, Hamel, Mesnil-Martinsart, Aveluy, Albert, Thiepval, Authuille, Ovillers, La Boiselle, Fricourt, Fricourt Wood, Mametz, Mametz Wood, Contalmaison, Pozières, Bazentin-le-Petit, Bazentin-le-Petit Wood, High Wood, Flers, Delville Wood, Longueval, Ginchy, Guillemont, Montauban, Maricourt, Morval, Combles, Maurepas, Hardecourt, Hem, Frise, Feuilléres, Herbecourt, Bray-sur-Somme, Cléry-sur-Somme, Ancre, Somme, Canal de la Somme)

PALESTINE DURING WORLD WAR I

1917 – 1918

PALESTINE OCTOBER 1917–OCTOBER 1918

World War I saw the end of the Ottoman Empire and the redrawing of the map of the Middle East, including the disputed lands of Palestine. The Ottoman Empire, which dated back to the 13th century and encompassed Palestine, aligned itself to the Germans and Austro-Hungarians during World War I. This proved to be a huge strategic error for the already enfeebled empire, as it allowed the Western powers to invade Palestine and impose their own strategic will on the region. On the eve of World War I the Zionists and Arab nationalists had very different ideas on how Palestine should be organized in the event of the fall of the Ottoman Empire. The Zionists hoped to attain support from one of the Western powers for increased Jewish immigration and eventual sovereignty in Palestine, whereas the Arab nationalists wanted an independent Arab state covering all the Ottoman Arab domains. The British decided to back the Zionist cause, convinced that a Jewish presence in the Middle East would be in their own strategic interests. In November 1917, British Foreign Secretary, Arthur Balfour, sent a letter to Lord Rothschild, President of the British Zionist Federation, expressing the British government's sympathies with the Zionist cause in the region. Just five weeks after the Balfour Declaration, as the letter became known, British troops led by General Sir Edmund Allenby took Jerusalem from the Turks; Turkish forces in Syria were subsequently defeated; an armistice was concluded with Turkey on October 31, 1918; and all of Palestine came under British military rule. The British governed Palestine until 1948, all the while backing Zionist ambitions for a sovereign homeland in the region, despite Arab objections.

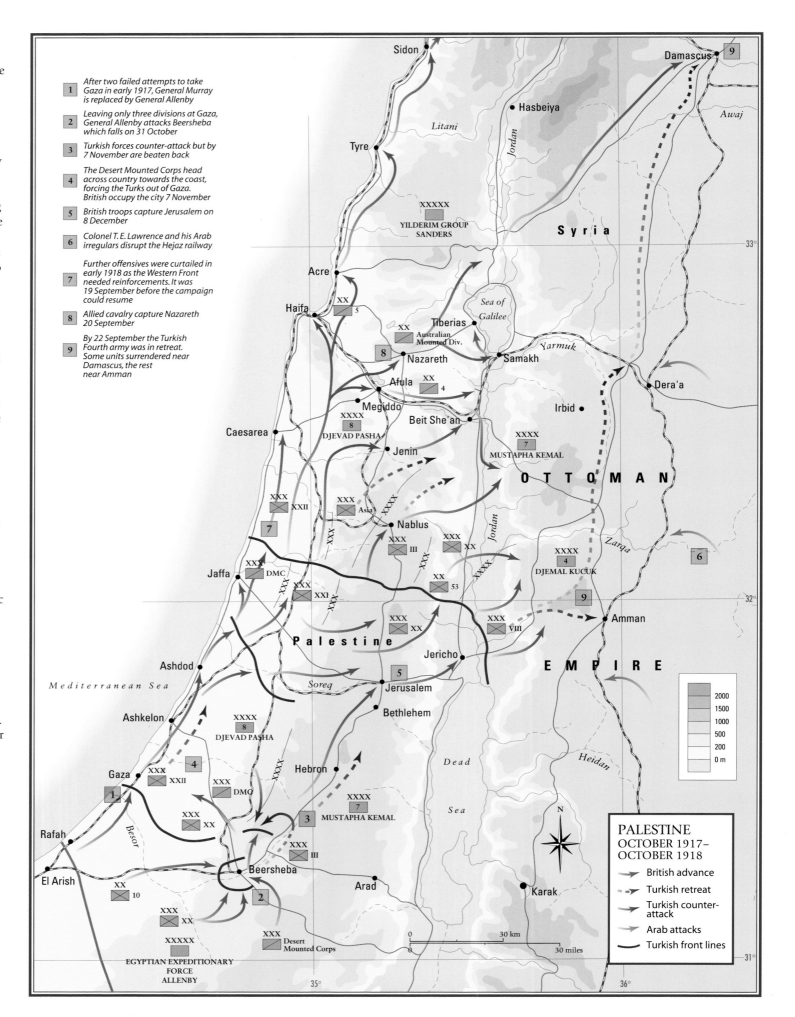

1. After two failed attempts to take Gaza in early 1917, General Murray is replaced by General Allenby

2. Leaving only three divisions at Gaza, General Allenby attacks Beersheba which falls on 31 October

3. Turkish forces counter-attack but by 7 November are beaten back

4. The Desert Mounted Corps head across country towards the coast, forcing the Turks out of Gaza. British occupy the city 7 November

5. British troops capture Jerusalem on 8 December

6. Colonel T. E. Lawrence and his Arab irregulars disrupt the Hejaz railway

7. Further offensives were curtailed in early 1918 as the Western Front needed reinforcements. It was 19 September before the campaign could resume

8. Allied cavalry capture Nazareth 20 September

9. By 22 September the Turkish Fourth army was in retreat. Some units surrendered near Damascus, the rest near Amman

**PALESTINE
OCTOBER 1917–
OCTOBER 1918**

→ British advance
⇢ Turkish retreat
→ Turkish counter-attack
→ Arab attacks
— Turkish front lines

2000
1500
1000
500
200
0 m

0   30 km
0   30 miles

ADVANCE TO VICTORY

ADVANCE TO VICTORY

The late summer had seen significant Allied gains and it was clear by October that as the Allies closed in, Germany could no longer mount a successful defense. Increasingly outnumbered, the German General Ludendorff put forward the view that Germany had just two ways out: total annihilation or an armistice. With six million casualties, Germany moved toward peace, but fighting continued right up to the end. The Kaiser abdicated, a republic was proclaimed and an armistice was signed in a railway carriage at Compiègne in France. This came into effect on the eleventh hour of the eleventh day of the eleventh month of the year 1918. In many parts of the world a two-minute silence to remember the dead is observed every year at 11 am on November 11.

**ADVANCE TO VICTORY
5 OCTOBER –
11 NOVEMBER 1918**

British advance
French advance
Belgian advance
British front lines
French front lines
Belgian front lines
German armistice line

1 Allied front line, 26 September 1918
2 Allied front line, 17 October 1918
3 Allied front line, 9 November 1918
4 Allied front line, 10 November 1918
5 German armistice line, 11 November 1918

1914 – 1921   THE RUSSIAN REVOLUTION

THE RUSSIAN REVOLUTION

By late 1916, after 14 months of war, Russia had lost nearly 5,000,000 men. There was considerable hardship, and widespread discontent was growing in all areas at the inefficiency and corruption of the Tsarist regime. Tsar Nicholas I was strongly advised to put a constitutional form of government in place, but he ignored this advice. The Russian Revolution of 1917 was a series of political and social upheavals beginning with the overthrow of the Tsar and ultimately leading to the establishment of Soviet power by the Bolshevik party led by Vladimir Lenin, thus paving the way for the formation of the USSR.

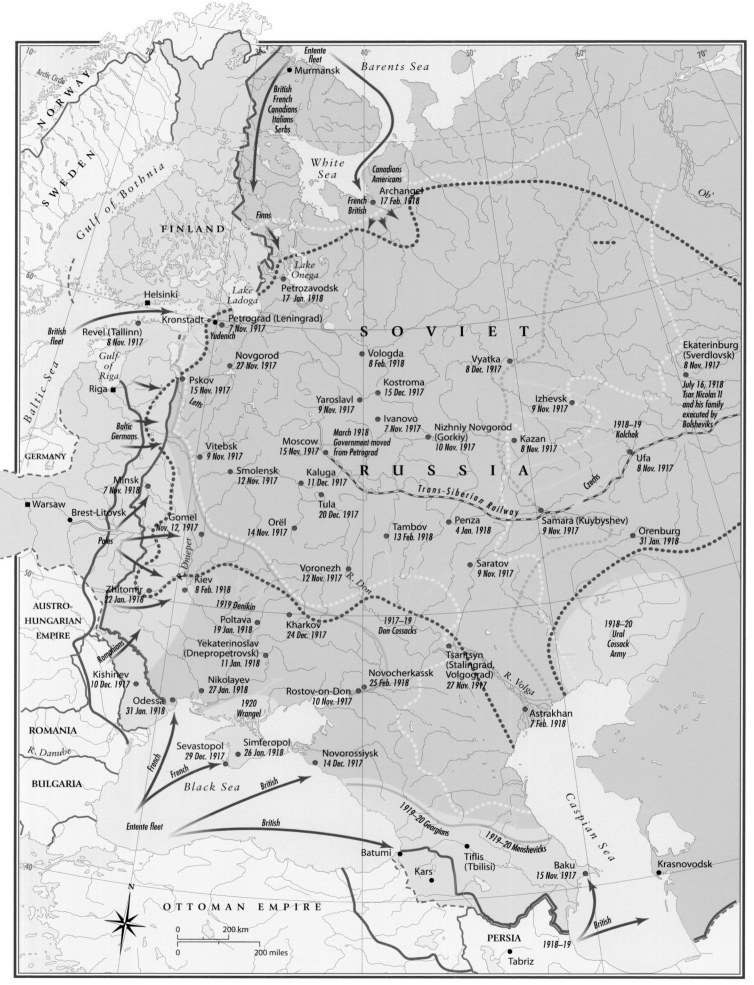

THE RUSSIAN REVOLUTION

- ⌐ ⌐ Russian territory, 1914
- —— Russian front, March 1917
- —— line set by Treaty of Brest-Litovsk, March 1918
- —— Soviet boundary, March 1921
- ⟶ White Russian armies
- ➡ non-Russian anti-Bolshevik forces
- • town taken over by Bolsheviks, Nov. 1917–Feb. 1918 (date given in new calendar)

boundary of areas controlled by Bolsheviks
- ⋯⋯ August 1918
- ⋯⋯ Eastern front, April 1919
- ⋯⋯ October 1919
- ▓ May 1920

EUROPE 1920 – 1921

EUROPE 1920–21

World War I was regarded as the "war to end all wars" and at the Peace Congress at Versailles in 1919, a prime aim was to prevent a similar war in the future. With scant concern toward its population, the map of Europe was redrawn. Germany and Russia were both reduced in size, as Poland was restored and the Baltic States and Finland regained independence. The vast, but crumbling, Austro-Hungarian Empire was broken up to create independent states such as Czechoslovakia, Hungary, and Austria. Yugoslavia also emerged, being a hotchpotch of smaller countries including the previously independent Serbia and Montenegro.

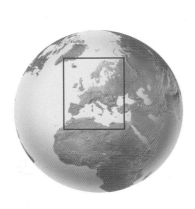

EUROPE 1920–21
Postwar Settlements

1922 – 1936 THE FASCIST STATES

THE FASCIST STATES
1922–1936

In the 1920s and 1930s there was a growth in right-wing political activity throughout Europe. A number of countries, such as the UK, Ireland, France, Czechoslovakia, the Benelux Countries and Scandinavia accepted this, but maintained their democratic traditions. Some countries like the Baltic and Balkan states and Poland were ultra conservative and inclined to be repressive. At the extreme end were Italy, Spain, Austria and Germany, which were ruled by fascist regimes. The USSR, being a communist dictatorship, had nothing to do with any of this.

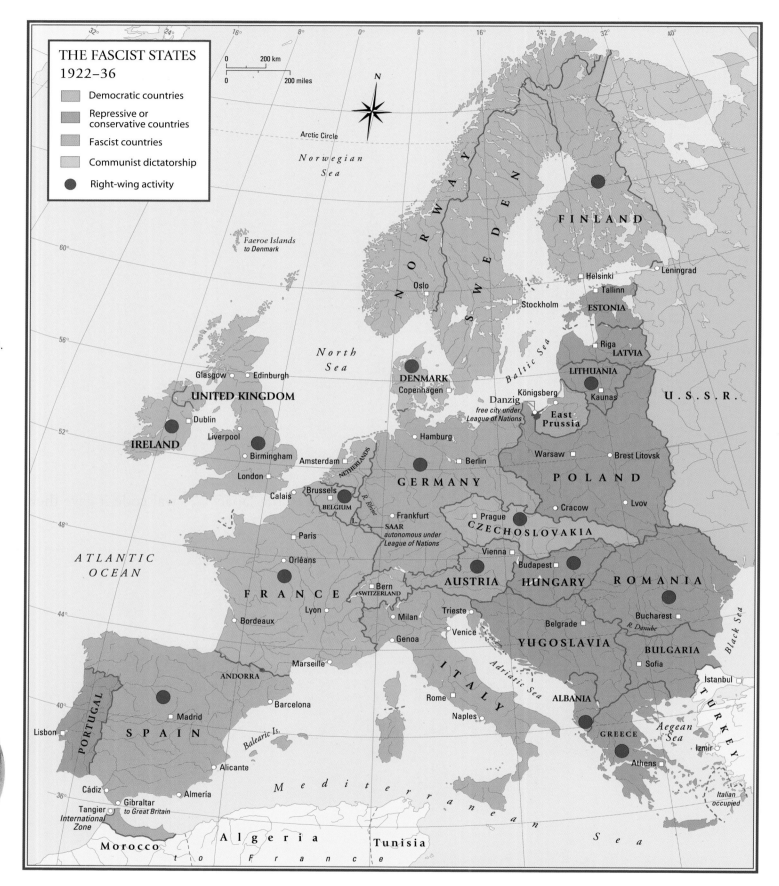

PART 6

WARFARE IN THE TECHNOLOGICAL AGE

WARFARE'S TECHNOLOGICAL AGE CAME ABOUT largely as a result of lessons and experience from World War I. By the start of World War II in 1939 the Germans had come up with the idea of *Blitzkrieg*, or "lightning war." This gave a fast-moving and heavy punch that would leave an enemy reeling before it realised what had hit it.

When Hitler wished to invade Britain, he knew that control of airspace was vital. The struggle by the Luftwaffe to gain this control has become known as the Battle of Britain. Another innovation was the use of airborne troops. The Germans used these during the invasion of Crete and suffered 7000 casualties. Hitler was so appalled that he forbade any future airborne operations. The Allies on the other hand were so impressed that they immediately began to expand their airborne forces.

On the Eastern Front it was clearly shown that good weapons and crack troops were no match for a combination of atrocious weather and a tenacious enemy who seemed to have an inexhaustible supply of reinforcements. Hitler's plans for a quick sharp finish foundered as his army got bogged down and his casualty rate peaked at three-quarters of a million.

Good intelligence is always vital. After the Allies had cracked the Japanese naval code it gave them a significant advantage in every operation. Advances in carrier-based aircraft enabled the Battle of the Coral Sea to be the first naval battle where neither side actually saw the other.

1939 – 1940   INVASION OF POLAND

**INVASION OF POLAND
SEPTEMBER 1–28, 1939**
Polish security had been guaranteed by a treaty between Germany, Britain, and France, so Germany's invasion of Poland on September 1, 1939 guaranteed a war between the western European powers. In August 1939 Germany and Russia had signed the secret Molotov-Ribbentrop Pact, which effectively outlined which parts of Europe both powers could invade. On September 17 the Red Army invaded Poland from the east and by the end of the month Poland had been completely overrun. The Polish government never surrendered and continued to function in exile. Most of the remaining air that managed to escape subsequently joined the Allied forces.

INVASION OF
POLAND
1–28 SEPTEMBER 1939

⌒	Polish border 1939
→	German advance
→	Russian advance
⇢	Polish retreat
⋏⋏	German fieldwork
⋎⋎	Polish defensive lines
⌒	Polish positions
⌒	German-Russian demarcation line

INVASION OF THE WEST; DUNKIRK

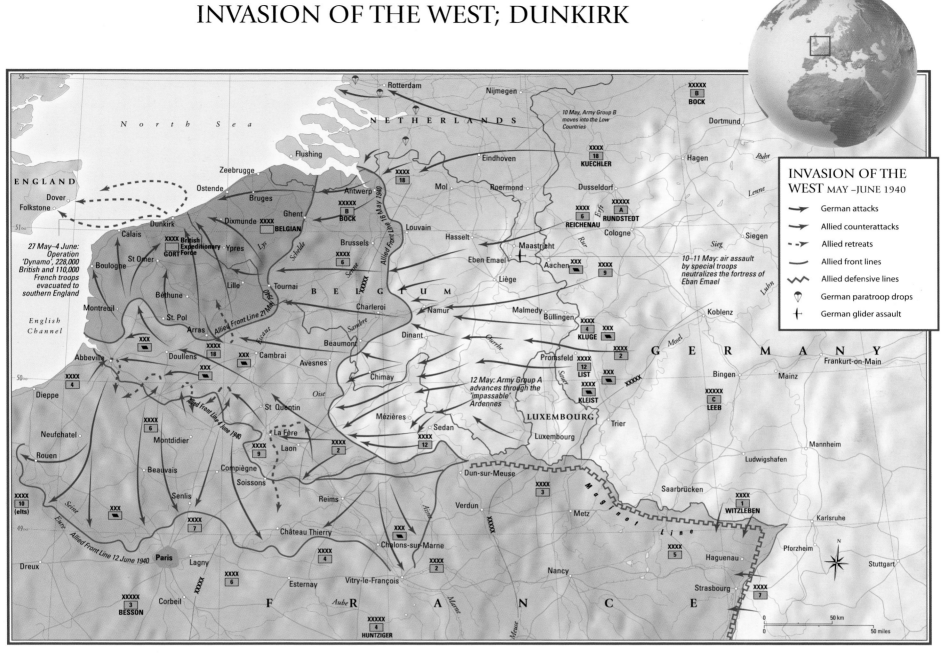

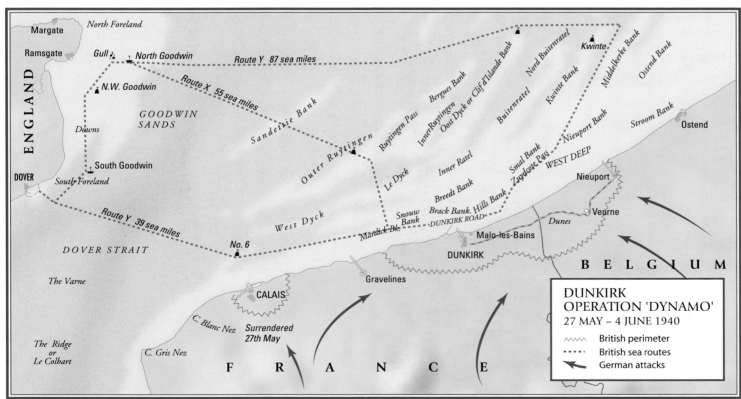

DUNKIRK – OPERATION DYNAMO
27 MAY–4 JUNE 1940

In May 1940 the Germans began their western advance, causing an Allied retreat towards the sea. Eventually the Allies could go no further and in nine days Operation Dynamo ensured the evacuation of 338,226 British and French soldiers from Dunkirk by a hastily assembled fleet of about 700 boats. These included a mixture of merchant marine boats, fishing boats, pleasure craft and RNLI lifeboats. The small craft ferried troops from the beaches to larger ships waiting offshore. In addition, 80 percent of the troops were evacuated onto 42 destroyers and other large ships by means of the harbor's protective mole.

1940 – 1941   THE BATTLE OF BRITAIN

THE BATTLE OF BRITAIN JUNE–SEPTEMBER 1940
This is the name commonly given to the effort made by the German Luftwaffe to gain air superiority over Britain's Royal Air Force before a planned sea invasion of Britain during World War II. The unsuccessful campaign is considered to be the first major defeat inflicted on Hitler's Germany. Initial attacks were on airfields, but eventually attention turned to urban areas in an attempt to break the resolve of the British people. By September it was clear that the opportunity for invasion had passed and the battle was effectively at an end. It resulted in some 27,450 civilian deaths and a further 32,000 civilian injuries.

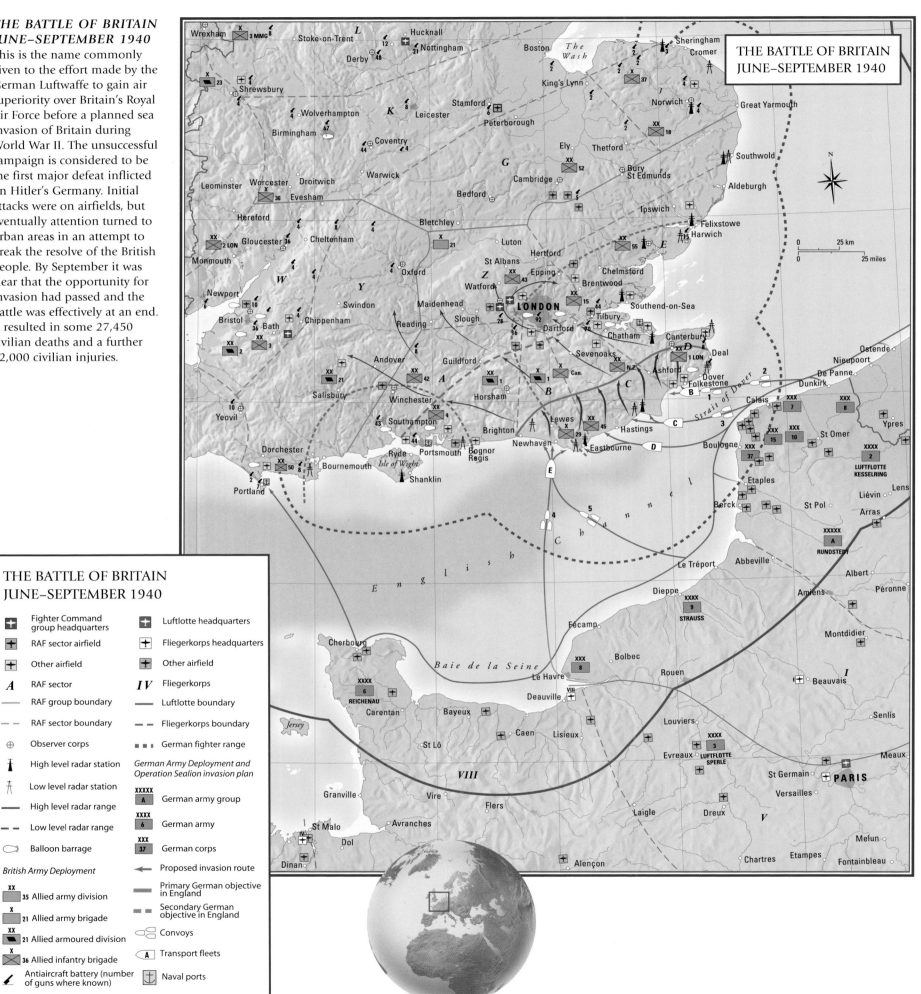

THE BATTLE OF BRITAIN
JUNE–SEPTEMBER 1940

THE BATTLE OF BRITAIN
JUNE–SEPTEMBER 1940

⊞ Fighter Command group headquarters	⊞ Luftlotte headquarters
⊞ RAF sector airfield	⊞ Fliegerkorps headquarters
⊞ Other airfield	⊞ Other airfield
A RAF sector	IV Fliegerkorps
— RAF group boundary	— Luftlotte boundary
– – RAF sector boundary	– – Fliegerkorps boundary
⊕ Observer corps	▪▪▪ German fighter range

German Army Deployment and Operation Sealion invasion plan

⊺ High level radar station	XXXXX A German army group
⊤ Low level radar station	XXXX 6 German army
— High level radar range	XXX 37 German corps
– – Low level radar range	← Proposed invasion route
◡ Balloon barrage	— Primary German objective in England

British Army Deployment

XX 35 Allied army division	– – Secondary German objective in England
X 21 Allied army brigade	◖ Convoys
XX 21 Allied armoured division	A Transport fleets
X 36 Allied infantry brigade	
⤡ Antiaircraft battery (number of guns where known)	⊞ Naval ports

THE CONQUEST OF GREECE AND CRETE; OPERATION MERKUR

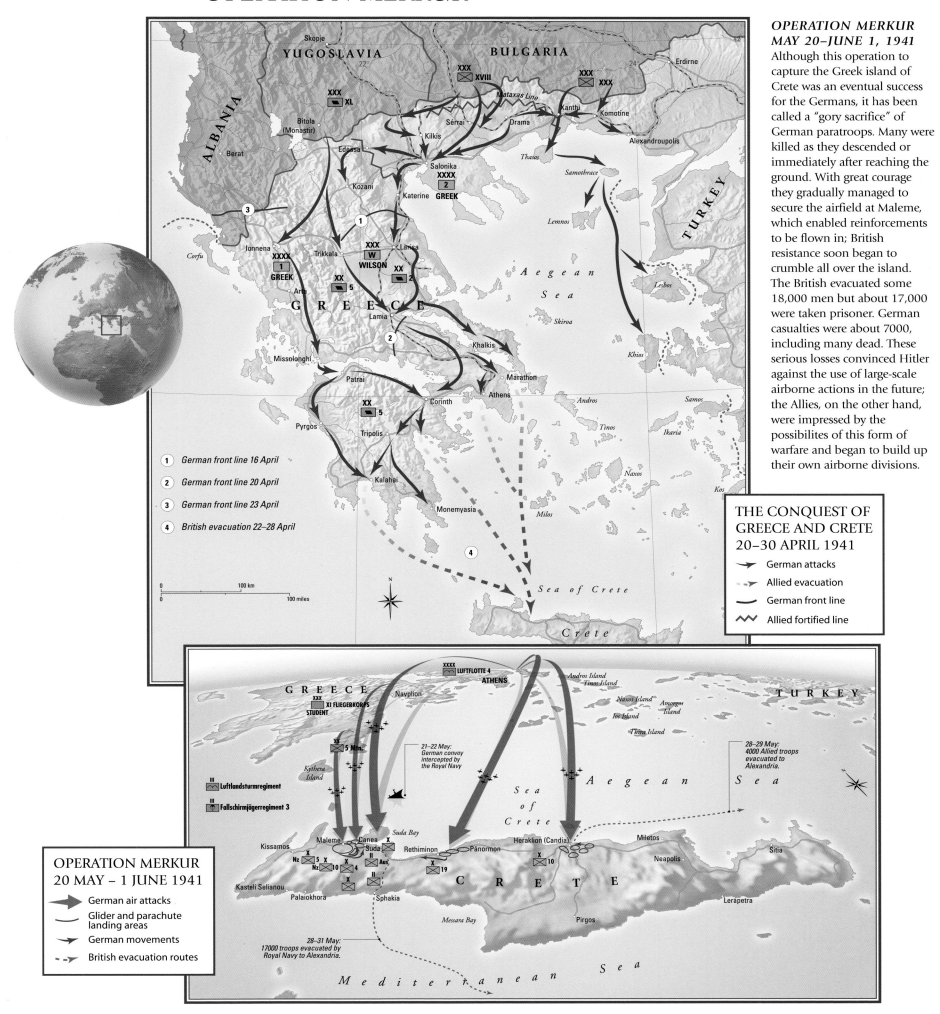

OPERATION MERKUR MAY 20–JUNE 1, 1941
Although this operation to capture the Greek island of Crete was an eventual success for the Germans, it has been called a "gory sacrifice" of German paratroops. Many were killed as they descended or immediately after reaching the ground. With great courage they gradually managed to secure the airfield at Maleme, which enabled reinforcements to be flown in; British resistance soon began to crumble all over the island. The British evacuated some 18,000 men but about 17,000 were taken prisoner. German casualties were about 7000, including many dead. These serious losses convinced Hitler against the use of large-scale airborne actions in the future; the Allies, on the other hand, were impressed by the possibilites of this form of warfare and began to build up their own airborne divisions.

1 *German front line 16 April*
2 *German front line 20 April*
3 *German front line 23 April*
4 *British evacuation 22–28 April*

0   100 km
0   100 miles

THE CONQUEST OF GREECE AND CRETE 20–30 APRIL 1941

→ German attacks
⇢ Allied evacuation
— German front line
⌇ Allied fortified line

OPERATION MERKUR 20 MAY – 1 JUNE 1941

➤ German air attacks
‿ Glider and parachute landing areas
→ German movements
⇢ British evacuation routes

21–22 May: German convoy intercepted by the Royal Navy

28–29 May: 4000 Allied troops evacuated to Alexandria.

28–31 May: 17000 troops evacuated by Royal Navy to Alexandria.

Luftlandesturmregiment

Fallschirmjägerregiment 3

1942 · AFRICA IN WORLD WAR II

AFRICA IN WORLD WAR II

Allied control of North Africa and the Mediterranean Sea was important because the British Empire depended on the Suez Canal for easy access to India and Australia. North Africa was finally secured in May 1943 after the "Torch" landings the previous November. Italian forces in East Africa attacked British territories in Somaliland, Kenya, and the Sudan. They were gradually driven back, eventually surrendering after Italy changed sides in 1943. The Vichy government in France retained firm control of the country's West African colonies until after the 1942 Torch landings. By that time the Free French forces already had control of French Equatorial Africa.

AFRICA IN WORLD WAR II

→ German and Italian advance from 1942

→ Allied movements

Colonial possessions

- British
- French
- Portuguese
- Spanish
- Italian
- Belgium

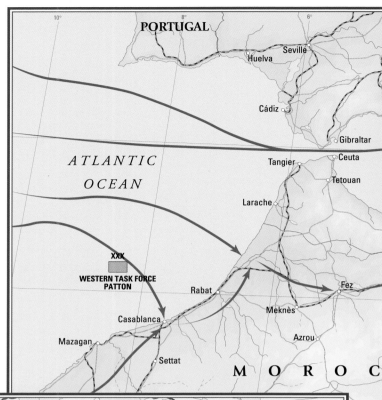

PORTUGAL
Seville
Huelva
Cádiz
Gibraltar
Ceuta
Tangier
Tetouan
Larache
ATLANTIC OCEAN
XXX
WESTERN TASK FORCE PATTON
Rabat
Meknès
Fez
Casablanca
Azrou
Mazagan
Settat
M O R O C

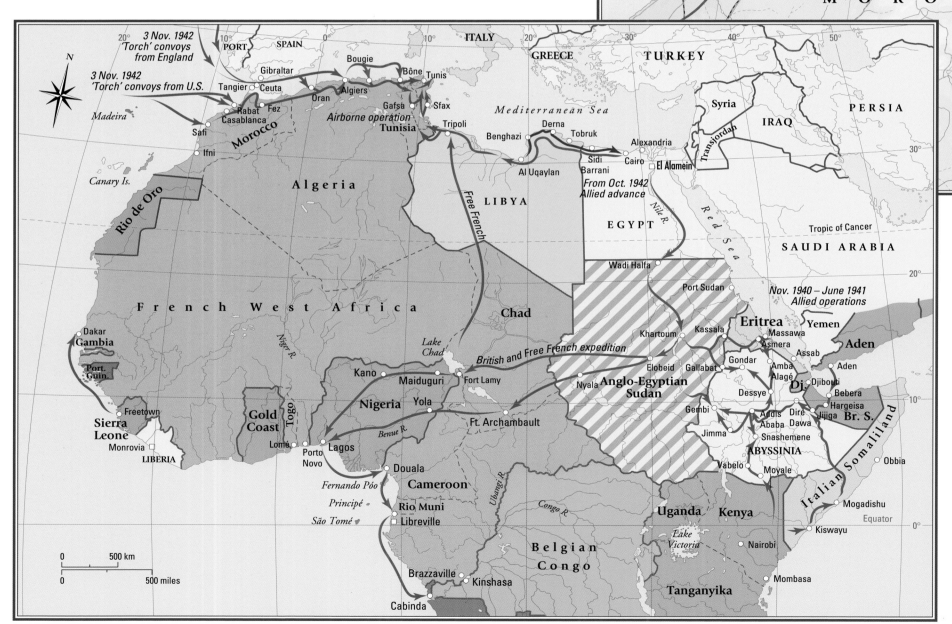

3 Nov. 1942 'Torch' convoys from England
3 Nov. 1942 'Torch' convoys from U.S.
N
Madeira
PORT.
SPAIN
ITALY
GREECE
TURKEY
Gibraltar
Bougie
Bône
Tunis
Tangier
Ceuta
Algiers
Oran
Rabat
Fez
Gafsa
Sfax
Casablanca
Safi
Ifni
Morocco
Airborne operation
Tunisia
Tripoli
Mediterranean Sea
Derna
Tobruk
Benghazi
Syria
IRAQ
PERSIA
Transjordan
Al Uqaylan
Sidi Barrani
Alexandria
Cairo
El Alamein
From Oct. 1942 Allied advance
Canary Is.
Rio de Oro
A l g e r i a
Free French
LIBYA
EGYPT
Nile R.
Red Sea
Tropic of Cancer
SAUDI ARABIA
Wadi Halfa
Nov. 1940 – June 1941 Allied operations
Port Sudan
F r e n c h   W e s t   A f r i c a
Chad
Khartoum
Kassala
Eritrea
Massawa
Asmera
Yemen
Aden
Dakar
Gambia
British and Free French expedition
Elobeid
Gallabat
Gondar
Amba Alagé
Assab
Aden
Port. Guin.
Lake Chad
Kano
Maiduguri
Fort Lamy
Nyala
Anglo-Egyptian Sudan
Dessye
Dire Dawa
Djibouti
Bebera
Hargeisa
Br. S.
Freetown
Sierra Leone
Monrovia
LIBERIA
Gold Coast
Togo
Nigeria
Yola
Ft. Archambault
Gembi
Jimma
Addis Ababa
Jijiga
Snashemene
Italian Somaliland
Niger R.
Benue R.
Lomé
Porto Novo
Lagos
Douala
Cameroon
ABYSSINIA
Vabelo
Moyale
Obbia
Fernando Póo
Principé
São Tomé
Rio Muni
Libreville
Ubange R.
Congo R.
Uganda
Kenya
Lake Victoria
Mogadishu
Equator
B e l g i a n   C o n g o
Nairobi
Kiswayu
Brazzaville
Kinshasa
Tanganyika
Mombasa
Cabinda
0   500 km
0   500 miles

OPERATION TORCH;
EL ALAMEIN – OPERATION LIGHTFOOT

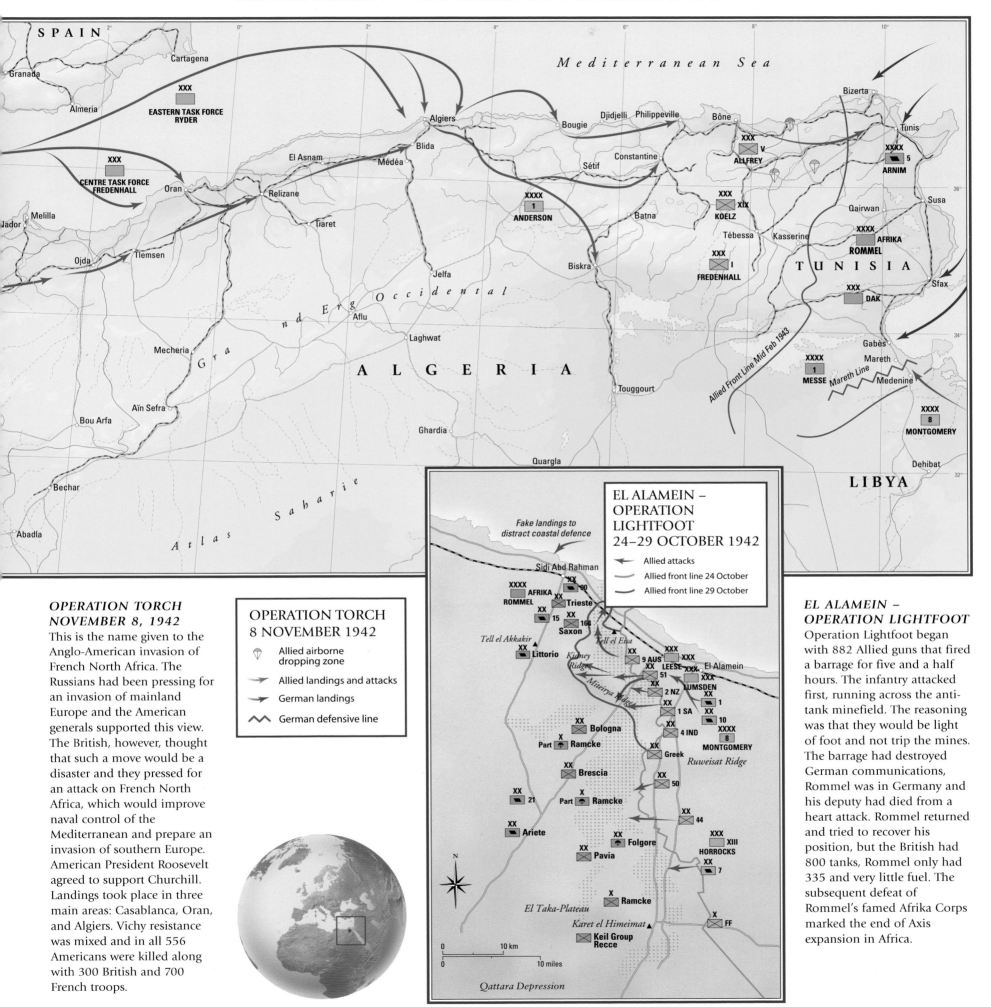

EL ALAMEIN – OPERATION LIGHTFOOT 24–29 OCTOBER 1942

➤ Allied attacks
〜 Allied front line 24 October
━ Allied front line 29 October

OPERATION TORCH 8 NOVEMBER 1942

⛉ Allied airborne dropping zone
➤ Allied landings and attacks
➤ German landings
〜 German defensive line

OPERATION TORCH NOVEMBER 8, 1942

This is the name given to the Anglo-American invasion of French North Africa. The Russians had been pressing for an invasion of mainland Europe and the American generals supported this view. The British, however, thought that such a move would be a disaster and they pressed for an attack on French North Africa, which would improve naval control of the Mediterranean and prepare an invasion of southern Europe. American President Roosevelt agreed to support Churchill. Landings took place in three main areas: Casablanca, Oran, and Algiers. Vichy resistance was mixed and in all 556 Americans were killed along with 300 British and 700 French troops.

EL ALAMEIN – OPERATION LIGHTFOOT

Operation Lightfoot began with 882 Allied guns that fired a barrage for five and a half hours. The infantry attacked first, running across the anti-tank minefield. The reasoning was that they would be light of foot and not trip the mines. The barrage had destroyed German communications, Rommel was in Germany and his deputy had died from a heart attack. Rommel returned and tried to recover his position, but the British had 800 tanks, Rommel only had 335 and very little fuel. The subsequent defeat of Rommel's famed Afrika Corps marked the end of Axis expansion in Africa.

OPERATION BARBAROSSA

1941 – 1942

OPERATION BARBAROSSA JUNE–OCTOBER 1941

The original goal of this German operation was the rapid conquest of the European part of the Soviet Union. Its failure was a turning point in the fortunes of Adolph Hitler and arguably resulted in the eventual defeat of Nazi Germany. Initially the Soviets were unprepared and the German advance was swift, but Hitler made the strategic error of ordering the army to stop short of Moscow in order to attack other targets. There were a number of brutal battles with bloody atrocities on both sides, and by the time the winter set in the invasion of the USSR had cost the Germans over 250,000 dead and 500,000 wounded.

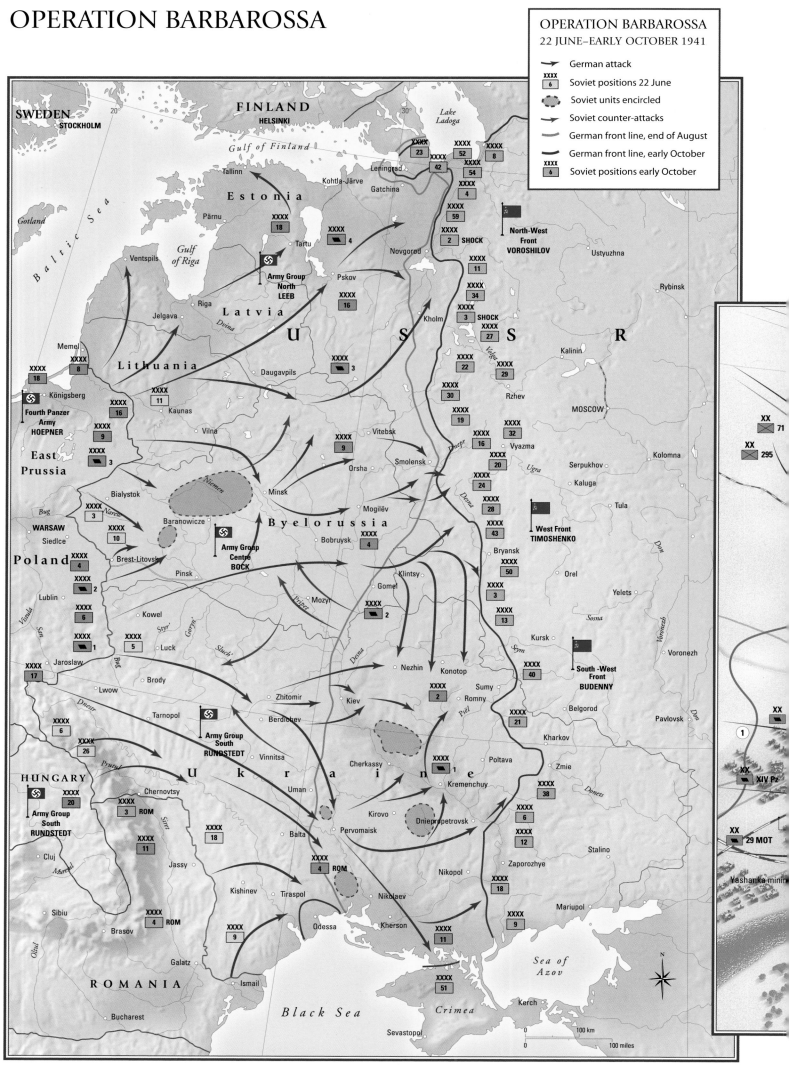

OPERATION BARBAROSSA
22 JUNE–EARLY OCTOBER 1941

- German attack
- Soviet positions 22 June
- Soviet units encircled
- Soviet counter-attacks
- German front line, end of August
- German front line, early October
- Soviet positions early October

THE BATTLE OF STALINGRAD

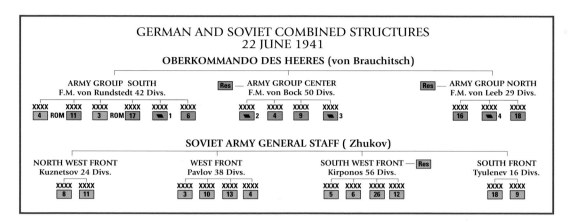

**GERMAN AND SOVIET COMBINED STRUCTURES
22 JUNE 1941**

OBERKOMMANDO DES HEERES (von Brauchitsch)

ARMY GROUP SOUTH F.M. von Rundstedt 42 Divs.	ARMY GROUP CENTER F.M. von Bock 50 Divs.	ARMY GROUP NORTH F.M. von Leeb 29 Divs.

SOVIET ARMY GENERAL STAFF (Zhukov)

NORTH WEST FRONT Kuznetsov 24 Divs.	WEST FRONT Pavlov 38 Divs.	SOUTH WEST FRONT Kirponos 56 Divs.	SOUTH FRONT Tyulenev 16 Divs.

THE BATTLE OF STALINGRAD SEPTEMBER–NOVEMBER 1942
This was arguably one of the bloodiest battles in human history. The combined casualty list amounted to about 1.5 million and the battle was marked by brutality and disregard for military and civilian casualties on both sides. It is taken to include the German siege of Stalingrad, the battle inside the city and the Soviet counteroffensive that eventually trapped and destroyed the German Sixth Army. Hitler ordered the defending General Paulus to stay and not to attempt to break out. Paulus obeyed but contrary to Hitler's expectation did not commit suicide and was the only Field Marshal in German history to surrender alive.

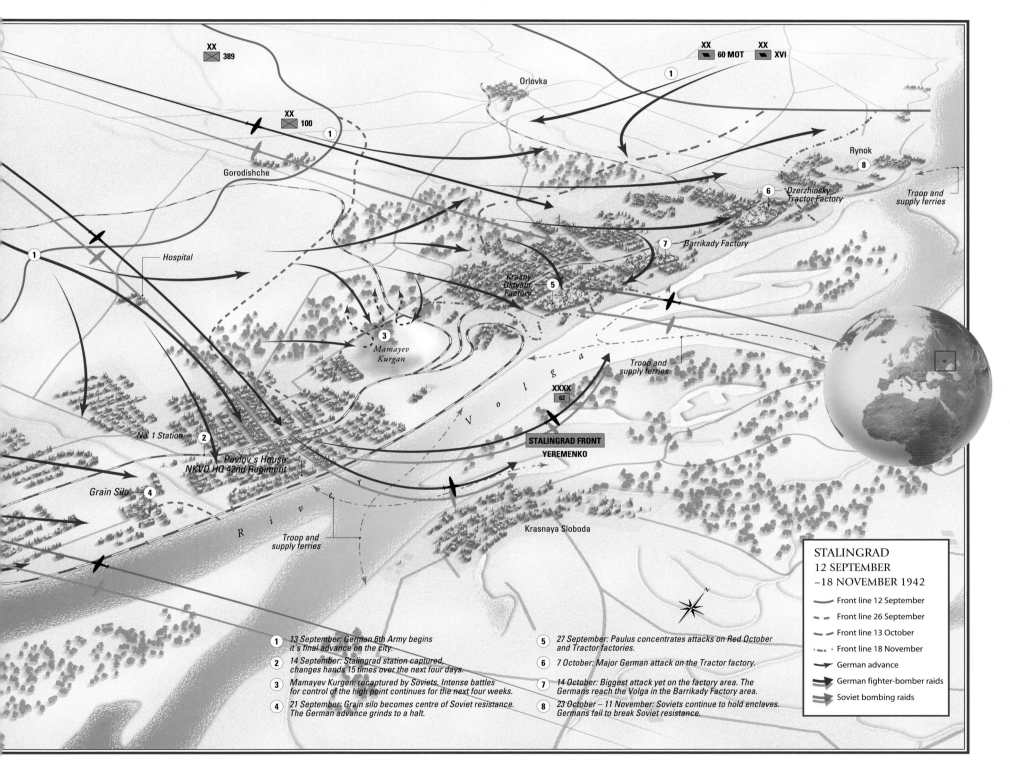

**STALINGRAD
12 SEPTEMBER
–18 NOVEMBER 1942**

Front line 12 September
Front line 26 September
Front line 13 October
Front line 18 November
German advance
German fighter-bomber raids
Soviet bombing raids

1. *13 September: German 6th Army begins it's final advance on the city.*
2. *14 September: Stalingrad station captured, changes hands 15 times over the next four days.*
3. *Mamayev Kurgen: recaptured by Soviets. Intense battles for control of the high point continues for the next four weeks.*
4. *21 September: Grain silo becomes centre of Soviet resistance. The German advance grinds to a halt.*
5. *27 September: Paulus concentrates attacks on Red October and Tractor factories.*
6. *7 October: Major German attack on the Tractor factory.*
7. *14 October: Biggest attack yet on the factory area. The Germans reach the Volga in the Barrikady Factory area.*
8. *23 October – 11 November: Soviets continue to hold enclaves. Germans fail to break Soviet resistance.*

1941 – 1942

JAPANESE EXPANSION

JAPANESE EXPANSION DECEMBER 1941–JULY 1942

In 1940 Japan signed a Tripartite Pact with Germany and Italy, thus becoming part of the "Axis." The United States imposed sanctions on Japan, hoping that it would withdraw from China and Manchuria. Japan countered by launching a surprise attack on Pearl Harbor in December 1941. The US promptly declared war on Japan and thus entered the European war. Japan achieved a long series of military successes, rapidly occupying much of South-east Asia, but the turning point came at the Battle of Midway in 1942. After heavy losses the Japanese fleet was turned back.

1940 Japanese established bases in the southern part of French Indo-China

JAPANESE EXPANSION
DECEMBER 1941–JULY 1942

- Japanese Empire early 1941
- Occupied by Japan December 1941 – July 1942
- China
- Aircraft carrier attack on Pearl Harbor
- Japanese offensive operations December 1941 – March 1942
- Approximate limit of Japanese advance July 1942

Colonial possessions 1941

- British (Commonwealth)
- Dutch
- French
- Portuguese
- Burma road

Khabarovsk

Aleutian Islands

Harbin

Vladivostok

Sea of Japan

JAPAN

Kyoto

Tokyo

asaki

Okinawa

PACIFIC OCEAN

Iwo Jima

Midway Is.

Hawaiian Is.

Wake Is.

Mariana Is.

Saipan

Guam

Yap

Marshall Is.

XXXX
SSD
SOUTH
SEAS DET.

Caroline Islands
Japanese mandate

Palau

Tarawa

Gilbert Is.

Hollandia

Indies

Bismarck
Arch.

Rabaul

New Guinea

Solomon Is.

Guadalcanal

Timor

Arafura Sea

Port Moresby

Darwin

Coral Sea

Cape
York

Fiji

Pearl Harbor

AUSTRALIA

150°

170°

190°

1942

BATTLE OF THE CORAL SEA

BATTLE OF THE CORAL SEA

Most of the action in this battle took place between May 4 and 8, 1942. It was a major battle in the Pacific, and it was the first naval battle in history where neither side's ships sighted or fired directly upon each other. It was also the first fleet action where aircraft carriers engaged each other. The battle is considered a tactical victory for Japan because American losses were greater, but it was a strategic victory for the Allies because it caused the Japanese to abandon attempts to land troops to take Port Moresby in New Guinea.

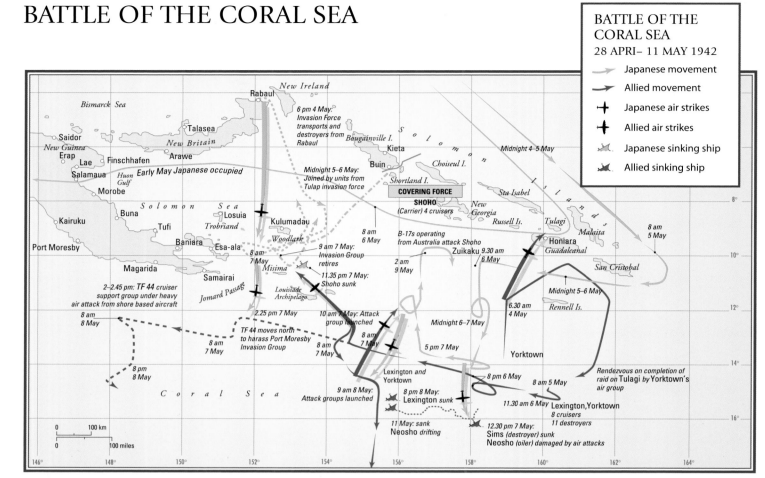

BATTLE OF THE CORAL SEA
28 APRI– 11 MAY 1942

→ Japanese movement
→ Allied movement
✛ Japanese air strikes
✛ Allied air strikes
⚓ Japanese sinking ship
⚓ Allied sinking ship

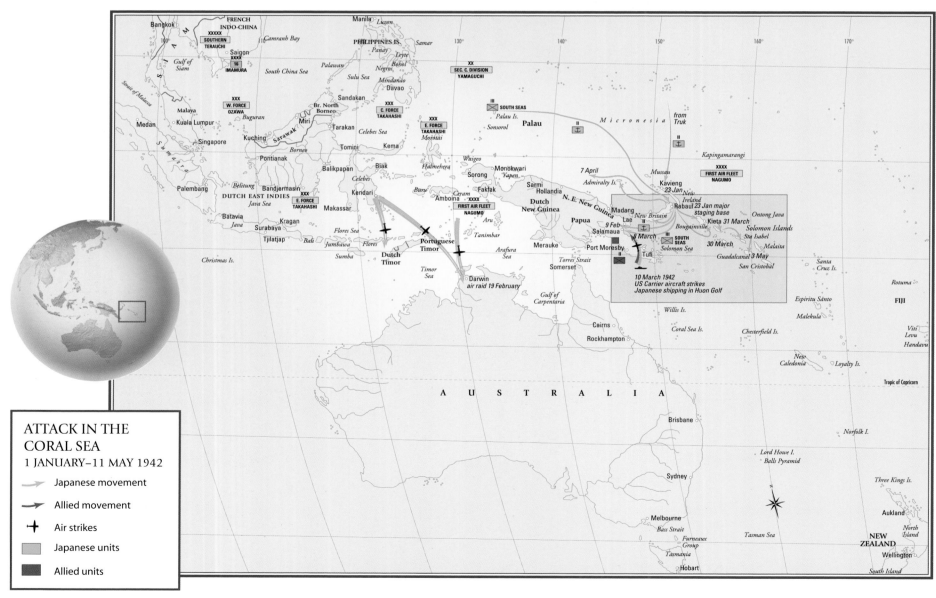

ATTACK IN THE CORAL SEA
1 JANUARY–11 MAY 1942

→ Japanese movement
→ Allied movement
✛ Air strikes
▨ Japanese units
▨ Allied units

BATTLE OF MIDWAY

BATTLE OF MIDWAY

Admiral Yamamoto wanted to knock the US Pacific Fleet out of action for long enough to allow Japan to fortify her defensive perimeter in the Pacific island chains.

His plan was that while the Fifth Fleet attacked the Aleutian Islands, the First Mobile-Force would attack Midway and destroy its air force. The Second Fleet would then land 5,000 troops and seize the atoll from the American Marines. This was expected to draw the American carriers west into a trap where the First Mobile-Force would engage and destroy them. The plan ended in disaster for the Japanese because the Americans knew of it in advance, having broken their naval code.

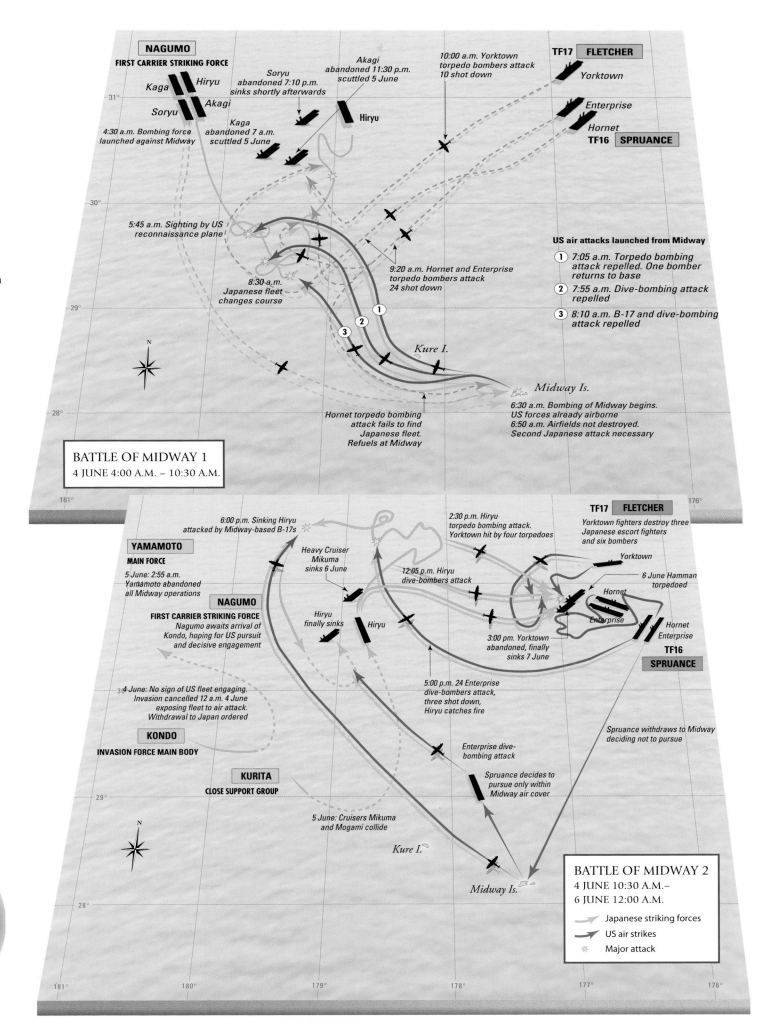

NAGUMO
FIRST CARRIER STRIKING FORCE

Kaga   Hiryu
Soryu   Akagi

4:30 a.m. Bombing force launched against Midway

Soryu abandoned 7:10 p.m. sinks shortly afterwards

Akagi abandoned 11:30 p.m. scuttled 5 June

Kaga abandoned 7 a.m. scuttled 5 June

Hiryu

10:00 a.m. Yorktown torpedo bombers attack 10 shot down

TF17 FLETCHER

Yorktown

Enterprise
Hornet

TF16 SPRUANCE

5:45 a.m. Sighting by US reconnaissance plane

8:30 a.m. Japanese fleet changes course

9:20 a.m. Hornet and Enterprise torpedo bombers attack 24 shot down

US air attacks launched from Midway

① 7:05 a.m. Torpedo bombing attack repelled. One bomber returns to base

② 7:55 a.m. Dive-bombing attack repelled

③ 8:10 a.m. B-17 and dive-bombing attack repelled

Kure I.

Midway Is.

Hornet torpedo bombing attack fails to find Japanese fleet. Refuels at Midway

6:30 a.m. Bombing of Midway begins. US forces already airborne
6:50 a.m. Airfields not destroyed. Second Japanese attack necessary

BATTLE OF MIDWAY 1
4 JUNE 4:00 A.M. – 10:30 A.M.

6:00 p.m. Sinking Hiryu attacked by Midway-based B-17s

Heavy Cruiser Mikuma sinks 6 June

2:30 p.m. Hiryu torpedo bombing attack. Yorktown hit by four torpedoes

Yorktown fighters destroy three Japanese escort fighters and six bombers

TF17 FLETCHER

Yorktown

6 June Hamman torpedoed

YAMAMOTO
MAIN FORCE

5 June: 2:55 a.m. Yamamoto abandoned all Midway operations

NAGUMO
FIRST CARRIER STRIKING FORCE
Nagumo awaits arrival of Kondo, hoping for US pursuit and decisive engagement

Hiryu finally sinks   Hiryu

12:05 p.m. Hiryu dive-bombers attack

Hornet
Enterprise

Hornet
Enterprise

TF16
SPRUANCE

3:00 pm. Yorktown abandoned, finally sinks 7 June

4 June: No sign of US fleet engaging. Invasion cancelled 12 a.m. 4 June exposing fleet to air attack. Withdrawal to Japan ordered

KONDO
INVASION FORCE MAIN BODY

KURITA
CLOSE SUPPORT GROUP

5:00 p.m. 24 Enterprise dive-bombers attack, three shot down, Hiryu catches fire

Enterprise dive-bombing attack

Spruance decides to pursue only within Midway air cover

Spruance withdraws to Midway deciding not to pursue

5 June: Cruisers Mikuma and Mogami collide

Kure I.

Midway Is.

BATTLE OF MIDWAY 2
4 JUNE 10:30 A.M.–
6 JUNE 12:00 A.M.

→ Japanese striking forces
→ US air strikes
✳ Major attack

BATTLE OF THE ATLANTIC

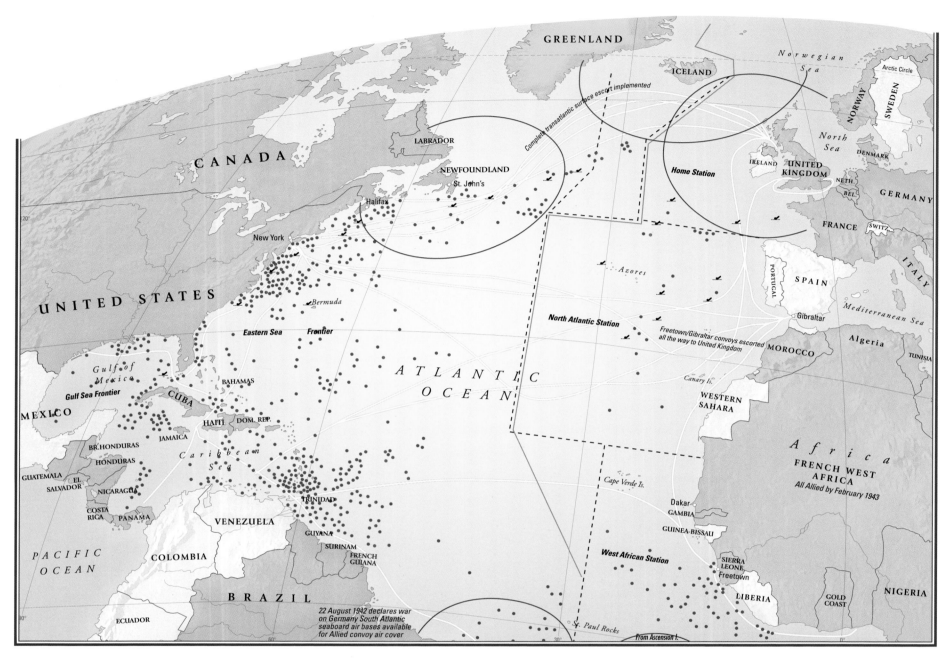

BATTLE OF THE ATLANTIC JUNE 1940 –MARCH 1941 AND JANUARY 1942 –FEBRUARY 1943

Between June and October 1940 German U-boats sank over 270 Allied ships. This was known as the "happy time" for the U-boat crews. At that time Britain was very much on its own. Convoys were used, but the Royal Navy had too few escort vessels and radar was in its infancy. Asdic (later known as sonar) could only detect underwater objects and was useless for detecting submarines on the surface. British losses were so great that there was a real concern that the country would be starved into submission, which of course was the prime objective

of the U-boat offensive.

When the Americans entered the war they failed to appreciate the importance of the convoy system or the importance of having a coastal blackout on their Atlantic seaboard. The result was that the U-boats simply sat offshore and picked off the lone merchant ships as they were silhouetted against the coastal lights. Once the Americans addressed these issues, losses to U-boats dropped dramatically. Eventually, with more escort ships and improved technology, the tide began to turn. By the end of the war, the Battle of the Atlantic had taken the lives of 28,000 U-boat crewmembers and 30,348 merchant seamen.

BATTLE OF THE ATLANTIC
JANUARY 1942–FEBRUARY 1943

——	Change of operational control UK to US, August 1942
——	Extent of air escort cover
– – –	UK Escort Stations to July 1942
	Major convoy routes
•	Allied merchant ships sunk by U-boats
	U-boats sunk
	Territory under Allied control
	Territory under Axis control
	Neutral territory

OPERATION BAGRATION

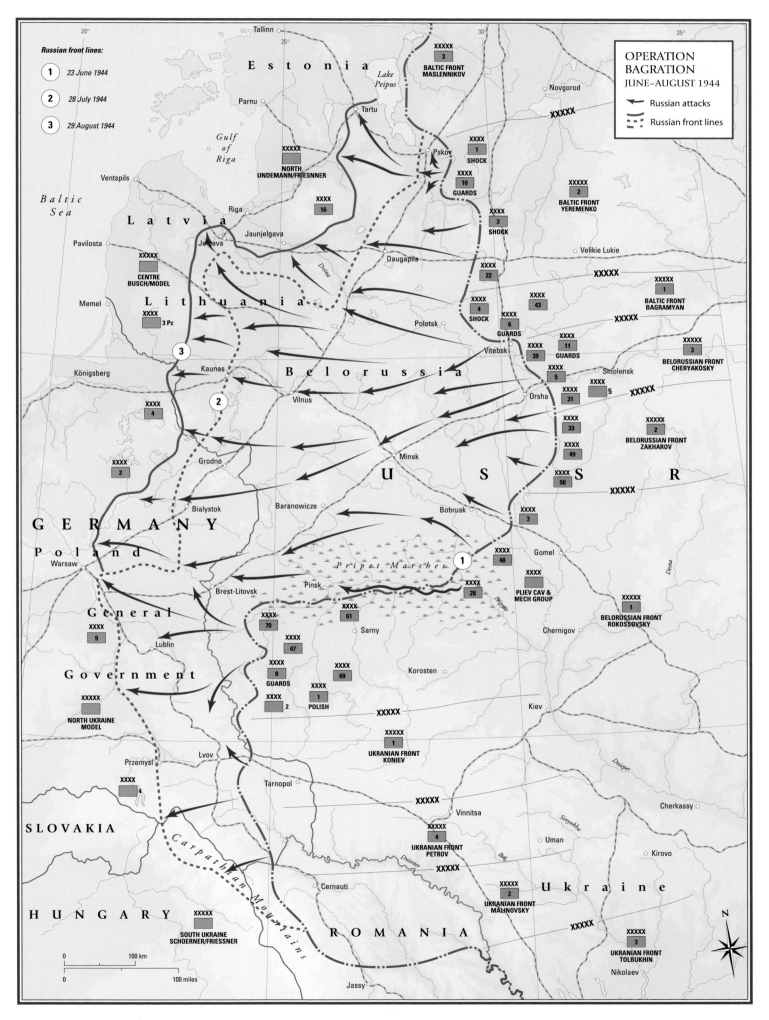

Russian front lines:
1. 23 June 1944
2. 28 July 1944
3. 29 August 1944

OPERATION
BAGRATION
JUNE–AUGUST 1944

→ Russian attacks
⋯ Russian front lines

This was the code name for the Russian Army Offensive that cleared the German army from Belorussia and Eastern Poland during the summer of 1944. The offensive resulted in the complete destruction of the German Army Group Centre and was arguably the greatest defeat for the Wehrmacht during World War II. Hitler underestimated the threat posed by Soviet troops facing Army Group Centre and had redeployed much of his resources to the Southern Front where he expected the next major offensive to come. Despite the huge forces involved, the Soviet army maintained complete co-ordination of all front movements and leaving the Germans completely confused.

1944 # D–DAY

ALLIED D-DAY LANDING PLAN & OBJECTIVES

Operation Overlord was the codename of the Allied invasion of northwest Europe. It was the largest seaborne invasion in history and involved three million troops crossing the English Channel from England to Normandy in a fleet of 6,938 vessels drawn from eight different navies. The invasion began with overnight parachute and glider landings, along with massive air attacks and naval bombardments. The amphibious phase began on June 6. There were five beachheads; three in the British Sector, codenamed Sword, Juno, and Gold; and two in the American Sector, codenamed Omaha and Utah. The object was to gain a foothold and then to advance into France and ultimately into Germany.

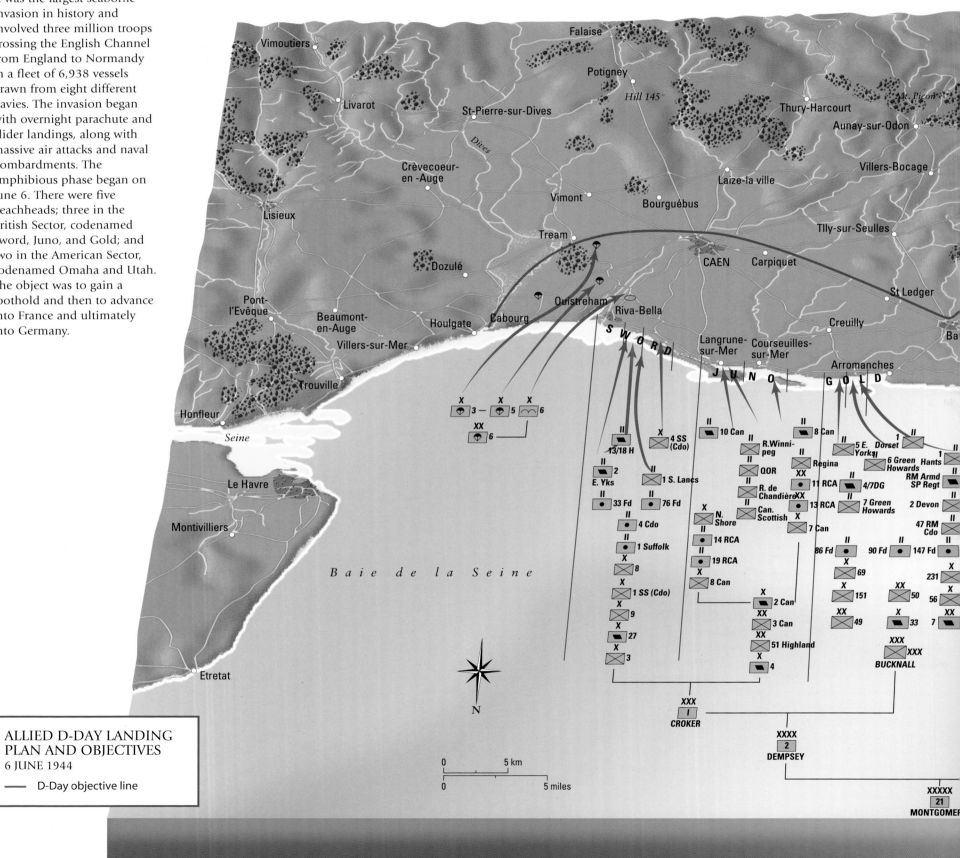

ALLIED D-DAY LANDING
PLAN AND OBJECTIVES
6 JUNE 1944

—— D-Day objective line

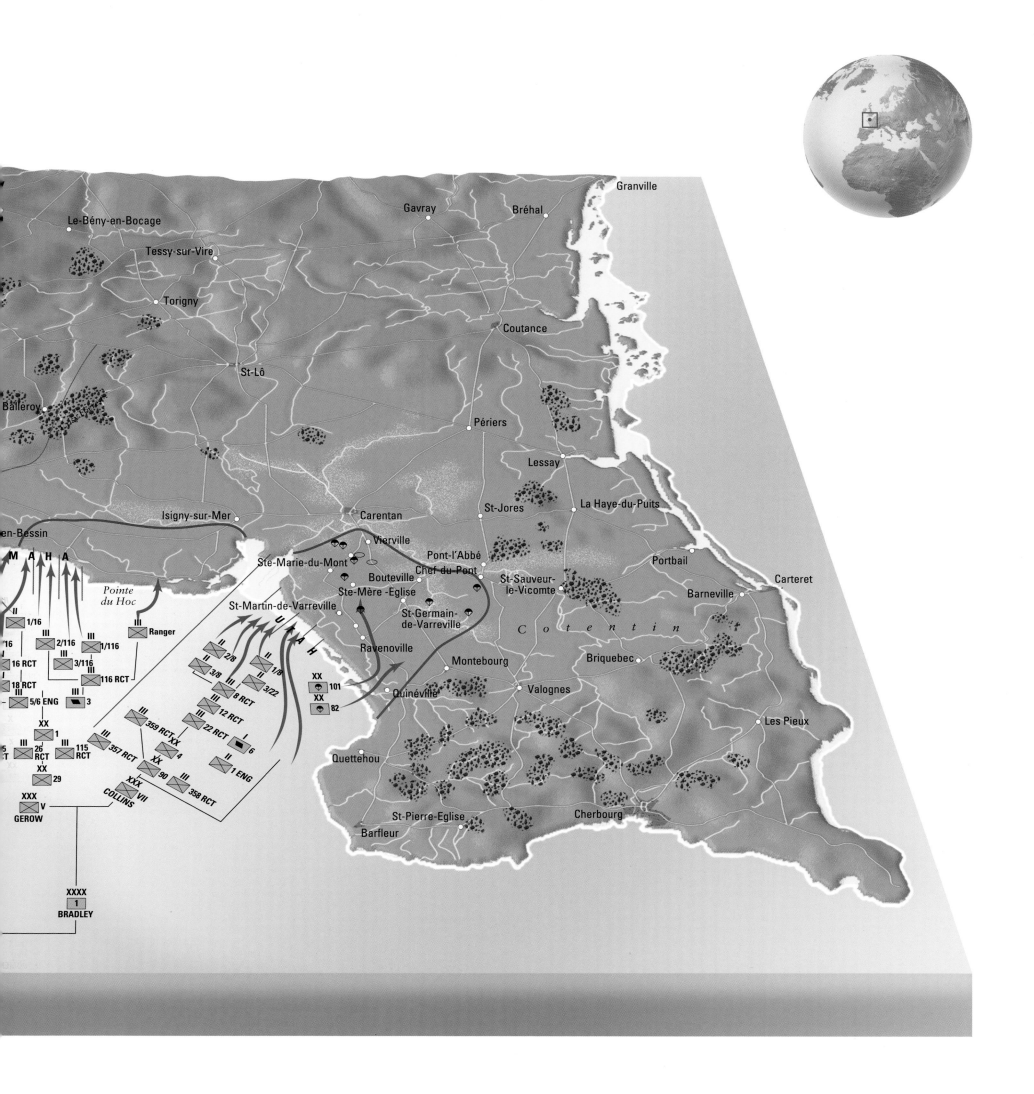

CROSSING THE RHINE

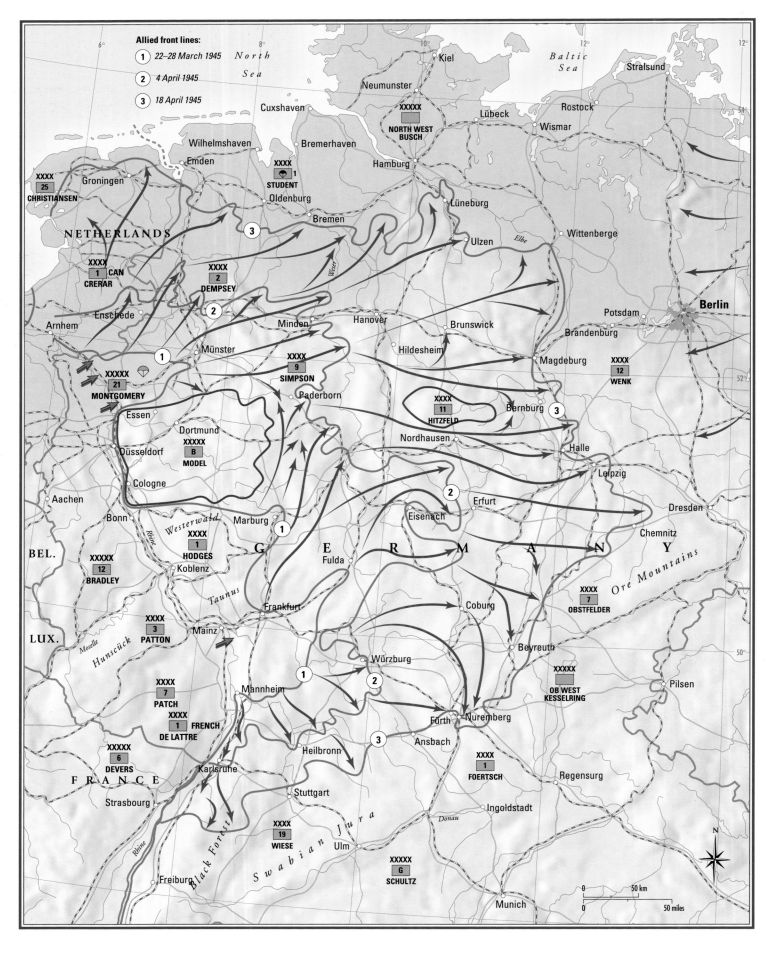

CROSSING THE RHINE MARCH 1945

Following the successful completion of the Battle of the Bulge in the Ardennes, Allied forces moved to the east, attacking German forces toward the Rhine. The 9th Armored Division to the north were able to capture the only intact bridge across the Rhine at Remagen, but the other Allied armies involved in the push toward the east had to bridge the river with their own resources. The first unit to cross was the 5th Infantry Division, using assault rafts to cross at Oppenheim. In the following days, three temporary bridges had been erected that allowed the Allies to move troops, vehicles, and supplies to the east side of the river. By March 27, five divisions with supporting troops and supplies had crossed the bridges at Oppenheim, allowing the Allies to begin their assault on the German military-industrial heartland.

CROSSING THE RHINE MARCH 1945

→ Allied Rhine crossings
→ Allied attacks
— Allied front line
◯ German pockets
⬙ Allied paratroop drop

BATTLE OF BERLIN

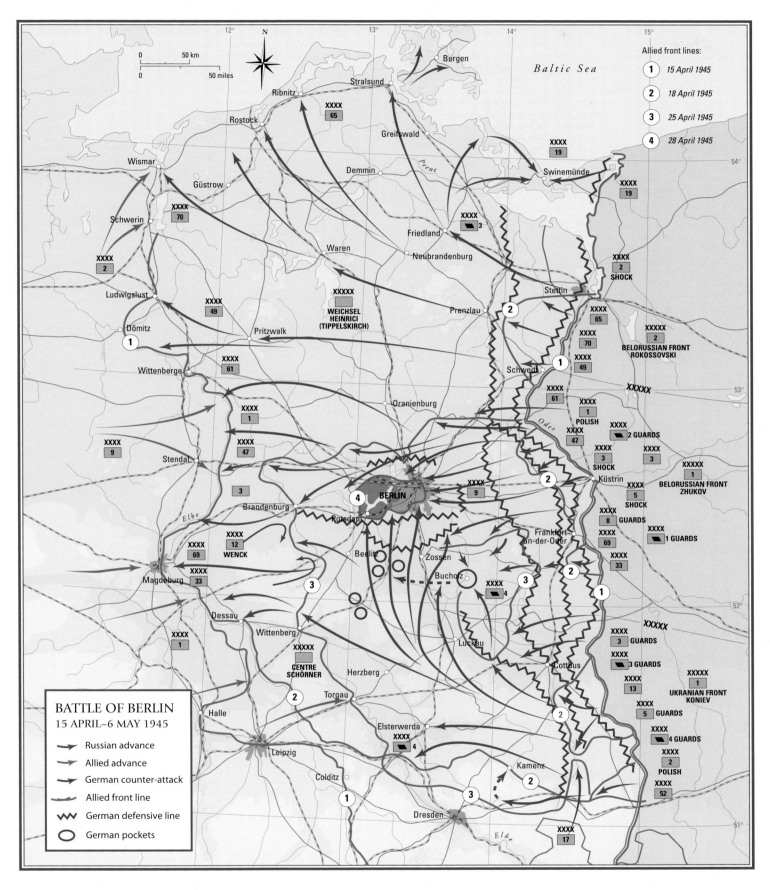

Allied front lines:

1. 15 April 1945
2. 18 April 1945
3. 25 April 1945
4. 28 April 1945

Baltic Sea

Bergen

Stralsund

Ribnitz

Rostock

XXXX
65

Greifswald

Wismar

Demmin

Güstrow

Swinemünde

XXXX
19

XXXX
70

Schwerin

Waren

Neubrandenburg

Friedland

XXXX
3

XXXX
19

XXXX
2

Ludwigslust

Neubrandenburg

XXXX
49

WEICHSEL
HEINRICI
(TIPPELSKIRCH)

Prenzlau

Stettin

XXXX
2
SHOCK

Dömitz

Pritzwalk

XXXX
65

Wittenberge

XXXX
61

Schwedt

XXXX
70

BELORUSSIAN FRONT
ROKOSSOVSKI

XXXXX
2

Oranienburg

XXXX
61

XXXX
1
POLISH

XXXXX

Stendal

XXXX
9

XXXX
47

XXXX
47

XXXX
2 GUARDS

XXXX
1

XXXX
3
SHOCK

XXXX
3

XXXXX
1

XXXX
3

BERLIN

XXXX
9

XXXX
5
SHOCK

BELORUSSIAN FRONT
ZHUKOV

Brandenburg

XXXX
8
GUARDS

Küstrin

Rotgdam

XXXX
12
WENCK

XXXX
69

XXXX
1 GUARDS

XXXX
69

Beelitz

Frankfurt
an-der-Oder

XXXX
33

Magdeburg

XXXX
33

Zossen

Buchholz

XXXX
4

XXXX
2

Dessau

Wittenberg

XXXX
1

XXXXX
3 GUARDS

Luckau

XXXX
3 GUARDS

Herzberg

XXXXX
CENTRE
SCHÖRNER

Cottbus

XXXXX
13

UKRANIAN FRONT
KONIEV

Torgau

XXXX
5
GUARDS

Halle

Elsterwerda

XXXX
4

XXXX
4 GUARDS

Colditz

Kamenz

XXXX
2

XXXX
2
POLISH

Dresden

XXXX
52

Elbe

XXXX
17

BATTLE OF BERLIN
15 APRIL–6 MAY 1945

→ Russian advance
→ Allied advance
→ German counter-attack
⌐ Allied front line
∨∨∨ German defensive line
○ German pockets

0   50 km
0   50 miles

N

12°   13°   14°   15°

54°
53°
52°
51°

Peene
Oder
Elbe

***BATTLE OF BERLIN
APRIL–MAY 1945***

Stalin was anxious to gain as
much ground as possible by
the end of the war, but his
overriding objective was to
capture Berlin. Two massive
Soviet army groups attacked
from the east and the south.
On April 20, Hitler's birthday,
the Soviet army started
shelling the city center and did
not stop until Berlin
surrendered. Gradually the
Soviet net tightened, but
fighting continued to be fierce
as the Germans defended with
everything that they had. On
April 29 Hitler dictated his last
Will and Testament and the
following day committed
suicide. On May 2 the city
surrendered.

SITUATION IN THE PACIFIC

PACIFIC SITUATION 1942–1945

By mid-1942 Allied code breakers were able to intercept Japanese naval communications and knew of a planned attack against New Guinea. In the Battle of the Coral Sea losses were fairly even, but the allies scored a strategic victory because the Japanese invasion of Port Moresby was thwarted. In

February 1943 Allied forces cleared the Japanese from Guadalcanal and this was the start of a long series of bloody battles as the Allies gradually moved from island to island. The Allies finally closed in on Japan and the Pacific War finally ended after the atomic bombing of Hiroshima and Nagasaki.

NAGASAKI 9 AUGUST, 1945

Although one of the largest sea ports in Southern Japan, with a wide range of industrial activity, Nagasaki had never been subjected to large-scale bombing; this changed on August 9 when an atomic bomb was dropped on the city. The bomb had originally been intended for Kokura but a cloudbank had moved in, obscuring the target—an appalling stroke of bad luck for Nagasaki.

It is estimated that 70,000 people (30 percent of the population) were killed instantly and up to 60,000 were injured. Several thousand more died later as a result of radiation poisoning.

The attack on Nagasaki occurred three days after another atomic bomb had been dropped on the Japanese city of Hiroshima. It is estimated that around 140,000 people had died by the end of the 1945 as a result of the Hiroshima bomb, either perishing immediately in the blast or dying later from their injuries.

Less than a week after the bombing of Nagasaki, Japan's Emperor Hirohito recorded his surrender, and this was broadcast on August 15.

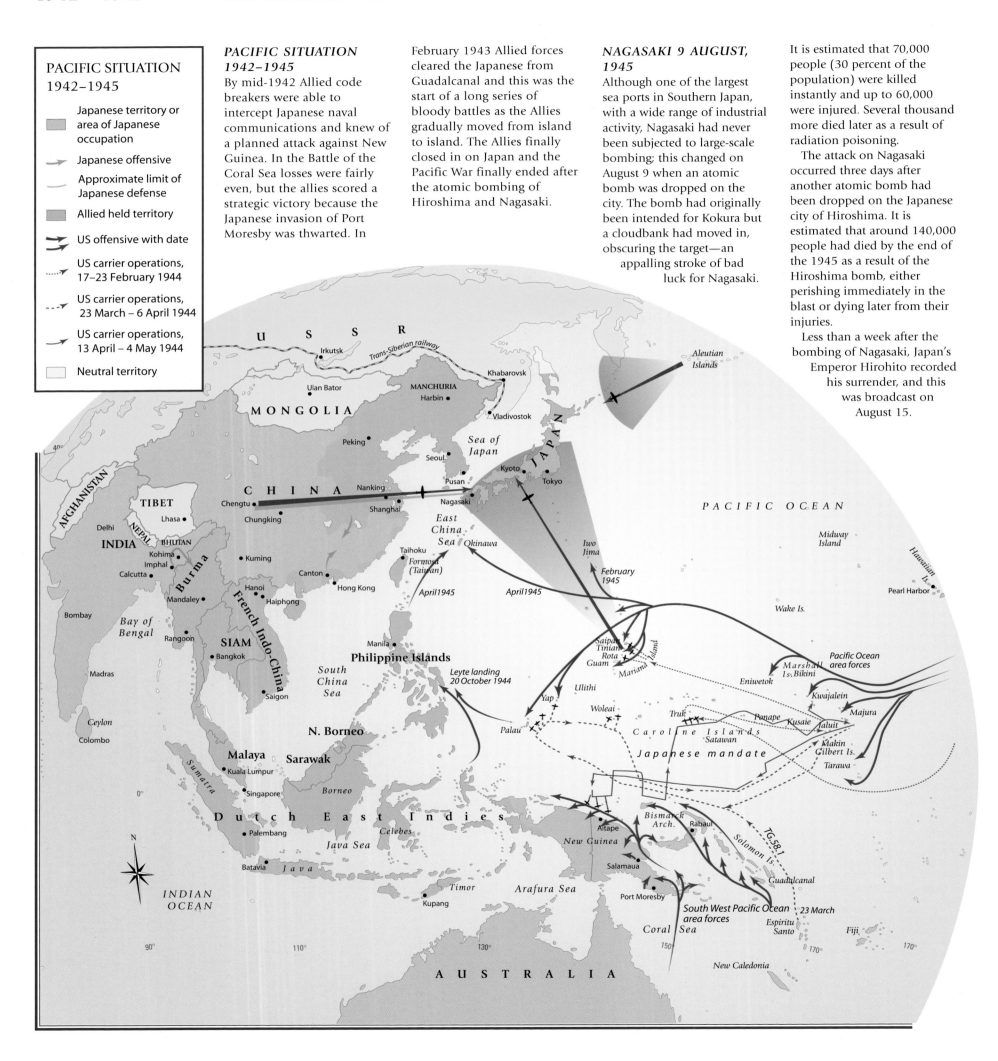

PACIFIC SITUATION 1942–1945

- Japanese territory or area of Japanese occupation
- → Japanese offensive
- Approximate limit of Japanese defense
- Allied held territory
- → US offensive with date
- ···→ US carrier operations, 17–23 February 1944
- --→ US carrier operations, 23 March – 6 April 1944
- → US carrier operations, 13 April – 4 May 1944
- Neutral territory

NAGASAKI

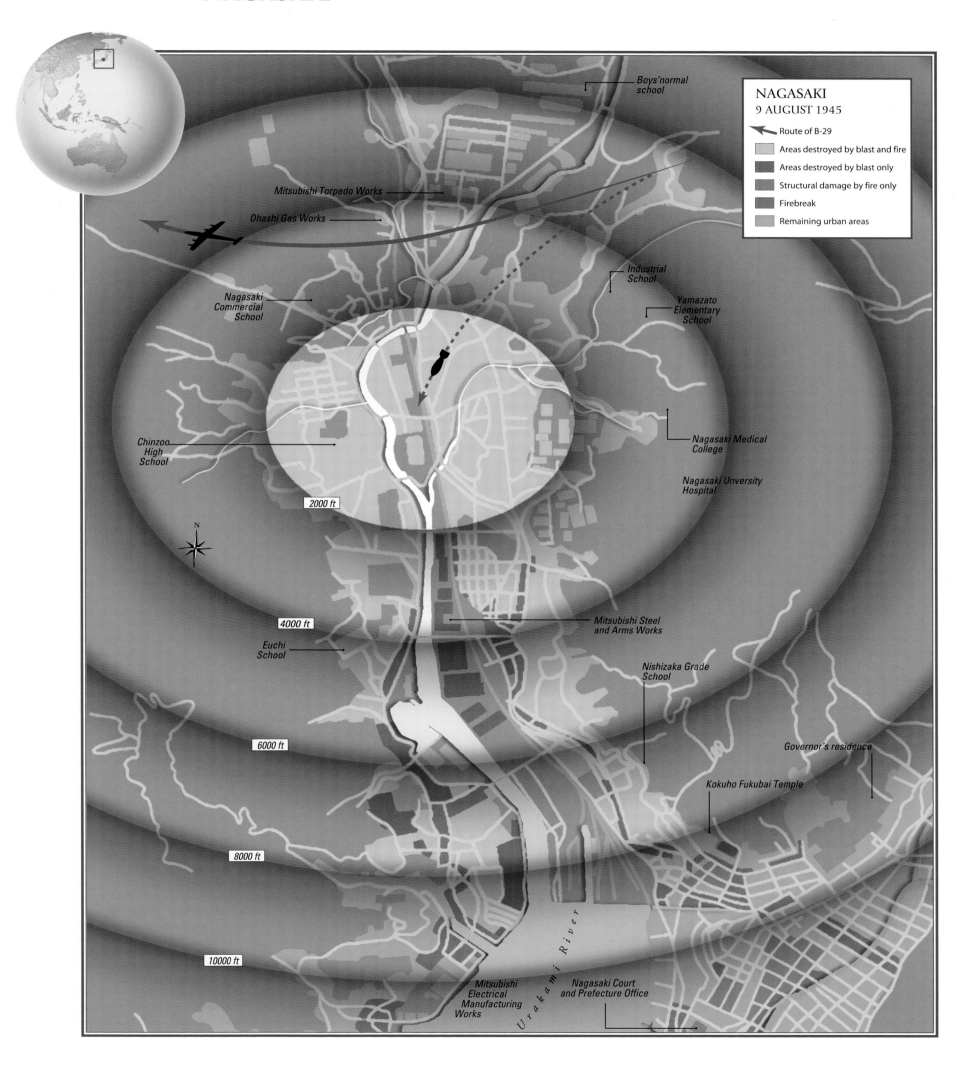

Boys'normal school

Mitsubishi Torpedo Works

Ohashi Gas Works

Nagasaki Commercial School

Chinzoo High School

Euchi School

Mitsubishi Electrical Manufacturing Works

Industrial School

Yamazato Elementary School

Nagasaki Medical College

Nagasaki Unversity Hospital

Mitsubishi Steel and Arms Works

Nishizaka Grade School

Governor's residence

Kokuho Fukubai Temple

Urakami River

Nagasaki Court and Prefecture Office

2000 ft

4000 ft

6000 ft

8000 ft

10000 ft

N

NAGASAKI
9 AUGUST 1945

Route of B-29
Areas destroyed by blast and fire
Areas destroyed by blast only
Structural damage by fire only
Firebreak
Remaining urban areas

1950 – 1973 THE KOREAN WAR

THE KOREAN WAR

The Korean War began as a civil war when the North Koreans moved south across the 38th parallel. The US immediately secured a United Nations resolution demanding that Northern forces withdraw. American forces landed but were pushed south to an area around Pusan. Massive reinforcements were rushed in and the Northern forces were gradually driven back. Towards the end of October the Chinese entered the fight and in November they attacked, scored a spectacular victory and moved south. In February 1951 the UN forces began to fight back. The war dragged on until a final ceasefire in July 1953.

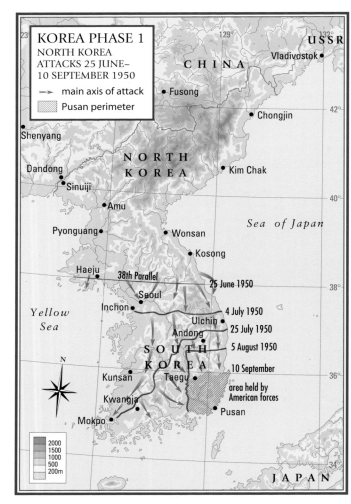

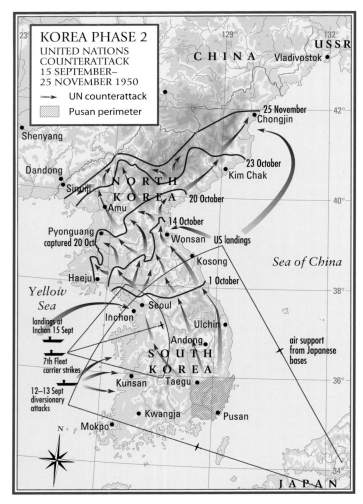

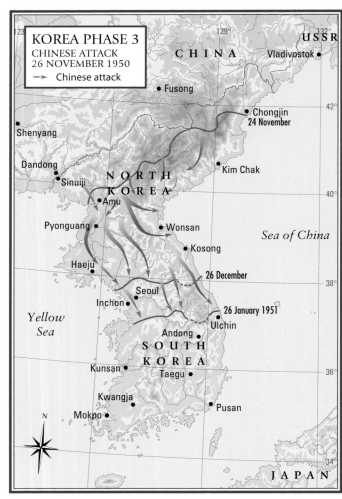

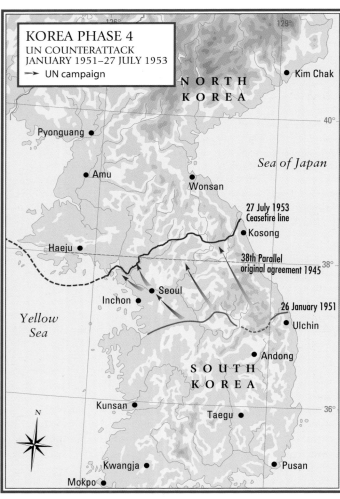

ARAB–ISRAELI WARS

THE SINAI CAMPAIGN OCTOBER–NOVEMBER 1956

In 1956 Egyptian President Nasser decided to nationalize the Suez Canal. The canal was considered to be vital since half of Western Europe's oil passed through it. Britain, France, and Israel came to an agreement whereby Israel would invade Sinai on the Egypt-Israel border. This resulted in a dramatic victory for Israel. However, a successful combined British and French attack from the north was opposed by the Americans, who demanded a ceasefire. Economic pressure was brought to bear and Britain and France withdrew.

THE SIX DAY WAR 1967

The Six Day War was fought between Israel and its Arab neighbors, Egypt, Jordan, and Syria. In the months leading up to the war Egypt had expelled the United Nations Emergency force from the Sinai Peninsula, increased military activity near the border, blocked the Straits of Tiran to Israeli ships, and called for unified Arab action against Israel. On June 5, fearing an imminent invasion, Israel launched a preemptive attack on Egypt's air force. At the end of the war Israel had gained control of Eastern Jerusalem, the Gaza Strip, the Sinai Peninsula, the West Bank, and the Golan Heights.

YOM KIPPUR WAR 1973

This war began on the Jewish holiday of Yom Kippur, when a coalition of Arab states led by Egypt and Syria crossed the ceasefire lines in the Sinai and Golan Heights. The Israelis were taken completely by surprise. For two days the Egyptians and Syrians made good progress, but by the second week the Syrians had been pushed out of the Golan Heights entirely and the Egyptians had been pushed back past the original ceasefire line. The Camp David Accord led to normalized relations between Egypt and Israel.

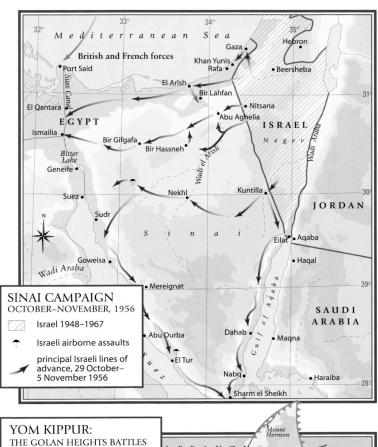

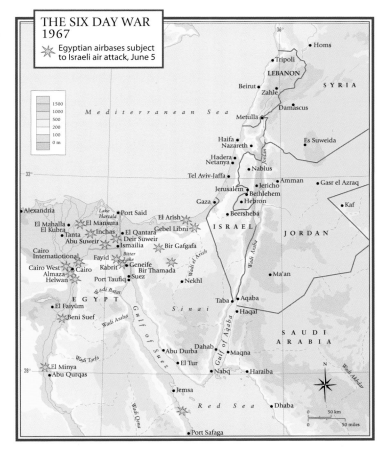

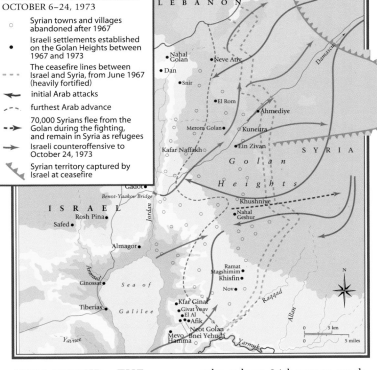

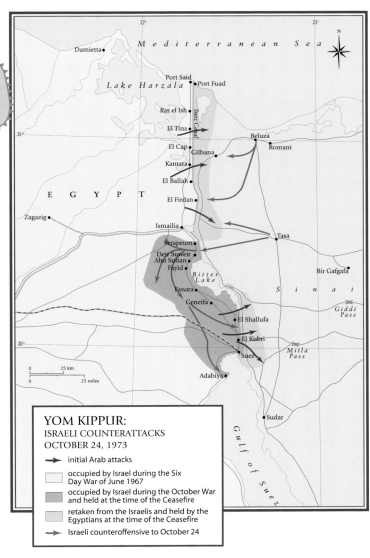

YOM KIPPUR—THE GOLAN HEIGHTS

Fighting in the Golan Heights was given top priority by Israel. The Sinai was considered to be a long way away, but if the Golan Heights fell, this would pave the way for the complete occupation of Israel. The Syrians had expected the Israeli reserves to take at least 24 hours to reach the front lines, but in fact they began arriving within 15 hours after the war began. As more reservists continued to arrive, the Syrians were gradually pushed back and the war ended with Israel having made additional territorial gains.

1945 – 1962   THE DIVISION OF EUROPE AFTER WORLD WAR II

THE DIVISION OF EUROPE AFTER WORLD WAR II 1945–1949

At the end of the War, among other border changes, Poland gained large areas that had formerly been part of Germany, and the Baltic States were returned to Russian rule. Stalin was adamant that he did not want to run the risk of yet another war with Germany and it was agreed that Germany and Austria should both be partitioned between Britain, France, the USA, and the USSR. The Soviet Zones would form part of a chain of "buffer states" that would protect the western border of the USSR. This division between the East and the West was a major cause of the Cold War.

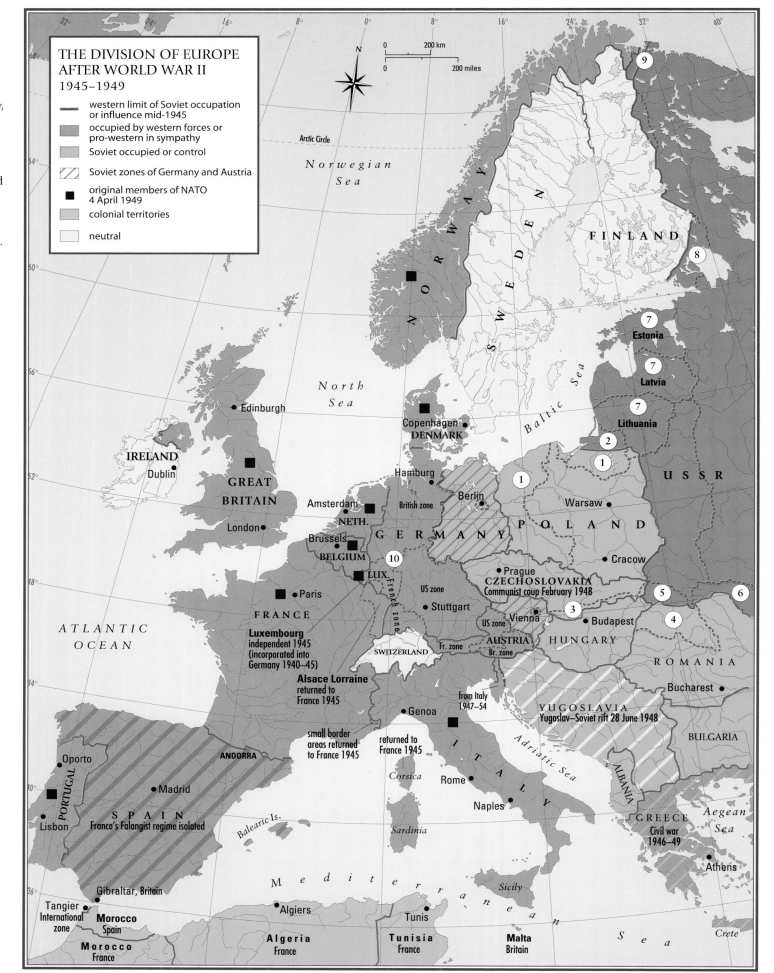

THE DIVISION OF EUROPE AFTER WORLD WAR II 1945–1949

— western limit of Soviet occupation or influence mid-1945

occupied by western forces or pro-western in sympathy

Soviet occupied or control

Soviet zones of Germany and Austria

■ original members of NATO 4 April 1949

colonial territories

neutral

① from Germany to Poland 1945

② from Germany to USSR 1945

③ returned to Czechoslovakia from Hungary 1945

④ returned to Romania from Hungary 1945

⑤ from Hungary to USSR 1945

⑥ from Romania to USSR 1945

⑦ to USSR 1940, lost 1941, retaken 1944

⑧ to USSR 1940, lost 1941–44, returned 1947

⑨ to USSR 1947

⑩ Federal Republic of Germany formed Sept. 1949

PACKAGES TO CUBA; THE CUBAN MISSILE CRISIS

PACKAGES TO CUBA 1962

Fidel Castro came to power in Cuba in 1959 after a revolution to oust military dictator General Fulgencio Batista. Castro was a trained lawyer with strong communist sympathies. Tensions between Castro's Cuba and the USA soon became apparent, and the United States stopped importing Cuban goods. Cuba responded by beginning to sell its sugar to the USSR. When Cuba confiscated all American property, the US broke off diplomatic relations. By then Cuba was already receiving economic aid from Russia. The US monitored the regular sea traffic between the Russian ports and Cuba, and a major crisis developed when it was realized that some of these ships were carrying ballistic missiles capable of destroying much of the eastern US.

THE CUBAN MISSILE CRISIS SEPTEMBER – NOVEMBER 1962

This event was arguably the high point of the Cold War. The US had installed ballistic missiles in Turkey that were 16 minutes' flying time from Moscow. The Soviets countered this by sending missiles to Cuba where Castro had become very close to the Soviet Union. The Americans threatened to invade Cuba and it seemed for a time as though there would be another world war. In the event, after intense diplomatic activity, both sides withdrew their missiles and the crisis was over. To help prevent similar incidents in the future a "hot line" was installed between the leaders of the USA and USSR.

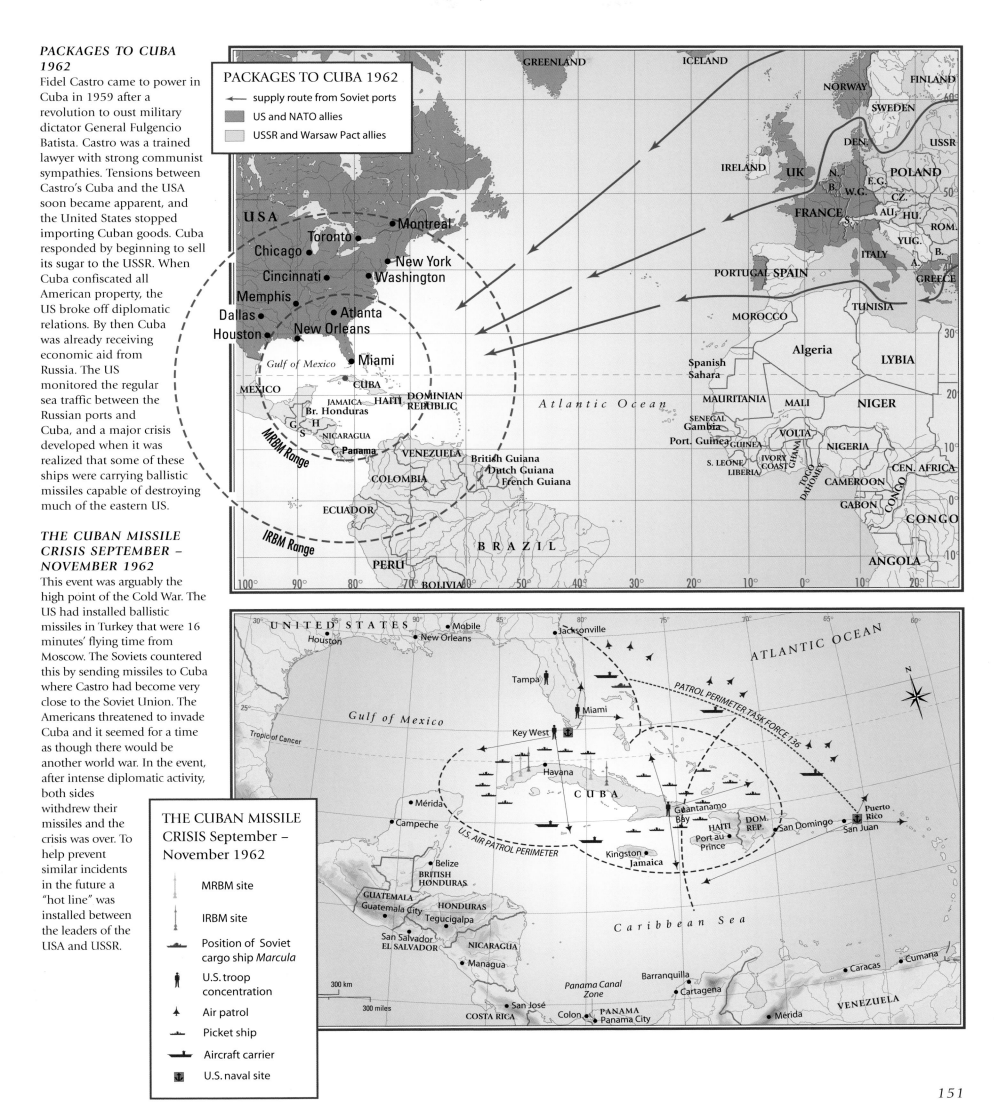

PACKAGES TO CUBA 1962

→ supply route from Soviet ports

US and NATO allies

USSR and Warsaw Pact allies

THE CUBAN MISSILE CRISIS September – November 1962

- MRBM site
- IRBM site
- Position of Soviet cargo ship *Marcula*
- U.S. troop concentration
- Air patrol
- Picket ship
- Aircraft carrier
- U.S. naval site

1946 – 1975   VIETNAM WARS

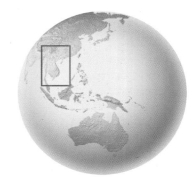

INDO-CHINA WAR

- ☐ French Indo-china
- ■ Viet-minh control, 1946–50
- • French garrison north of 16th parallel after "free state" agreements, March 1946
- ▨ Viet-minh control, 1950–54
- → French expeditionary corps movement, October 1945 – January 1946
- → French expeditionary corps movement, March – July 1946
- ✕ major battle

THE INDOCHINA WAR

The Indochina War took place between 1946 and 1954 between the French, supported by the Vietnamese National Army, and the Viet Minh led by Ho Chi Minh. Most of the fighting occurred in the north, in Tonking, but the conflict engulfed the entire country. Originally a Viet Minh rebellion against French authority it only became a full-scale war after the arrival of the Chinese Communists in 1949. In 1954 the French were defeated and the country was provisionally divided by the 17° parallel. Talks were due to take place regarding

nationwide elections, but these never materialised and this contributed to the subsequent Vietnam War.

THE VIETNAM WAR

There was no formal declaration of this war. US advisers started arriving in the South in 1955, but it was not until 1965 that the US openly declared its involvement. Casualties were high and it became increasingly unpopular in the United States. The Tet offensive in 1968 was a major victory for the south, but it was a turning point in public support. By 1970 the US was already withdrawing troops

and most had left by the time of the Paris Peace Accord in 1973. On its own the South Vietnamese army was no match for its opponent and the war ended with the capture of Saigon in April 1975.

VIETNAM WAR

- → Ho Chi Minh Trail
- → Sihanouk Trail
- ⇢ sea supply routes
- ▨ Communist-held area, 1959–60
- ✳ main attacks of the Tet offensive, 30–31 January 1968
- ▨ Communist-held area, January 1973 'ceasefire'
- –·– US corps command area
- ✳ North Vietnam subject to air attack
- ▤ Communist-controlled area in Laos and Cambodia, 1950–75
- ▨ controlled by Khmer Rouge, c. 1975
- ▨ controlled by Pathet Lao, c. 1975
- ▨ area of Communist guerrilla activity, c. 1975

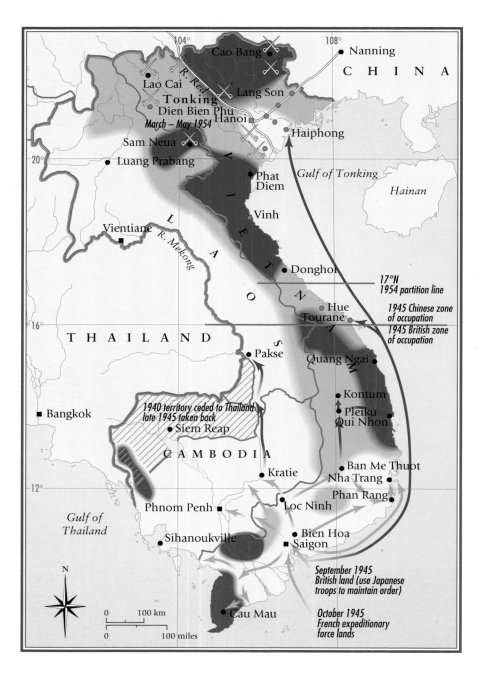

THE BATTLE OF AP BAC

THE BATTLE OF AP BAC 1963

This was a small-scale action that took place on January 2, 1963 in the early stages of the Vietnam War. It was the first major combat victory by the Viet Cong guerrillas over the South Vietnamese forces. Although the Viet Cong were hopelessly outnumbered, 350 as opposed to 1400, they scored a spectacular victory. The Viet Cong lost 18 killed and 39 wounded, but the Southern forces lost 80 dead and 100 wounded, with 3 US advisors killed and 8 wounded, and 5 helicopters also lost. Following the success of Ap Bac, the North immediately began planning for a full-scale war against the South.

1 Original Viet Cong positions.

2 1st Battalion of civil guard arrives. Concealed Viet Cong open fire. Civil guard falls back in disorder, their commanding officer among the dead.

3 US advisor flying overhead in spotter plane orders helicopter- borne infantry reinforcements.

4 These reinforcements land too close to the Viet Cong positions. Many are wounded and survivors withdraw.

5 Sky raider fighter-bombers launch napalm attack but hit villages and miss Viet Cong positions.

6 In an attempt to rescue the downed helicopter crews, armored personnel carriers are ordered forward. Thought invulnerable to small arms fire the carriers approach the eastern tree line. At point-blank range the Viet Cong open fire killing the machine gunners riding on top of the vehicles. The Viet Cong then rush forward throwing grenades and the carriers withdraw.

7 The senior American advisor still flying overhead persuades the South Vietnamese Commander to order a parachute drop to seal in the Viet Cong. The drop is badly handled and the troops land in front of the Viet Cong positions and come under heavy fire. They are unable therefore to launch an attack.

8 7th South Vietnamese infantry division approaching from the north are unable to cooperate with dispersed and pinned down airborne troops.

9 During the night the Viet Cong withdraw, having tied down a force many times their size and vastly better equipped. In the process only eighteen of their own men were killed.

THE BATTLE OF AP BAC

1978 – 1991   SOVIET-AFGHANISTAN WAR; FALKLANDS WAR

FALKLANDS WAR 1982

The Falklands are a group of around 200 islands of various size that lie about 770 miles from the Argentine coast. They have been claimed by Argentina since 1820, but have been administered and occupied by Britain since 1833. In April 1982 an Argentine military force invaded. As a result Britain launched a task force to retake the islands. The British were successful, but the result was 258 British killed and 777 wounded with 649 Argentine deaths and 1068 wounded. Air and sea losses on both sides were considerable. In spite of the British victory Argentina has never relinquished its claim of sovereignty over the islands.

AFGHANISTAN 1978–1984

The Marxist regime of Afghanistan had been receiving economic support from the USSR. When Mujahideen insurgents began fighting to overthrow the Communist rule, a request was made to the Soviet Union for military assistance. This was given, but since the US had been supporting the rebels, the West saw it as an invasion. It was a very difficult war for the Soviets to fight. They were not used to fighting in such terrain and their equipment was often ineffective or vulnerable. The result was a military stalemate. Casualties were high in this very unpopular war. It was impossible to win and is often referred to as "Russia's Vietnam."

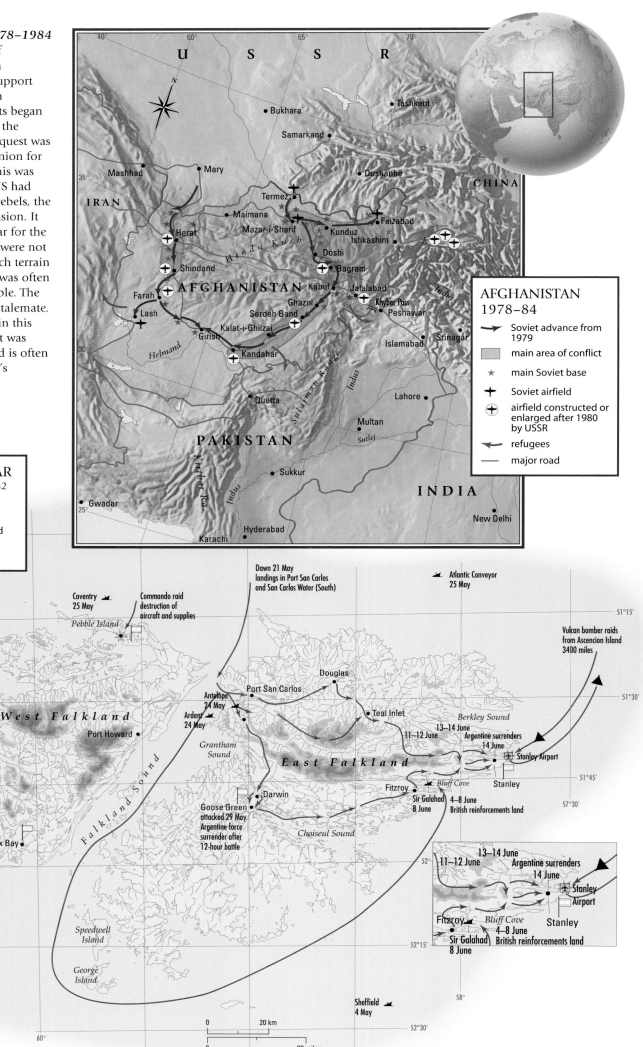

AFGHANISTAN 1978–84

→ Soviet advance from 1979

▮ main area of conflict

★ main Soviet base

✚ Soviet airfield

⊕ airfield constructed or enlarged after 1980 by USSR

← refugees

— major road

FALKLANDS WAR
2 APRIL–15 JUNE 1982

▯ main Argentine positions

→ British attacks and advances

↖ British ships sunk

OPERATION DESERT STORM

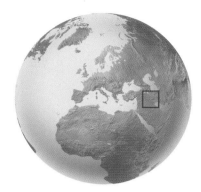

DESERT STORM FEBRUARY 24– MARCH 2, 1991
Following Iraq's invasion of Kuwait on August 2, 1990, the United Nations introduced immediate economic sanctions against the aggressor. The UN authorized a coalition of approximately 30 nations to liberate Kuwait and armed intervention began in early 1991. Operation Desert Storm

was the name for the air and land operation, but the conflict is also known as the Gulf War. Aerial and ground conflict was confined to Iraq, Kuwait, and bordering areas of Saudi Arabia. It resulted in a decisive and quick victory for the US-led coalition forces, driving the Iraqi forces out of Kuwait with a minimal number of coalition deaths.

DESERT STORM 24 FEBRUARY– 2 MARCH 1991	
	French army unit
	US army unit
	British army unit
	Arab army unit
	Allied advance
	Iraqi retreat
	Allied bombing
	airbase

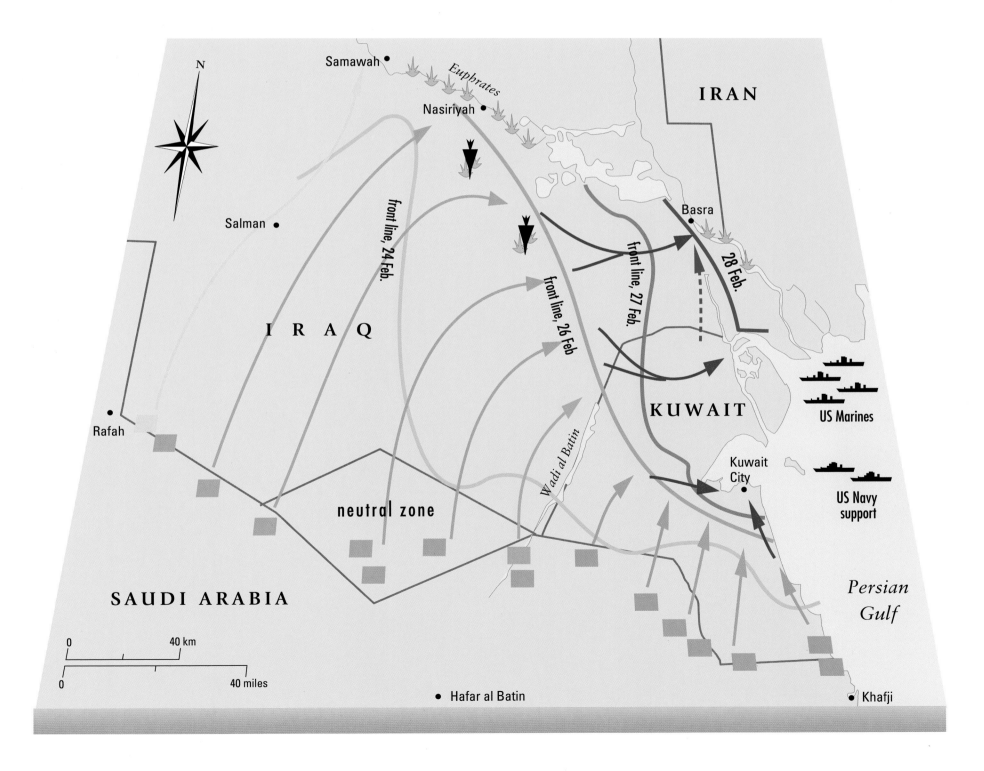

2003 – TODAY INVASION OF IRAQ; AFGHANISTAN

INVASION OF IRAQ
MARCH 21–APRIL 9, 2003

The United States-led invasion of Iraq began in March 2003. US President George W. Bush claimed that the objectives of the invasion were linked to the ongoing War Against Terror. The stated aims of the war were to disarm Iraq of the weapons of mass destruction that it was said to be in possession of, end the tyrannical rule of Saddam Hussein, and free the Iraqi people. One hundred thousand US troops were assembled in Kuwait prior to the invasion. No weapons of mass destruction were subsequently found and although Saddam Hussein was speedily deposed, attempts to form an effective Iraqi government have not come to fruition and the country is riven by internal conflict between Shia and Sunni Muslim groups.

AFGHANISTAN UNDER
NATO CONTROL 2006

The Taliban maintained a repressive regime in Afghanistan from 1996 to 2001, based on a very strict interpretation of Islamic teachings. September 2001 saw the terrorist attacks on the United States and the destruction of the World Trade Center in New York. It was widely accepted that the force behind these attacks was the terrorist group Al-Qaeda and that the Taliban provided a safe haven for Al-Qaeda and its leader Osama bin Laden in Afghanistan. In 2002 the US and Britain invaded Afghanistan

on the basis that by destroying the Taliban it would be possible to obliterate Al-Qaeda. Although the Taliban have been removed, Al-Qaeda has proved to be more elusive, and bin Laden is still in hiding. Democratic elections were held in 2004 and NATO forces are now endeavoring to keep the peace in Afghanistan in the hope of gradually returning the country to normality.

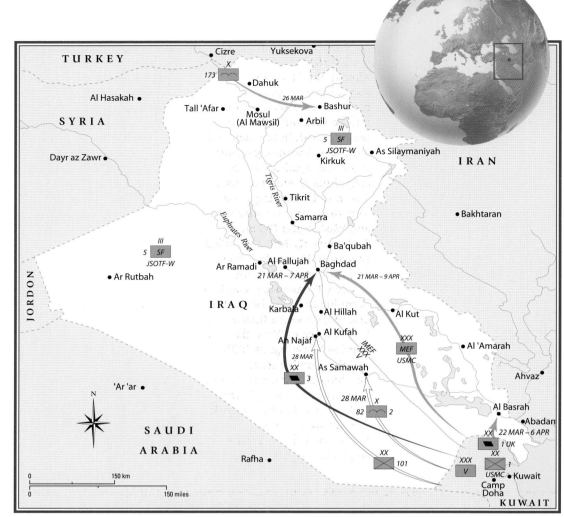

INVASION OF IRAQ
21 MARCH–9 APRIL 2003

→ Main axis of advance with date

→ Supporting axis of advance with date

⇒ Securing line of communications with date

AFGHANISTAN UNDER NATO CONTROL 2006

Provincial Reconstruction Teams

○ Existing PRTs
● Existing forward support base
◆ Regional command capital
✈ Airports
• US facilities
· Minor facilities

CONFLICTS IN THE 21ST CENTURY

CONFLICTS IN THE 21ST CENTURY
Already, the 21st century has seen a series of armed conflicts, particularly in the Middle East, but it has also seen a growth in international terrorism. A worrying feature is the rise in suicide attacks carried out around the world. The most devastating so far were the attacks on New York and Washington DC on September 11, 2001 that killed around 3000 people. Other major attacks include the Moscow Theater siege and Bali bombing in 2002, the Madrid bombings and the Beslan School Siege in 2004, the London bombings of 2005 and the Mumbai train bombing of 2006. These alone have accounted for a further 1200 deaths, but this figure is dwarfed by the many thousands killed in suicide attacks in Iraq since 2003.

CONFLICTS IN THE 21ST CENTURY

🌿 Major terrorist attacks

⬤ Armed conflicts

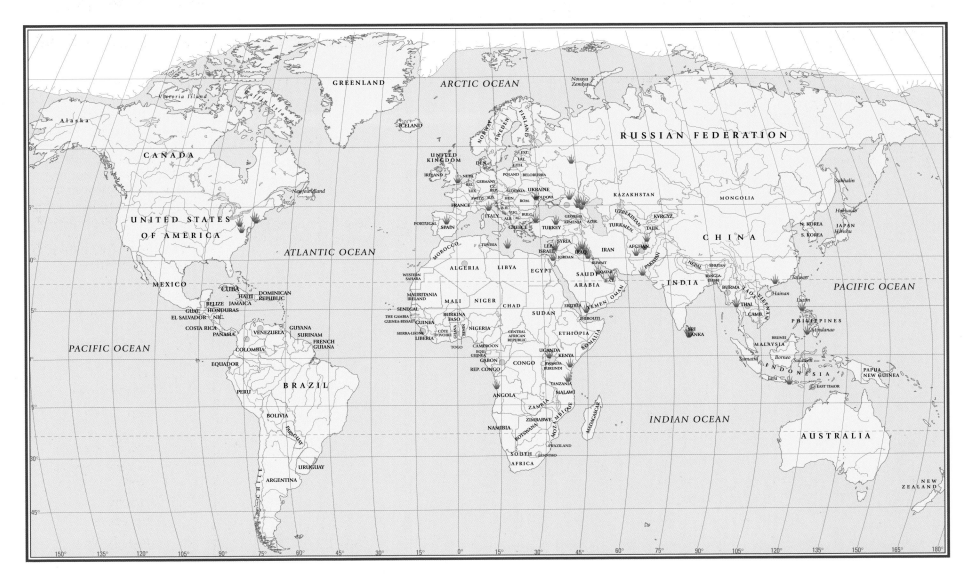

MAPS AND RECONSTRUCTIONS

Part 1: Warfare in the Classical Age

The Empire of Hammurabi c. 1750 BC   26

The Defenses of Egypt c. 1500 BC   27

The Battle of Kadesh 1274 BC   28-29

The Middle East c. 2000 BC   30

The Collapse of Mycenae c.1200 BC   31

The Persian Empire 550-330 BC   32-33

Battle of Marathon   34

Xerxes' Invasion 480 BC   35

Peloponnesian War I 431-337 BC   36

Campaign in Sicily   36

The Rise of Macedonia   37

The Empire of Alexander the Great 336-323 BC   38-39

The Battle of Gaugemela   38-39

The Celts   40

The Battle of Telamon 225 BC   41

Hannibal's Campaigns in Italy 218- 203 BC   42

Punic Wars 264-146 BC   43

Battle of Zama   43

The Battle of Magnesia   44

The Roman Empire 55 BC   44-45

Caesar's Campaigns in Gaul 58- 50 BC   46

The Siege of Alesia   47

The Battle of Actium   48

Civil Wars 49-31 BC   48

The Roman Empire AD 68   49

Parthian Wars AD 114-117   49

The Roman Empire AD 214   50

The Roman Empire c. AD 395   51

Enemy at the Gates   52

The Battle of Strasbourg   53

Frontiers of Northern Britain   54

Germanic Kingdoms c. 500   55

The Empire in the East   56-57

The Emergence of Hungary   58

Battle of Lechfeld 10 August 955   58

Part 2: Dark Ages to the Rise of Islam

Viking, Magyar, Abbasid Invasions   60

The Swedes in the East 800-913   61

Normandy and British Isles 1035-92   62

Battle of Hastings   62

Conquest of England to 1069   63

The Battle of Yarmuk   64

The Expansion of Islam to 750   64-65

The Seljuk Era   66

Battle of Manzikert August 1071   67

The Crusades 1096-1204   68-69

The Siege of Jerusalem 1099   69

The Empire and Campaigns of Saladin 1173- 1185   70

Part 3: Medieval to Renaissance Warfare

Mongol Conquests 1206-59   72-73

The Battle of Liegnitz 1241   73

Mongol Campaigns in Europe 1240-45   74

The Battle of Mohi 1241   75

The Baltic 1200-1400 BC   76

The Battle of Tannenberg   77

The Hussite Crusades 1420-1431   78

Eastern Europe c. 1460   79

Battle of Pavia 1525   80-81

Expansion of the Ottoman Empire 1328-1566   82

The Siege of Antwerp September 1584-August 1585   83

The Battle of Lepanto 7 October 1571   84

The Spanish Armada May-September 1588   85

The Siege of Vienna 1683   86

Part 4: Kings and Revolutions

The Thirty Years' War 1618-29   88

The Thirty Years' War 1630-39   89

The Battle of Breitenfield 1631   90

The Thirty Years' War 1640-48   91

English Civil War 1642-43   92

English Civil War 1644   92

English Civil War 1645-6   93

Cromwell in Ireland   93

Battle of Naseby   94

Dahlberg's Fortifications at Gothenburg   95

Vauban's Trench Attack with Fields of Fire   95

Colonial Frontiers 1700-60   96

Discontent in the colonies on the Eve of War 1764-76   97

The Battle of Trenton 26 December 1776   98

Siege of Yorktown 6- 19 October 1781   99

The Treaty of Paris 1783   100

India, Invasions, and Regional Powers 1739- 60   101

Battle of Plassey 23 June, 1757   101

French Revolution 1789-1795   102

Europe 1789   103

The Battle of Marengo 14 June 1800   104

Part 5: Wars of the Industrial Age

French Empire 1810   106

Battle of Waterloo 10:00 hrs 18 June 1815   107

Battle of Waterloo 13:30 hrs 18 June 1815   107

The Campaigns of 1861- 1863 (American Civil War)   108

The Battle of Antietam   109

Gettysburg   110- 111

The Occupied South   112

The Battle of Appomatox April 3- 9 1865   113

Franco Prussian War 1870- 71   114

Sedan 1870   114

Russo- Japanese War 1904- 5   115

Europe in 1914   116

The Schlieffen Plan 1914   117

The Eastern Front 1914   118

Battle of the Marne 5- 10 September 1914   119

Battle of Verdun February-June 1916   120- 121

Battle of the Somme July-November 1916   120- 121

Palestine October 1917-October 1918   122

Advance to Victory   123

The Russian Revolution   124

Europe 1920- 21   125

The Fascist States 1922- 36   126

Part 6: Warfare in the Technological Age

Invasion of Poland 1- 28 September 1939   128

Invasion of the West May- June 1940   129

Dunkirk Operation 'Dynamo' 27 May- 4 June 1940   129

The Battle of Britain June-September 1940   130

The Conquest of Greece and Crete 20-30 April 1941   131

Operation Merkur 28 May-1 June 1941   131

Africa in World War II   132

Operation 'Torch' 8 November 1942   133

El Alemein- Operation Lightfoot 24- 29 October 1942   133

Operation Barbarossa 22 June-early October 1941   134

Stalingrad 12 September-18 November 1942   135

Japanese Expansion December 1941-July 1942   136- 37

Battle of the Coral Sea 28 April-11 May 1942   138

Attack of the Coral Sea 1 January-11 May 1942   138

Battle of Midway 1 4 June 4.00am-10.30am   139

Battle of Midway 2 4 June 10.30 am-6 June 12.00 am   139

Battle of the Atlantic January 1942- February 1943   140

Operation Bagration June-August 1944   141

Allied D- Day Landing Plan and Objectives 6 June 1944   142-143

Crossing the Rhine March 1945   144

Battle of Berlin 15 April-6 May 1945   145

Pacific Situation 1942-1945   146

Nagasaki 9 August 1945   147

The Korean War   148

Arab- Israeli Wars   149

The Division of Europe after World War II 1945- 1949   150

Packages to Cuba 1962   151

The Cuban Missile Crisis September- November 1962   151

Indochina War   152

Vietnam War   152

The Battle of Ap Bac   153

Afghanistan 1978-84   154

Falklands War 2 April-15 June 1982   154

Desert Storm 24 February-2 March 1991   155

Invasion of Iraq 21 March-9 April 2003   156

Afghanistan under NATO control   156

Conflicts in the 21st Century   157